VERLAG
ÖSTERREICH

Franz Steiner Verlag

Dietmar Sternad
Eithne Knappitsch
Christina Mundschütz

Cross-Border Cooperation: European Institutional Framework and Strategies of SMEs

VERLAG ÖSTERREICH

Franz Steiner Verlag

FH-Prof. Dr. Dietmar Sternad
Dr. Eithne Knappitsch
Mag. Christina Mundschütz

Carinthia University of Applied Sciences, Villach, Austria

www.verlagoesterreich.at
Printed in Germany

Typesetting: Jung Crossmedia Publishing GmbH, Lahnau, Germany
Printing: Strauss GmbH, Mörlenbach, Germany

Printed on acid-free and chlorine-free bleached paper

With 21 Figures

CIP data applied for

ISBN 978-3-515-10260-5 Franz Steiner Verlag
ISBN 978-3-7046-6313-9 Verlag Österreich

Contents

Figures

Tables

List of abbreviations

AEBR	Association of European Border Regions
AER	Assembly of European Regions
AMSC	American Superconductor
BAS	Business Advisory Services
BATNA	best alternative to the negotiated agreement
BGB	Bürgerliches Gesetzbuch (German Civil Code)
CARDS	Community Assistance for Reconstruction, Development and Stabilisation
CBC	cross-border cooperation
CCCTB	Common Consolidated Corporate Tax Base
CDLR	Committee for Local and Regional Democracy
CEO	chief executive officer
CIP	Competitiveness and Innovation Framework Programme
CLA	Conference of Local Authorities
CPA	certified public accountant
DMIS	Developmental Model of Intercultural Sensitivity
EBRD	European Bank for Reconstruction and Development
ECG	Euroregional Cooperation Grouping
EEA	European Economic Area
EEIG	European Economic Interest Group
EEN	Enterprise Europe Network
EGTC	European Grouping of Territorial Cooperation
EIB	European Investment Bank
EIF	European Investment Fund
EIP	Entrepreneurship and Innovation Programme
ENPI	European Neighbourhood and Partnership Instrument
ENSR	European Network for SME Research
EPMF	European Progress Microfinance Facility
ESF	European Social Fund
ERDF	European Regional Development Fund

EU	European Union
FDI	foreign direct investment
FEMIP	Facility for Euro-Mediterranean Investment and Partnership
GDP	gross domestic product
GIF	High Growth and Innovative SME Facility
ICT-PSP	Information and Communication Technologies Policy Support Programme
IEE	Intelligent Energy Europe Programme
IFRS	International Financial and Reporting Standards
IJV	international joint venture
IPA	Instrument for Pre-Accession Assistance
ISAs	International Standards on Auditing
JASMINE	Joint Action to Support Micro-finance Institutions in Europe
JEREMIE	Joint European Resources for Micro and Medium Enterprises
MEDA	financial and technical measures to accompany (Mésures d'Accompagnement) the reform of economic and social structures in the framework of the Euro-Mediterranean partnership
METP	Managers Exchange and Training Programme
NIF	Neighbourhood Investment Facility
NGO	non-governmental organisation
NUTS	Nomenclature of Territorial Units for Statistics
OECD	Organisation for Economic Co-operation and Development
PHARE	Poland and Hungary: Aid for Restructuring of the Economies
RBV	resource-based view
R&D	research and development
SBA	Small Business Act
SE	Societas Europaea
SME	small and medium-sized enterprise
SPE	Statute for a European Private Company
TACIS	Technical Assistance to the Commonwealth of Independent States
TAM	turn around management
UfM	Union for the Mediterranean
U.K.	United Kingdom
U.S.	United States
VAT	Value Added Tax
VC	venture capital

Introduction

Welch and White (1981) state that "a small business is not a little big business" (p. 18). Small and medium-sized enterprises (SMEs) are characterised by a relative lack of resources, including capital, an adequately qualified workforce, or simply time. This leads to possible disadvantages in terms of global competition. Nevertheless, the benefits of smaller businesses may include a higher degree of flexibility or overall closeness to customers. SMEs have the ability to utilize their innate size advantages as well as compensate for their resource shortcomings if they cooperate with complementary partners. In cross-border cooperation (CBC), partners from different countries can share specific resources and capabilities in order to achieve a common goal. These goals may include introducing products and services to new markets, increasing efficiency, or co-creating new knowledge or capabilities.

Cross-border cooperation in Europe is not a recent phenomenon albeit one that has attracted growing interest over recent years, also as a response to European integration processes and an increasing number of policies, programmes and initiatives aimed at promoting international SME cooperation. As Anne Thevenet (2011) aptly expresses, "the European idea cannot be dissociated from cooperation" (p. 15). Whether considered within the framework of the European Union consisting of 27 members or the Council of Europe with its 47 members, cross-border cooperation is a complex and diverse phenomenon. It has a variety of forms and occurs in various contexts. Adding to its complexity, there are also several "players" in this field, from policy makers on European, national, or regional levels to government agencies, academic institutions, and SME managers. To accurately convey this complexity, we aim to provide a multi-perspective discussion of cross-border cooperation.

For this purpose, we divide the book into three parts:

In **Part I**, we begin by discussing the importance of cross-border cooperation for European SMEs and giving insight into the fundamentals of SME cooperation as well as the key factors that influence cooperation success.

Chapter 1 ("Cooperation and the internationalisation of SMEs") highlights the role of cross-border cooperation for the internationalisation of SMEs, in particular for gaining access to new markets.

Cross-border cooperation is a broad term that encompasses many forms of collaborative endeavours between two or more firms. In **Chapter 2 ("Characteristics and forms of SME cross-border cooperation: A classification approach")**, various forms of cooperation are classified, taking into account some of the key SME cooperation characteristics, namely the direction of the cooperation, the geographic scope, the number of partners, the level of integration, and the form of governance. Further, the most common types of SME cross-border cooperation are discussed.

Regardless of the form of cooperation, the decision of whether or not it is sensible for an SME to cooperate is not a straightforward one. Following such a strategy involves challenges and risks. Weighing them with the potential benefits of cooperating is the main goal of **Chapter 3 ("Benefits and challenges of SME cross-border cooperation")**.

Chapter 4 ("Success factors for cross-border cooperation") summarises and integrates the vast literature on critical success factors for cooperation, especially in a cross-border context. Finding the right cooperation partner, defining realistic joint goals and strategies, developing a governance structure that helps to prevent uncertainty, opportunism, and conflict, forming a clear division of tasks and outcomes, and having effective operational cooperation management, monitoring, and controlling systems are as important in this context as are relationship-oriented factors such as developing and maintaining trust and commitment, and learning from cooperation experience. Furthermore the partner firms' backgrounds also have considerable impact on cooperation performance.

Chapter 5 ("External success factors of cross-border cooperation") provides an overview of the external conditions influencing the development and success of SME cross-border cooperation. These external conditions can be described as laws, rules, policies, and regulations defining the boundaries of and conditions for SME cooperation, the technological development, the partners' cultural backgrounds, and the business environment influencing the development of cooperation.

Part II of this book focuses on the institutional environment influencing cross-border cooperation in Europe. This section presents the development of cross-border collaborations in Europe against a backdrop of increasing regionalisation tendencies and dynamic as well as transforming European regional policy and initiatives. Understanding the web of institutions, initiatives and programmes promoting and facilitating cross-border cooperation in Europe is a daunting task for many, for SMEs in particular. As a result of their size and resource constraints, SMEs often lack the impulse essential for dismantling this web in order to gain access to the support offered for cooperation activities. Hence, this section aims to provide a comprehensive understanding of the European framework context for cross-border cooperation in general, for SME collaborations in particular, and simultaneously outline the development of various actions underpinning the now widespread phenomenon of cross-border cooperation in Europe.

Chapter 6 ("A history of cross-border cooperation in Europe") traces the history and evolution of cross-border cooperation policies in Europe. It provides an account of the development of programmes and activities relating to cross-border cooperation, thereby contributing to a better understanding of the broader framework conditions for SME cooperation. Specifically, the salient role of the Council of Europe and the European Union (EU) for promoting cross-border cooperation is emphasised in **Chapter 7 ("The European institutional dimension")**, setting the scene for later chapters discussing the wider (inter-) regional context of cooperation, policy implications for SMEs, and EU initiatives specific to SME cross-border cooperation.

From an EU perspective, when cross-border cooperation is linked to economic development, it tends to fall within the more recently popularised spectrum of territorial cohesion. This concept of territorial cohesion has become embedded in the new trend of introducing macro-regional planning as part of the new regional policy and cohesion policies of the EU. This will be discussed in **Chapter 8 ("The European regional dimension")**. In keeping with regionalisation tendencies, European policies promoting and facilitating cross-border cooperation now tend to focus extensively on local and regional factors; these play an increasingly important role in policy making for economic development. In many cases, this has led to cooperation across state borders as a means of solving common local or regional problems, maximising local/regional potential and ensuring sustainable development.

Considering the substantial territory of the EU covered by border regions, the importance of the economic development of these regions for the overall economic well-being of the Union should not be underestimated. Policies promoting cross-border cooperation are also regarded as a valuable tool in boosting economic development for border regions, or more specifically, regional economic development. Xheneti and Smallbone (2008) suggest that "such policies need to be viewed in the wider context of increasing internationalisation forces, which are presenting new sources of threats and opportunities, for businesses of all sizes" (p. 3). **Chapter 9 ("SME policy of the EU")** and **Chapter 10 ("EU initiatives supporting SME cross-border cooperation")** delve deeper into EU policy for SMEs and concrete EU initiatives supporting cross-border cooperation of SMEs.

In **Part III** of this book, we change our focus from the institutional environment to individual actors in SMEs. Adequate institutions form the backbone of cross-border cooperation. In order to be successful, however, cross-border cooperation also needs to be effectively managed. It is inherently more complex and therefore more challenging to engage in cross-border cooperation than to work with domestic partners. Such an endeavour involves varying cultural, legal, political, social, and economic contexts, as well as higher information asymmetries between partners (Hennart and Zeng 2002).

In the final part of the book, we explore cooperation management from the partner firm's perspective, following a sequence of the most important decisions that need to be made as cross-border alliances pass through various stages. Several authors provided phase models of cooperation (e.g., Hoffmann and Schlosser 2001; Kale and Singh 2009). We use a combination and extension of those models and present the development of cross-border cooperation in six stages:

1. ***Selecting the right cooperation partner*** **(Chapter 11)**: after the general decision to engage in a cross-border partnership, the right partner needs to be chosen in a search and selection process.
2. ***Cooperation negotiations in an intercultural context*** **(Chapter 12)**: the potential partners need to undertake negotiations pertaining to collaboration, taking their cultural differences into account.
3. ***Choosing a governance structure*** **(Chapter 13)**: considering the advantages and disadvantages of different forms of governance, a decision has to me made on whether cooperation will be equity-based, contract-based, or solely relationship-based.
4. ***Managing the cooperative relationship*** **(Chapter 14)**: once a formal agreement is reached, the partnership needs to be operatively arranged and maintained. It is necessary to manage the tasks and relationship, as well as to establish adequate control systems.
5. ***Adaptive cooperative strategy*** **(Chapter 15)**: as environments rapidly change, so do partner strategies. Therefore, the cooperative strategy needs to adapt to evolving circumstances.
6. ***Terminating cooperation*** **(Chapter 16)**: if the partnership has either reached all its goals or has lost its basis, it needs to be terminated in a structured and organized manner.

As Europe concurrently follows both paths of integration and regionalisation, cross-border cooperation of SMEs as a strategy to overcome resource constraints and to capture new business development potential will continue to increase in relevance. By combining institutional and managerial perspectives on cross-border cooperation in one book, we aim to provide a better mutual understanding for policy makers and entrepreneurs, and to create a more integrated picture of external and internal factors contributing to the success of cross-border cooperation.

References

Hennart, J. F. and Zeng, M. (2002) Cross-cultural differences and joint venture longevity. *Journal of International Business Studies* 33(4), 699–716

Hoffmann, W. and Schlosser, R. (2001) Success factors of strategic alliances in small and medium-sized enterprises – an empirical survey. *Long Range Planning* 34(3), 357–381

Kale, P. and Singh, H. (2009) Managing strategic alliances: What do we know now, and where do we go from here? *Academy of Management Perspectives* 23(3), 45–62

Thevenet, A. (2011) Why a colloquy on the European dimension of cross-border cooperation? In: Wassenberg, B. and Beck, J. (eds.) Living and researching cross-border cooperation, Vol. 3: The European dimension. Stuttgart: Franz Steiner Verlag, 13–16

Welch, J. and White, J. (1981) A small business is not a little big business. *Harvard Business Review* 59(4), 18–32.(4), 18–32

Xheneti, M. and Smallbone, D. (2008) The role of public policy in entrepreneurship development in post-socialist countries: a comparison of Albania and Estonia. *EBS Review* 1(24), 24–37

Part I: Fundamentals of SME cross-border cooperation

Christina Mundschütz

1 Cooperation and the internationalisation of SMEs

As a consequence of the globalisation of markets and in light of the constantly intensifying international competition, the number of small and medium-sized enterprises (SMEs) operating in foreign markets has been growing steadily (Nummela 2002). Specifically the removal of trade barriers within the European Union has led to an increased internationalisation of SMEs within the common European market. Besides that the time span between the formation of a firm and its first steps towards internationalisation is decreasing (Nummela 2002). However, SMEs make, in proportion, a much smaller contribution to value added in global markets than large firms and are generally less active on international markets. The reason for this imbalance can be attributed to their inherent size and resource constraints. Due to these characteristics, SMEs traditionally face more and different challenges in their internationalisation endeavours than larger firms.

The aforementioned increase in the number of SMEs active in global markets has been linked to their ability to create and join networks, a concept rapidly gaining importance in internationalisation process research (Holmlund and Kock 1998). According to Johanson and Vahlne (1990), firms develop and distribute products in foreign markets through business networks that, through providing local market knowledge, lower uncertainty and allow for faster internationalisation. Contemporary research on the relationship between SMEs has long focused on these networks "while the research on the co-operation between one enterprise and its partners is far less rich and homogenous" (European Commission 2003c, p. 13). This is noteworthy, as SMEs could overcome their individual resource constraints especially by entering long-term strategic alliances. Strategic alliances among enterprises, which can be seen more as intense cooperation rather than loose network ties can play a key role for the successful internationalisation of SMEs (Brouthers 2002; Robson et al. 2006). By bundling resources, strategic cooperation can enable SMEs to achieve a "critical mass" for internationalisation (Welge and Borghoff 2005). This argument is supported by Fink et al. (2008), who confirm that cooperation can foster the internationalisation of SMEs, as combining complementary resources allows them to engage in internationalisation activities from which they would otherwise be excluded.

1.1 SME characteristics

Before exploring the role of cooperation in the internationalisation of SMEs, we need to identify (a) the main characteristics of SMEs and (b) the specifics of their internationalisation process.

As there is no universally accepted definition of an SME, we use the term as defined by the European Commission, which is widely used in European literature. As defined by the European Commission (2003a), an SME is a private company with fewer than 250 employees, a turnover not exceeding € 50 million, and/or a balance sheet size less than € 43 million. Table 1.1 summarises the details of the EU definition of micro, small, and medium-sized enterprises, all subsumed under the term "SME".

Table 1.1 European Union SME definition

		and/or	
Category	**Staff headcount (annual work units)**	**Annual turnover**	**Annual balance sheet total**
Medium-sized enterprise	< 250	≤ € 50 million	≤ € 43 million
Small enterprise	< 50	≤ € 10 million	≤ € 10 million
Micro enterprise	< 10	≤ € 2 million	≤ € 2 million

Source: European Commission (2003a)

Table 1.2 illustrates the key role that SMEs in all three categories play in the European economy.

Table 1.2 Key indicators by enterprise size

	Micro	**Small**	**Medium**	**SME total**	**Large**
Number of enterprises (in 1000), 2010 (estimates)	19,2	1 378	219	20 796	43
Employment (in 1000), 2010 (estimates)	38 906	26 605	21 950	87 461	43 257
Persons employed by the enterprise (average), 2010 (estimates)	2	19	100	4,2	1 005

	Micro	Small	Medium	SME total	Large
Persons employed (%), 2010 (estimates)	29,8	20,4	16,8	66,9	33,1
Value added (%), 2010 (estimates)	21,6	18,9	17,9	58,4	41,6
Labour productivity (EUR 1 000/person), 2008	34,3	41,2	47,9	45,5	56,6

Source: European Commission (2011) and Eurostat European Commission (2011)

The annual report on EU small and medium-sized enterprises published by the European Commission (2011) shows that SMEs represent more than 99% of businesses in the European Union (EU) and form the backbone of the European economy. In 2010, there were nearly 20.8 million SMEs in the EU; most of them (19.2 million or 92.1% of all EU businesses) were micro-firms. In the private sector, SMEs account for more than two-thirds of all employment opportunities and contribute around 58.4% of the total gross value added.

However, owing to their limited resource base and little support from governments, SMEs are facing various challenges, especially in this uncertain economic period. The 2008–09 financial crisis and subsequent debt crisis had a considerable impact on the performance of European SMEs. Globalisation and increasing international competition have forced SMEs to search for innovative and flexible survival strategies in a negative economic environment. Increasing globalisation has affected SMEs in two important ways (OECD 2004): On the positive side, SMEs that (a) have high growth rates, (b) are niche exporters, or (c) are able to tie in with global supply chains, can benefit from the opportunities created by globalisation. On the other hand, globalisation also poses a threat to SMEs that are not able (or do not try) to compete in the international market. A study published by the European Commission (2007) shows that most European SMEs believe that the competition in their markets has increased over the past two years. In response to this competition, SMEs have taken different approaches to overcome these hurdles. According to the study, SMEs have tried to improve the quality of their products and services, widen their product differentiation, look for market niches, extend their marketing activities, reduce costs, or form strategic partnerships. Given their resource constraints and risk awareness, looking for new foreign markets is seen as a strategy of last resort (European Commission 2007).

1.2 SME internationalisation

Owing to their particular characteristics, SMEs face specific challenges in the process of internationalisation and their smaller firm size is often regarded as a disadvantage. Westhead et al. (2002) argue that internationalisation usually involves high risks and SMEs are less able to manage risks and uncertainties than larger firms, as they do not have the same financial background and international experience. Moreover, SMEs often lack other resources necessary to enter foreign markets (Meyer and Skak 2002), such as human resources, time resources, and knowledge. This lack of resources constitutes a substantial obstacle to their ability to perform in an international environment. However, SMEs also possess advantages, which can be used in the process of internationalisation, such as their flexibility, their closeness to the market, and their ability to quickly adapt to changes within the environment (Chen and Hambrick 1995; Peters 1992). Technological and structural changes have made it less difficult for SMEs to participate in the international economy, as these changes facilitate information flows and support the expansion of the market potential of small enterprises (OECD 2004). Further, SMEs are often more innovative, as they have a more informal and flexible behaviour (Alvarez and Barney 2001).

Theoretical work on the internationalisation process of SMEs was dominated, for a long time, by incremental models originating from the Uppsala School (Johanson and Vahlne 1977; Johanson and Wiedersheim-Paul 1975). These models were characterised as "tempting because of their simplicity and logic" (Nummela 2002, p. 6). The focus of the Uppsala approach is to explain the increasing internationalisation of a firm through the interplay between knowledge development through experiential learning and international commitment building. According to this theory, enterprises gradually intensify their involvement in international markets over time, as a firm will usually first enter a market with the lowest possible commitment, expanding its activities only after having gained experience and trust in the market (Johanson and Vahlne 1977). Consequently, the model suggests that firms will start the internationalisation process by choosing culturally similar markets, strengthening their commitment over time with increasing experience by gradually entering physically and culturally distant markets.

This model of internationalisation, however, has received ample criticism. Andersen (1993), for example, argues that the Uppsala approach does not explain the start of the internationalisation processes nor provides clear information about the working of the mechanism linking knowledge with commitment. Further criticism addresses the model's limited applicability for entrepreneurial SMEs. In the 1990s, several studies identified a significant number of firms that did not follow the steps of the traditional stage model of internationalisation. Such companies, often referred to as "born globals" (Oviatt and McDougall 1994), were able to leapfrog some stages of the internationalisation process. This phenomenon has been attributed to (1) advances in technology, production, transportation, and communication, (2) increased competition in a firm's domestic market, and (3) entrepreneurs' acquisition of an increasing amount of international experience and foreign market knowledge (Madsen and Servais 1997; Oviatt and McDougall 1994).

Acknowledging the rapid internationalisation of born globals, the incremental models were combined with the network theory (Johanson and Mattson 1988; Johanson and Vahlne 1990; Meyer and Skak 2002). According to this theoretical approach, firms use both domestic and international business networks to develop and distribute products for foreign markets. These networks aid in lowering uncertainty by providing local market knowledge, thus enabling faster internationalisation.

In addition to networks, firm-specific resources, such as a firm's assets, capabilities, information, knowledge, and technologies, may constitute a source of differential advantage in foreign markets (Collis 1991; Porter 1991), thus fostering accelerated internationalisation. The resource-based view (RBV) has gained considerable influence in recent internationalisation research (Peng 2001). Following RBV thinking, the main reason that firms are able to internationalise lies in their firm-specific resource advantages, which are transformed into competitive advantage in the international market place. It is essential for SMEs planning to go international to consider the resource needs for this process, as a lack of adequate resources was found to be the main barrier to SME internationalisation (Wright et al. 2007).

1.3 The role of cooperation in the internationalisation of SMEs

We identified the possession of relevant resources and capabilities and being a part of relevant networks as key factors for rapid internationalisation. One of the main characteristics of SMEs, however, is their resource limitation. Most SMEs have less financial capital, human resources, and managerial capabilities than large corporations. Owing to these inherent constraints, smaller firms often seek cooperation, bundling resources with partners in order to secure their survival and development (Simons and Royer 2006). "Strategic alliances may in fact serve as a strategy to neutralize the disadvantages of small-scaled organizations [...] achieving a competitive advantage while maintaining a higher degree of organizational flexibility" (Johansson and Ylinenpää 2006, p. 3). The formation and management of external relationships is therefore an important strategy in the development of small businesses (Street and Cameron 2007) and can help SMEs exploit new market opportunities across borders.

SMEs face specific challenges when it comes to cooperation. In addition to controlling more resources, larger corporations usually have more relationships and are able to obtain more information about their operating environments (Yasai-Ardekani and Nystrom 1996). Both these factors can be seen as considerable advantages in building cooperation. The resource constraints of SMEs limit their ability to contribute specific resources to an alliance and lower their potential of attracting partners and establishing alliances (Dickson and Weaver 2011). This might also be one of the reasons of why SMEs are less likely to engage in cooperation than large-scale corporations (Frank 1994).

Nevertheless, cooperating across borders is still a strategic option for SMEs to strengthen their competitive position in the international marketplace (Kotha et al. 2001) as they can also exploit their size-specific advantages, such as their higher degree of flexibility, lower level of rigidity (Greve 2011), and reduced bureaucratic inertia (Haveman 1993), for cooperative ventures.

The definition of SME cooperation

In accordance with the definition in the 2003 Observatory of European SMEs report by the European Commission, we refer to the term "SME cooperation" in this book as "the interaction between independent SMEs for a specific purpose that extends beyond a single task" (European Commission 2003c, p. 7). Specifically, SME cooperation is characterised by:

(1) the objective of improving the potential of each partner enterprise to attain a specific purpose;
(2) long-term commitments rather than a limitation to a certain milestone or event (although we see joint project work also as a viable form of cooperation);
(3) different degrees of formalisation of the cooperation agreement, and
(4) collaboration between SMEs rather than between an SME and large enterprises (European Commission 2003c).

Reasons to cooperate

Firms have different motives for entering into an alliance, such as the desire to increase market power, to obtain efficiency gains, to reduce risk, to obtain access to key resources and capabilities, or to enter new markets (Johansson and Ylinenpää 2006; Kale and Singh 2009). The reasons for SME cooperation were also investigated in the ENSR (European Network for SME Research) Enterprise Survey 2003. The sample for this survey included SME managers from 19 EU countries and Switzerland.

Table 1.3 Reasons for SME cooperation in Europe

	Micro enterprises	**Small enterprises**	**Medium-sized enterprises**
Nr 1 reason	Access to new and larger markets	Access to new and larger markets	Reduced costs
Nr 2 reason	Broader supply of products	Additional production capacity	Access to know-how and technology
Nr 3 reason	Access to know-how and technology	Reduced costs	Access to new and larger markets
Lowest ranked reason	Access to capital	Access to capital	Access to capital

Source: ENSR Enterprise Survey, European Commission (2004)

The ENSR Enterprise survey results reveal that the main reason for cooperation, particularly for micro and small enterprises, is gaining access to new and larger markets (see also Table 1.3). This supports the view of cross-border cooperation with partners in a target market as an important internationalisation path for SMEs.

The definition of cross-border cooperation

Building on the definition of cooperation in this chapter, we see cross-border cooperation as a process of working together for a specific common purpose or benefit, in which two or more partners from at least two countries are involved.

The term "cross-border cooperation" is often used in a macro context, linked to cooperation among countries and regions rather than to collaboration of private entities. In this book, we follow Doz's definition of cross-border alliances (1996) and use the term "cross-border cooperation" for describing a partnership between two or more SMEs from different countries for the purpose of pursuing mutual interests by sharing resources and capabilities.

As geographical distance constitutes an important factor in internationalisation, we focus on the cooperation among SMEs within a smaller geographical space. This acknowledges that SMEs in their internationalisation efforts often tend to orient themselves towards neighbouring or nearby countries. Resource constraints and a lack of experience in foreign markets can limit the ability of SMEs to systematically explore and evaluate target countries or regions and their opportunities (Wood et al. 2009). Many small firms thus focus on regions that are geographically and culturally close rather than evaluating their options globally (Buckley and Casson 1996). Huber (2003, p. 4) argues that "[i]f different forms of co-operation require different intensities of personal interaction and distance between two partners is a measure of the cost of such interaction, the choice of form of co-operation will depend on distance".

In the European context, the opening of borders as a consequence of political and economic integration has positively influenced the internationalisation of SMEs. As a result of reduced border impediments, enterprises can profit from the lower transaction costs of cross-border trade. Combined with geographic proximity, SMEs have a higher market potential in international near-border markets. Studies show that the removal of internal borders within the EU has indeed resulted in an increased inclination of SMEs to internationalise, leading to a higher chance of profiting from the new market opportunities (Smallbone et al. 2007).

Although it is important to stress that cross-border partnerships are not a universal remedy for SMEs (ibid), they are definitely a major strategy by which SMEs may overcome their size-related disadvantages, uncovering opportunities they would not have been able to detect or exploit on their own.

Internationalisation through cross-border cooperation

Exporting, which has been the traditional path for the internationalisation of SMEs, still plays an important role. According to an EU Observatory Report on European SMEs (European Commission 2003b), however, internationalisation with its crucial importance for the competitiveness of SMEs has become much more differentiated. In addition to exporting, cooperation with foreign partners and membership in cross-border clusters are viable alternatives for strengthening the international performance capacity of a small firm, especially through exchanges of knowledge and technology, as "[c]o-operations are an avenue for learning and internalisation of new skills" (European Commission 2003c, p. 18). According to Kaufmann (1995), cross-border cooperation is frequently even the only possible form of SME internationalisation.

Besides exporting, using suppliers from abroad, or establishing subsidiaries in another country through foreign direct investment, cross-border cooperation adds to the repertoire of strategies for SMEs' initial internationalisation steps (Wolff and Pett 2000). Cross-border cooperation not only facilitates access to new and larger markets but can also support SMEs in their effort to gain new inputs and become more successful in the home market.

Cooperation can also help SMEs alleviate the following three liabilities they typically face when trying to enter foreign markets:

1. The *liability of foreignness*, having no experience of the local business environment;
2. the *liability of newness* to a foreign market, and
3. the *liability of smallness*, manifesting itself in their limited resource endowments, difficulties in obtaining critical resources such as capital and qualified people, and a vulnerability to environmental change (Lu and Beamish 2006).

Cooperation can accelerate the acquisition of knowledge through learning from partners and the creation of relationships and networks in foreign markets. Having local partners with knowledge about and existing relationships in the desired market can therefore be a means of overcoming the *liability of foreignness*. For younger enterprises, the *liability of newness* can be alleviated through alliances with established companies having a strong market reputation (Fink et al. 2008). Cross-border cooperation that combines resources, capabilities, and knowledge of partners can overcome the *liability of smallness* (ibid). Bundling resources is also a way of achieving a "critical mass" for internationalisation (Welge and Borghoff 2005). Although internationalisation is often considered contingent on firm-specific advantages, firms can develop new joint competitive advantages by combining complementary resources and capabilities with foreign firms, especially with those who are either more technologically advanced or more knowledgeable about or connected to the target market (Shan and Song 1997).

A summary on cooperation as an internationalisation strategy for SMEs

1. Despite the growing number of small and medium-sized enterprises operating in foreign markets and the generally shortening time lag between a firm's formation and its first steps towards internationalisation, SMEs are still less active in international markets than are large firms.
2. SMEs cooperate mainly to gain access to new and larger markets. Cross-border cooperation can thus be seen as an important SME internationalisation strategy.
3. SMEs face specific challenges while internationalising due to their inherent resource constraints. They are also often unwilling to or incapable of dealing with the high risks of internationalisation. Cross-border cooperation can help neutralise these disadvantages.
4. Globalisation and increased international competition force SMEs to search for innovative and flexible strategies for surviving in a challenging economic environment. Cross-border cooperation allows firms to combine the advantages of being small (such as their flexibility) with the size-related benefits (such as achieving the critical mass needed to compete in a new market).
5. Cooperation helps SMEs alleviate the burdens they typically face while internationalising, such as the liabilities of (1) foreignness, (2) newness, and (3) smallness.

References

Alvarez, S. A. and Barney, J. B. (2001) How entrepreneurial firms can benefit from alliances with large partners. *Academy of Management Executive* 15(1), 139–148

Andersen, O. (1993) On the internationalization process of firms: A critical analysis. *Journal of International Business Studies* 24(2), 209–232

Brouthers, K. D. (2002) Institutional, cultural, and transaction cost influences on entry mode choice and performance. *Journal of International Business Studies* 33(2), 203–211

Buckley, P. J. and Casson, M. (1996) An economic model of international joint venture strategy. *Journal of International Business Studies* 27(5), 849–876

Chen, M.-J. and Hambrick, D. C. (1995) Speed, stealth, and selective attack: How small firms differ from large firms in competitive behavior. *Academy of Management Journal* 38(2), 453–482

Collis, D.J. (1991) A resource-based analysis of global competition: The case of the bearings industries. *Strategic Management Journal* 12 (Special Issue *Summer*), 49–68

Dickson, P. H. and Weaver, K. M. (2011) Institutional readiness and small to medium-sized enterprise alliance formation. *Journal of Small Business Management* 49(1), 126–148

Doz, Y. L. (1996) The evolution of cooperation in strategic alliances: Initial conditions or learning alliances. *Strategic Management Journal* 17(1), 55–83

European Commission (2003a) Commission Recommendation of 6 May 2003 concerning the definition of micro, small and medium-sized enterprises. *Official Journal of the European Union L 124/36*

European Commission (2003b) Internationalisation of SMEs. *Observatory of European SMEs* Vol. 4

European Commission (2003c) SMEs and cooperation. *Observatory of European SMEs* Vol. 5

European Commission (2004) *ENSR enterprise survey 2003*. Luxembourg: Office for Official Publications of the European Communities

European Commission. (2007) Observatory of European SMEs. Summary. *Flash Eurobarometer* Vol. 196

European Commission (2011) *Are EU SMEs recovering? Annual report on EU SMEs 2010/2011*. Rotterdam and Cambridge: European Commission

Eurostat European Commission (2011) Key figures on european business with a special feature on SMEs 2011 edition, http://epp.eurostat.ec.europa.eu/cache/ITY_OFFPUB/KS-ET-11-001/EN/KS-ET-11-001-EN.PDF (date accessed 27 July 2012)

Fink, M., Harms, R., and Kraus, S. (2008) Cooperative internationalization of SMEs: Self-commitment as a success factor for international Entrepreneurship. *European Management Journal* 26(6), 429–440

Frank, C. (1994) Strategische Partnerschaften in mittelständischen Unternehmen. Wiesbaden: Deutscher Universitäts Verlag

Greve, H. R. (2011) Positional rigidity: Low performance and resource acquisition in large and small firms. *Strategic Management Journal* 32(1), 103–114

Haveman, H. (1993) Organizational size and change: Diversification in the savings and loan industry after deregulation. *Administrative Science Quarterly* 38(1), 20–50

Holmlund, M. and Kock, S. (1998) Relationships and the internationalization of Finnish small and medium-sized companies. *International Small Business Journal* 16(4), 46–64

Huber, P. (2003) On the determinants of cross-border cooperation of Austrian firms with Central and Eastern European partners. *Regional Studies* 37(9), 947–955

Johanson, J. and Mattsson, L-G. (1988) Internationalization in industrial systems – a network approach. In: Hood, N. and Vahlne, J.-E. (eds.). Strategies for Global Competition. London: Croom Helm, 287–314

Johanson, J. and Vahlne, J. E. (1977) The internationalization process of the firm: A model of knowledge development and increasing foreign market commitment. *Journal of International Business Studies* 8(1), 23–32

Johanson, J. and Vahlne, J. E. (1990) The mechanism of internationalization. *International Marketing Review* 7(4), 11–24

Johanson, J. and Wiedersheim-Paul, F. (1975) The internationalisation process of the firms: four Swedish case studies. *Journal of Management Studies* 12(3), 305–322

Johansson, J. and Ylinenpää, H. (2006) SME alliance motives and knowledge modes. Paper presented at the 14th Nordic Conference on Small Business Research, Stockholm/Sweden

Kale, P. and Singh, H. (2009) Managing strategic alliances: What do we know now, and where do we go from here? *Academy of Management Perspectives* 23(3), 45–62

Kaufmann, F. (1995) Internationalisation via co-operation – Strategies of SME. *International Small Business Journal* 13(2), 27–33

Kotha, S., Rindova, V., and Rothaermel, F. T. (2001) Assets and actions: Firm-specific factors in the internationalisation of U.S. internet firms. *Journal of International Business Studies* 32(4), 769–791

Lu, J. W. and Beamish, P. W. (2006) Partnering strategies and performance of SMEs' international joint ventures. *Journal of Business Venturing* 21(4), 461–486

Madsen, T. K. and Per Servais (1997) The internationalization of born globals: an evolutionary process? *International Business Review* 6(6), 561–583

Meyer, K. and Skak, A. (2002) Networks, serendipity and SME entry into Eastern Europe. *European Management Journal* 20(2), 179–188

Nummela, N. (2002) Change in SME internationalisation: A network perspective. Paper presented at the 28th EIBA Conference, Athens/Greece

OECD (2004) Facilitating SMEs' access to international markets. Paper presented at the 2nd OECD conference of ministers responsible for small and medium-sized enterprises (SMEs), Istanbul, Turkey

Oviatt, B. M. and McDougall, P. P. (1994) Toward a theory of international new ventures. *Journal of International Business Studies* 25(1), 45–64

Peng, M. W. (2001) The resource-based view and international business. *Journal of Management* 27(6), 803

Peters, T. (1992) Rethinking scale. *California Management Review* 35(1), 7–29

Robson, M. J., Skarmeas, D., and Spyropoulou, S. (2006) Behavioral attributes and performance in international strategic alliances: Review and future directions. *International Marketing Review* 23(6), 585–609

Porter, M. E. (1991) Towards a dynamic theory of strategy. *Strategic Management Journal* 12 (Special Issue *Winter*), 95–117

Shan, W. and Song, J. (1997) Foreign direct investment and the sourcing of technological advantage: Evidence from the biotechnology industry. *Journal of International Business Studies* 28(2), 267–284

Simons, R. H. and Royer, S. (2006) Building bridges to successful alliance formation: Extending our understanding of performance related determinants focusing on small- and medium-sized businesses. *International Journal of Globalisation and Small Business* 1(3), 244–257

Smallbone, D., Labrianidis, L., Venesaar, U., Welter, F., and Zashev, P. (2007) Challenges and prospects of cross border cooperation in the context of EU enlargement, Deliverable 7: State of the Art Literature Review http://www.crossbordercoop.net/Publications/Integrated_lit_review.pdf (date accessed 15 Februar 2012)

Street, C. T. and Cameron, A.-F. (2007) External relationships and the small business: A review of small business alliance and network research. *Journal of Small Business Management* 45(2), 239–266

Welge, M. K. and Borghoff, T. (eds.) (2005) The strategic position of SMEs in the internationalisation process. Wiesbaden: Gabler

Westhead, P., Binks, M., Ucbasaran, D., and Wright, M. (2002) Internationalization of SMEs: A research note. *Journal of Small Business and Enterprise Development* 9, 38–48

Wolff, J. A. and Pett, T. L. (2000) Internationalization of small firms: An examination of export competitive patterns, firm size, and export performance. *Journal of Small Business Management* 38(2), 34–47

Wood, V. R., Pitta, D. A., and Franzak, F. J. (2009) Successful strategic alliances with international partners: Key issues for small- to medium-sized enterprises. *Journal of Business Innovation and Research* 3(3), 232–251

Wright, M., Westhead, P., and Ucbasaran, D. (2007) Internationalization of small and medium-sized enterprises (SMEs) and international entrepreneurship: A critique and policy implications. *Regional Studies* 41(7), 1013–1030

Yasai-Ardekani, M. and Nystrom, P. (1996) Designs for environmental scanning: Tests of a contingency theory. *Management Science* 42(2), 187–204

2 Characteristics and forms of SME cross-border cooperation: A classification approach

The forms and structure of international cooperation vary greatly, and, as "the prerequisites of successful co-operation are emphasized differently in different types of co-operation" (Varamaki and Vesalainen 2003, p. 27), SMEs planning or building a cooperative arrangement must know from the start the kind of cooperation they aim for. Describing the different forms of SME cross-border cooperation requires that we first specify what is meant by "cooperation", as a consistent conception of the term does not exist in either the literature or in practice. Different limitations have been discussed depending on the object of study, and overlaps between the concepts of "cooperation", "alliances", "partnerships", and "coalitions" have frequently appeared (Benkenstein and Beyer 2003).

We have broadly defined SME cross-border cooperation as a partnership between two or more SMEs from different countries created to pursue mutual interests by sharing resources and capabilities. In contrast, some authors define international cooperation more specifically, from a long term, formalised, and strategic perspective. Holtbrügge (2003) states, for example, that international cooperation can be seen as a formalised long-term collaboration between two or more firms from different countries with the purpose of realising individual goals in a joint manner, in which the legal and economic autonomy of all the partners is preserved. This long-term, formalised, and strategic form of cooperation in the international context is premised on the fact that the conditions for cooperating across borders differ from those of national cooperation.

In this book, we will use the terms "cooperation", "partnership", and "alliance" synonymously and will not limit cross-border cooperation to contract-based, formal, and long-term forms of cooperation but will focus on a broader perspective of partnership agreements.

In order to be able to fully understand the different forms of cooperation, we start by describing cooperation as an organisational form between market and hierarchy, followed by a systematisation of the possible classifications of cooperation, and finally presenting the typical forms of SME cross-border cooperation.

2.1 Cooperation, an organisational form between market and hierarchy

Transaction cost theory has had a profound influence on the analysis of inter-firm cooperation, as many analyses of the formalisation of domestic and international cooperation use key concepts drawn from this theory (Chen and Chen 2003) according to which, cooperation can be seen as a form of organisation lying between the two poles of market and hierarchy and able to minimise transaction costs for the firms. The transaction cost theory tries to explain why institutional structures other than markets or hierarchies may more efficiently govern economic activities (ibid). Williamson (1996) identifies transactions that (1) have uncertain outcomes, (2) occur frequently, and (3) require substantial investments that cannot be easily transferred normally take place within a hierarchy (i.e., within one firm). Exchanges that are (1) non-repetitive and (2) for which no transaction-specific investment is required normally take place in the market. As Powell (1990) argues, however, "I do not share the belief that the bulk of economic exchange fits comfortably at either of the poles of the market-hierarchy continuum" (p. 298). He furthermore describes cooperative forms of organisation, with their reciprocal patterns of communication and exchange, as alternatives to hierarchical or market-based governance structures.

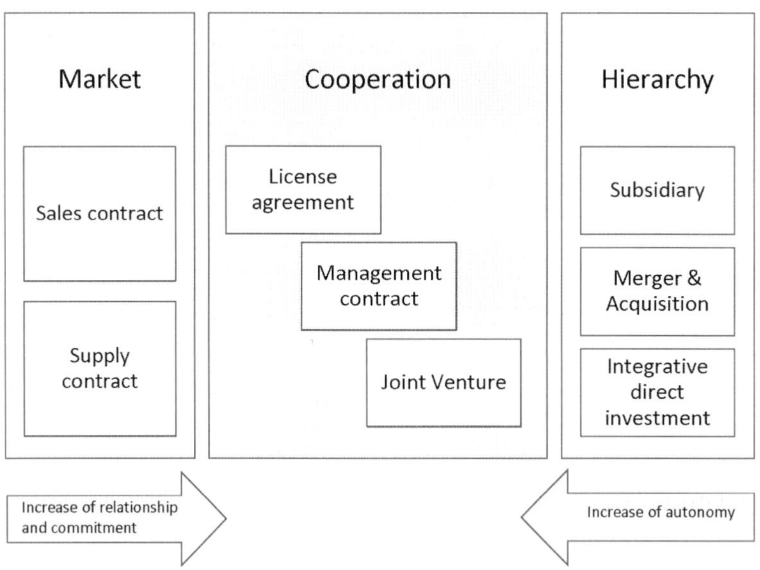

Fig. 2.1 Cooperation – between market and hierarchy

Source: Author, based on Weder (1989, p. 74), Powell (1990)

The figure above illustrates the different forms of SME cooperation (showing some typical forms of cooperation) on a continuum bounded by two contrary poles – market and hierarchy. In *market*, transactions are carried out by independent market players and coordinated by price mechanisms. In *hierarchy*, the market players cannot act independently given their economic positions, and their interactions are thus coordinated through instructions. Between these extreme poles lies *cooperation*. As the figure above shows, the dichotomy between market and hierarchy represents the primary exchange alternatives; cooperation and alliance are either closer to the market or to the hierarchy, depending on the magnitude of the transaction cost involved. The higher the transaction costs, the more hierarchical the cooperation will be in tendency (Chen and Chen 2003). According to transaction cost theory, firms should cooperate when the cooperation costs are perceived to be lower than the costs that would occur through the full integration of the given activity within the existing hierarchy and also lower than the costs on the market.

2.2 Characteristics of cooperation

Cooperation among SMEs can take different forms, ranging from very informal information- and knowledge-sharing cooperation to extremely formalised forms such as joint ventures. But to understand the different shapes cooperation can assume it is first necessary to understand the certain characteristics of cooperation types. In this section we therefore describe the characteristics of cooperation between SMEs based on five dimensions: (1) the direction of the cooperation, (2) the number of partners involved, (3) the geographic scope of the partnership, (4) the level of integration, and (5) the chosen form of governance.

Table 2.1 Characteristics of cooperation

Dimension	Characteristics		
Direction	Horizontal	Vertical	Lateral
Geographic scope	Regional	National	International
Number of partners	Bilateral	Multilateral/Network	
Level of integration	Type I (informal)	Type II (often informal)	Type III (formal)
Form of governance	Equity-based	Contract-based	Relationship-based

Source: Author

Direction of the cooperation

Cooperation between competing firms is different from cooperation between either firms working in the same value chain or those that are unconnected. We thus need to distinguish among three directions cooperation can take: (1) vertical cooperation, (2) horizontal cooperation, and (3) lateral cooperation.

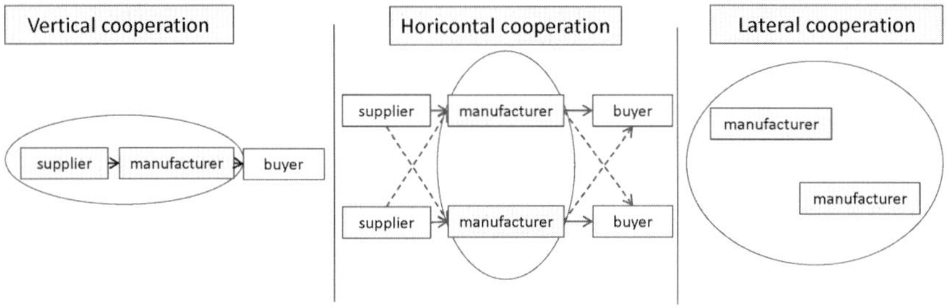

Fig. 2.2 Vertical, horizontal, and lateral cooperation

Source: Adapted from Hungenberg (1998), p. 482 (reprinted with permission of the publisher Fachverlag der Verlagsgruppe Handelsblatt GmbH zfbf/sbr)

There are important differences among vertical, horizontal, and lateral cooperation concerning the relations between the partners involved and the outcomes they seek (Rindfleisch 2000).

Vertical cooperation implies a buyer-seller relationship among the cooperation partners; their activities, which are subject to the cooperative agreement, are carried out by one of the parties, who then transfers output to the other parties in exchange for cash (García-Canal 1996). There are two types of vertical cooperation: (1) forward oriented, in which the cooperation initiative springs from the supplier who seeks to secure his sales, and (2) backward oriented, in which the cooperation is initiated by the manufacturer, who seeks to secure the supplies. Vertical cooperation can occur on different levels of a supply chain.

Horizontal cooperation can be described as the collaboration among firms active at the same level of the value chain. In this case, it is also possible that competitors cooperate. Horizontal cooperation involves identifying and exploiting win-win situations among firms active at the same level of the supply chain that aim to increase their performance jointly (Cruijssen et al. 2007). Bengtsson and Kock (1999) identified four different types of horizontal relationship: (1) co-existence between companies, which means that the relationship does not include economic exchange and the companies' goals are reached separately; (2) cooperation, where tight bonds exist between companies with common goals; (3) competition, characterised by an action-reaction pattern wherein companies rely on the same or comparable suppliers and target the same group of customers; and (4) coopetition, where goals are jointly stipulated for areas in which they cooperate while the firms continue to compete in other areas. If cooperation between competitors (coopetition) occurs, the firms need to jointly identify and exploit win-win situations to increase their performance despite being market competitors. A study by Rindfleisch (2000) suggests that firms who participate in horizontal alliances appear to be less trusting of their partners than firms in vertical alliances. The findings also show that trust plays a facilitating role in enhancing cooperation if there is low competitive intensity, as in vertical cooperation, but has little effect under highly competitive conditions, as in horizontal cooperation.

Lateral cooperation, sometimes referred to as "diagonal cooperation", is the third form of cooperation, and describes the partnership among firms that are not working in the same value chain and are sometimes not even coming from the same industry. This kind of cooperation is established if firms offer products or services that complement each other and for which common marketing might be useful.

The number of partners involved

Another way to classify cooperation is looking at the number of partners involved. The size of the cooperation can be seen as a decisive factor in how cooperation should be organised, as the legal and organisational forms of partnerships depend on the size of the cooperation (European Commission 2003). The number of partners is influenced by factors such as the reason to cooperate, the form of cooperation, and the organisational capacity of the cooperating firms. The importance of cooperation for an SME also influences the number of partners involved, as studies show that SMEs usually have fewer than three partners in their most important projects (ibid).

Bilateral cooperation between two firms can be characterised by the fact that the two partners directly coordinate the partnership and react straight to each other's behaviour. Examples of bilateral cooperation agreements include technological and patent exchange agreements (Morschett 2003). A study carried out by Hoffmann and Schlosser (2001) indicates that the rate of cooperation success lowered when more than one partner was involved; they assume that *multilateral cooperation* is more difficult to manage and that SMEs, which usually have less experience in alliance management than large companies, are therefore particularly prone to problems in extensive cooperation. There appears to be a practical limit to the number of partners with which SMEs can efficiently interact. Too many partnerships can lead to an overdose of partnership relationships, as sufficient time is needed for cooperation to be effective (European Commission 2003). The results of the ENSR survey (ibid) confirm that most SMEs cooperate with only a few partners; two thirds of the firms had fewer than seven partners, and about 30% had one or two partners; only about 20% cooperated with more than ten. The study also shows that larger SMEs typically have more partners than small SMEs, which can be attributed to the amount of time and capacity large SMEs can dedicate to the cooperation. Their larger administrative capacity might be another reason why large SMEs can more easily handle a higher number of partners (ibid).

Although the bulk of alliances are bilateral, it is important to take the broader context of multilateral collaboration into account (Doz and Hamel 1998), as bilateral cooperative agreements form the basis for *multilateral networks*. Multilateral networks are becoming more and more important for SMEs; according to the OECD (2004), cooperation within networks is by far the most important channel of knowledge sharing and exchange. Cooperation also leads to further cooperation: many firms start with bilateral cooperation and then develop their cooperation into other fields and with other partners. According to Baird et al. (1993), "[s]mall firms may have special challenges in finding amenable network members due to lack of contacts in the industry or international environment" (p. 19). Thus, for SMEs entering into a first cooperative agreement, it is much easier to get involved in other cooperative agreements.

Most SME cooperation classifications have occurred on a general level, rather than with a focus on multilateral cooperation (Varamaki and Vesalainen 2003). Varamäki and Vesalainen propose the five different types of multilateral SME cooperation shown below.

Table 2.2 Different types of multilateral SME cooperation

Types of multilateral SME cooperation	
Development circle Development circles are regular and purposeful meetings of entrepreneurs with the intention to learn from each other and transfer knowledge through discussions and practical examples. There are no strategic aims, and almost no financial involvement is necessary. This kind of cooperation can be described as highly informal.	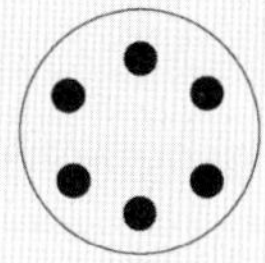
Loose cooperative circle In loose cooperation circles, the participating enterprises share some resources (i.e. human resources, equipment). The SMEs use this joint resource but do not run a joint business. Cooperative efforts are realised only at the operative level. This loose cooperation type requires a certain level of trust among the partners.	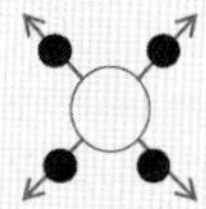
Strategic alliance (project group) A strategic alliance is a project group aiming to develop a joint business by combining the resources and capabilities of the SMEs involved; this is therefore an intensive arrangement. A project group is usually based on a written contractual agreement, the partners' strong commitment is essential.	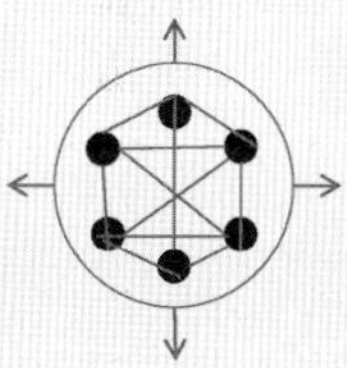
Joint venture In a joint venture, a jointly owned firm is set up by the cooperation partners with the aim of starting, developing, and running a new joint business and finding new business opportunities together. One advantage lies in the ability to share risks. A joint venture is very formal, and a careful partner selection is essential. Trust and commitment are also very important.	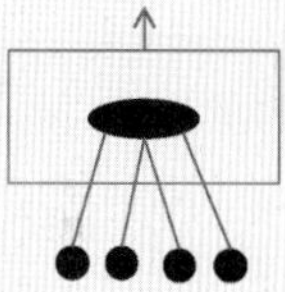
Joint unit A joint unit is the most formal type of cooperation. The cooperating enterprises set up a new firm and place themselves inside it, meaning that the firms allow their own images as independent companies to fade, though the companies still exist. Trust and commitment have to be very high, and a careful partner selection is the critical success factor in building a joint unit.	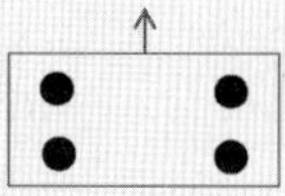

Source: Figures based on Varamäki and Vesalainen (2003, p. 34); text summarised from Varamäki and Vesalainen (2003, p. 34–40)

Varamäki and Vesalainen (2003): Modelling different types of multilateral co-operation between SMEs. Entrepreneurship & Regional Development 15(1), p. 34. Reprinted with permission of the publisher Taylor & Francis Ltd, http://www.tandf.co.uk/journals.

Table 2.2 shows the different forms of multilateral SME cooperation. The authors propose that there is a constant development across these cooperation types and that each type thus has the potential to eventually develop into a more (or less) intense form of cooperation.

The geographic scope

Cooperation can be regional, national, or international in scope, depending on the origin of the partners. Currently, SMEs prefer *national cooperation* and usually cooperate with partners from the same region or country. The ENSR study reveals that more than 80% of all cooperating SMEs are cooperating only with SMEs from their own country (European Commission 2003). Also *regional clusters* are becoming increasingly prominent. These clusters are geographic agglomerations of firms in the same or related industries, often seen in the form of (1) industrial SME districts, (2) concentrations of high technology firms characterised by the development and use of joint technologies, and (3) production systems that bundle around large hub firms and their local suppliers and spin-offs (Smallbone et al. 2007). Clusters can include horizontal and vertical cooperation types. The advantages of taking part in clusters include access to specialised human resources and suppliers, knowledge spillovers, the pressure to achieve higher performance through head-to-head competition, and learning from close interaction with cooperation partners and customers (ibid).

However, especially in the last few years, *international cooperation* has become increasingly important due to changing economic and legal conditions, the globalisation of markets, and new information and communication technologies. Nevertheless, even firms involved in international cooperation often stick to partners in close geographic proximity. Thus, Smallbone observes, "[w]ith respect to internationalisation of SMEs, geographical distance is of importance, as firms tend to internationalise within their region" (Smallbone et al. 2007, p. 17). Huber found that the probability of not cooperating increases with the distance to the closest potential cooperation partner (Huber 2003). In general, though, the role of geographic distance in cross-border networks should not be overemphasised, as Huber's study also highlighted that the importance of geographic distance is minor relative to that of other factors, such as cooperation experience and firm size (2003).

The level of integration

To structure cooperation according to the level of integration, we stick to the classification of Lambert et al. (1999), who identify three main types of cooperation depending on the level of integration. Although these types were designed for vertical supply chain relationships, they can be translated to accommodate cooperation in general. *Type I* cooperation consists of mutually recognised partners who jointly coordinate their activities and planning. Duration, strength, and closeness are limited within this form of cooperation, which is short-term and mostly involves a single activity. *Type II* is a cooperation in which the partners do not merely coordinate but also start to integrate part of their business planning. It is mostly long-term and involves multiple functions and segments of each company. *Type III*, often referred to as a "strategic alliance", is a form of cooperation where the partners have integrated their operations significantly. It usually has no fixed end date. Whereas types I and II are often characterised by informal agreements between the cooperation partners, type III is usually rather formal, with a stronger sense of common goals and challenges than the other types. In explaining the terms "formal" and "informal", it can be said that transactions and commitments within a cooperation based on the written word and contracts are formal and, when based on the spoken word and trust, are informal. The ENSR Survey (European Commission 2003) shows that, although half of European SMEs are currently involved in some form of cooperative relationships with other enterprises, only about 25% have established some kind of formal agreement. The smaller companies are, the more they favour informal and loose forms of cooperation, especially those forms of cooperation characterised by low intensity, such as bidding consortia or the joint use of equipment or machinery (Schmidt and Kiefer 2003). Intense forms of cooperation like joint ventures are often less interesting for SMEs due to their resource constraints and their fear of losing independence.

The governance form

As we have seen, cooperation need not always take the form of a contractual agreement signed by all partners involved; informal, relationship-based cooperation, and other arrangements can also be feasible modes of international cooperation. In this book, we classify cooperation into three broad categories: (1) equity-based, (2) contract-based, and (3) relationship-based forms of cooperation (Kale and Singh 2009): In *equity-based cooperation* such as joint ventures, all partners hold shares in a separate and jointly owned firm, and the cooperating partners jointly share the profits and losses of the business. In a *non-equity or contract-based partnership*, the cooperating firms agree to work together to develop, manufacture, or sell products or services, but they do not hold equity positions in each other. Instead, the cooperation is managed through the use of various forms of contract (Barney 2002). The contract-based form of cooperation generally preserves the independence of the firms involved but still formalises the terms of interaction, the contributions of the parties involved, and the procedures for terminating the cooperation. The third form of governance mechanism is a sole reliance on trust, with no formal equity exchange or contractual arrangement. Such a *relationship-based cooperation* has specific advantages for SMEs, as its transaction costs are often lower compared to equity or contract-based partnerships.

When cooperation is formed, the partnering firms need to decide on their governance structure; they need to determine the general arrangements of working together and the mechanism they want to use to coordinate and monitor their common venture. Therefore, choosing a governance form is one of the main tasks in cooperation management and will be explained in more detail in Chapter 13.

2.3 Forms of SME cross-border cooperation

Changes in the business environment and a trend towards internationalisation have forced SMEs to consider forms of integration deeper than mere international trade. This leads to the development of different forms of international cooperation (OECD 2001). The aforementioned characteristics of cooperation influence the form in which partnerships occur and also have an effect on which form of partnership is chosen by the cooperating firms.

As we focus on cross-border cooperation, we present a short description of the typical forms of SME cooperation specific to the international context in the following table.

Table 2.3 Forms of international SME cooperation

Form	Characterisation
Indirect export and export cooperation	Firms using indirect export try to find partners abroad with the necessary market knowledge to help them gain access to new markets. Partners can be exporting

Form	Characterisation
	agents, sales agents or trading houses. The advantages of this form of cooperation include the takeover of export risks, the reduction of necessary personal and financial resources, and the chance to overcome a lack of knowledge of the foreign market. Drawbacks include leaving part of the profit with the export agent and lacking direct contact with the foreign customers, which could harm subsequent direct market cultivation. Another possibility is building export cooperation through the pooling of firms with a similar or complementary array of products or services who have decided to promote their offers jointly in the new market. The benefits of the joint use of export and distribution channels are cost reduction and knowledge sharing. A disadvantage is the dependence on the cooperation partner and the risk that one's product will not be promoted adequately.
International licensing	Licensing means granting permission to use intellectual property rights such as trademarks, patents, or technology to a cooperation partner under defined conditions. The licensee takes over the production and is obliged in return to pay licensing fees to the licensor. Licensing provides an efficient organisation of technology transactions and the protection or building of competitive advantages for both cooperation partners. On the positive side, licensing helps save management and capital resources and can open up new or blocked foreign markets. One key disadvantage is that, once the license agreement is over, the licensee may become a direct competitor who may use the gained know-how against the former cooperation partner. It is also difficult for the licensor to control the quality of the licensee's product.
International subcontracting agreements	In this form of cooperation, a partner in a foreign country (usually from a low-wage region) produces products on behalf of another company. The advantages of international subcontracting lie in the lower costs of labour and material in the foreign country and the avoidance of high costs of export to the foreign market and of high production costs in the home country. The possible loss of know-how to a potential competitor is one major threat of international subcontracting.

Form	Characterisation
International project cooperation	International project cooperation is mostly seen in infrastructure development, industrial plant construction, institutional foundations, and common service provision. Especially in the European context, project-based SME cooperation in research and development is becoming more common. A project can be carried out by either a general contractor or a consortium structure. A general contractor determines all business activities and the cooperation itself and is liable for the success of the cooperation project. In a consortium, all partners work together independently but under the control of a consortium manager, who is held responsible only for his own liabilities.
International strategic alliances	International strategic alliances can be seen as a typical form of international cooperation. Spekman et al. (1998) define strategic alliances as "a close, long-term, mutually beneficial agreement between two or more partners in which resources, knowledge, and capabilities are shared with the objective of enhancing the competitive position of each partner" (p. 748). International strategic alliances enable firms to exploit economies of scale through the joint use of know-how, resources, and capabilities. On the negative side, strategic alliances require intensive cooperation, and a partner's ability to act independently can be restricted. Furthermore, the cooperating firms need to consider the potential for opportunistic behaviour.
International joint ventures	Joint ventures are alliances with the highest grade of partner commitment. A joint venture is an agreement by which cooperation partners agree to develop, for a certain time, a new entity and new assets by contributing their own capital. The venture can be set up for one specific aim or a continuing form of business cooperation. Joint ventures can be seen as a promising market entry strategy for SMEs, given their limited resources and knowledge of foreign markets. According to a study carried out among German and UK SMEs with joint ventures in China, a joint venture is primarily a device for obtaining access to resources from other organisations and is particularly favoured in countries whose national governments are attempting to restrict foreign ownership and where local expertise and con-

Form	Characterisation
	nections are seen as particularly important for facilitating market entry (Kirby and Kaiser 2003).
International virtual enterprises	A virtual enterprise can be defined as a temporary alliance in which businesses come together to share resources, skills, and competences to better respond to business opportunities. This form of cooperation is supported by computer networks. Consisting with the characteristics of SMEs, it is usually informally organised and often adopts non-hierarchical, lean, and modular configurations wherein every member makes some proprietary sub-process available to the cooperation partners. Virtual enterprises are driven by specific market opportunities and often falter after the business opportunity is over.

Source: Summary by the author adapted from Perlitz and Seger (2003)

Summary on the characteristics and forms of SME cross-border cooperation

1. Familiarizing oneself with the different forms of cooperation can help in better understanding their respective requirements.
2. Transaction cost theory can be used to analyse the different forms of cooperation. According to this theory, cooperation can be seen as a form of organisation lying between the two poles: market and hierarchy. In markets, transactions are carried out by independent market players and are coordinated by a price mechanism. In hierarchy, the market players are bound to each other, unable to act independently, and are coordinated through instruction. Cooperation is either closer to market or to hierarchy, depending on the magnitude of the transaction costs involved.
3. Cooperative ventures are shaped by different characteristics. It is necessary to understand these different characteristics because they influence the organisation of each partnership. The characteristics of cooperation can be described by five dimensions: (1) the direction of cooperation, (2) the geographic scope, (3) the number of partners involved, (4) the level of integration, and (5) the chosen form of governance.
4. As cooperation between competing firms is different from cooperation between firms working on different levels of the same value chain or between

formerly unconnected firms, it is necessary to distinguish between the three directions cooperation can take: (1) vertical, (2) horizontal, or (3) lateral. Another way to classify cooperation is by examining the number of partners involved. Also, the distinction between regional, national, and international cooperation is necessary. When forming a cooperation, the partners further need to decide on the level of integration and the governance structure of their cooperative venture.

5. Cooperation among SMEs can take different forms, depending on the circumstances that led to their creation. They can range from very informal information- and knowledge-sharing cooperation to extremely formalised varieties, such as joint ventures. Typical forms of international SME cooperation are indirect export and export cooperation, licensing, subcontracting agreements, project cooperation, strategic alliances, joint ventures, and virtual enterprises.

References

Baird, I. S., Lyles, M. A., and Orris, J. B. (1993) Alliances and networks: cooperative strategies for small businesses. *Mid-American Journal of Business* 1(1), 17–23

Barney, J. B. (2002) Gaining and sustaining competitive advantage, 2nd edn. New Jersey: Prentice Hall

Bengtsson, M. and Kock, S. (1999) Cooperation and competition in relationships between competitors in business networks. *Journal of Business and Industrial Marketing* 14(3), 178–194

Benkenstein, M. and Beyer, T. (2003) Kooperationen im Marketing. In: Zentes, J., Swoboda, B., Morschett, D. (eds.), Kooperationen, Allianzen und Netzwerke: Grundlagen-Ansätze-Perspektiven. Wiesbaden: Gabler, 705–726

Chen, H.-L. and Chen, T.-J. (2003) Governance structures in strategic alliances: Transaction cost versus resource-based perspective. *Journal of World Business* 38(1), 1–14

Cruijssen, F., Dullaert, W., and Fleuren, H. (2007) Horizontal cooperation in transport and logistics: A literature review. *Transportation Journal* 46(3), 22–39

Doz, Y. L. and Hamel, G. (1998) Alliance advantage: The art of creating calue through partnering. Boston, MA: Harvard University Press

European Commission (2003) SMEs and cooperation. In European Commission (ed.), Observatory of European SMEs (Vol. 5). http://ec.europa.eu/enterprise/policies/sme/files/analysis/doc/smes_observatory_2003_report5_en.pdf (date accessed 1 July 2012)

García-Canal, E. (1996) Contractual form in domestic and international strategic alliances. *Organization Studies* 17(5), 773–794

Hoffmann, W. and Schlosser, R. (2001) Success factors of strategic alliances in small and medium-sized enterprises – An empirical survey. *Long Range Planning* 34(3), 357–381

Holtbrügge, D. (2003) Management internationaler strategischer Allianzen. In: Zentes, J., Swoboda, B., Morschett, D. (eds.), Kooperationen, Allianzen und Netzwerke. Grundlagen – Ansätze – Perspektiven. Wiesbaden: Gabler, 1182–1201

Huber, P. (2003) On the determinants of cross-border cooperation of Austrian firms with Central and Eastern European partners. *Regional Studies* 37(9), 947–955

Hungenberg, H. (1998) Strategische Allianzen in der Telekommunikation. *Schmalenbachs Zeitschrift für Betriebswirtschaftliche Forschung* 50(5), 479–498

Kale, P. and Singh, H. (2009) Managing strategic alliances: What do we know now, and where do we go from here? *Academy of Management Perspectives* 23(3), 45–62

Kirby, D. A. and Kaiser, S. (2003) Joint ventures as an internationalisation strategy for SMEs. *Small Business Economics* 21(3), 229–242

Lambert, D., Emmelhainz, M., and Gardner, J. (1999) Building successful logistics partnerships. *Journal of Business Logistics* 20(1), 165–181

Morschett, D. (2003) Formen von Kooperationen, Allianzen und Netzwerken. In: Zentes, J., Swoboda, B., Morschett, D. (eds.), Kooperationen, Allianzen und Netzwerke: Grundlagen – Ansätze – Perspektiven. Wiesbaden: Gabler, 387–413

OECD (2001) Enhancing SME competitivness. OECD proceedings of the OECD Bologna Minsterial Conference. Paris: OECD Publishing

OECD (2004) Networks, partnerships, clusters and intellectual property rights: Opportunities and challenges for innovative SMEs in a global economy. Paper presented at the 2nd OECD conference of ministers responsible for small and medium-sized enterprises (SMEs), Istanbul, Turkey

Perlitz, M. and Seger, F. (2003) Internationalisierung durch Kooperation. In: Zentes, J., Swoboda, B., Morschett, D. (eds.), Kooperation, Allianzen und Netzwerke: Grundlagen – Ansätze – Perspektiven. Wiesbaden: Gabler, 515–542

Powell, W. (1990) Neither market nor hierarchy: Network forms of organization. *Research in Organizational Behavior* 12(3), 295–336

Rindfleisch, A. (2000) Organizational trust and interfirm cooperation: An examination of horizontal versus vertical alliances. *Marketing Letters* 11(1), 81–95

Schmidt, A. and Kiefer, C. (2003) Kooperation zwischen mittelständischen Unternehmen. In: Zentes, J., Swoboda, B. and Morschett, D. (eds.), Kooperationen, Allianzen und Netzwerke. Grundlagen – Ansätze – Perspektiven. Wiesbaden: Gabler, 1259–1282

Smallbone, D., Labrianidis, L., Venesaar, U., Welter, F., and Zashev, P. (2007) Challenges and prospects of cross border cooperation in the context of EU enlargement. Deliverable 7: State of the art literature review, http://www.crossbordercoop.net/Publications/Integrated_lit_review.pdf (date accessed 15 February 2012)

Spekman, R. E., Forbes, T. M., Isabella, L. A., and Macavoy, T. C. (1998) Alliance management: A view from the past and a look to the future. *Journal of Management Studies* 35(6), 747–772

Varamaki, E. and Vesalainen, J. (2003) Modelling different types of multilateral co-operation between SMEs. *Entrepreneurship and Regional Development* 15(1), 27–47

Weder, R. (1989) Joint Venture. Rüegger Verlag Zürich/Chur

Williamson, O. E. (1996) Transaction cost economics and organizational theory. In: Smelser, N. J. and Swedberg, R. (eds.), The Handbook of Economic Sociology. Princeton: Princeton University Press, 77–107

3 Benefits and challenges of SME cross-border cooperation

Cross-border cooperation is preceded by the decisions of at least two partners in different countries to enter into a collaborative venture. While deciding, managers first need to be clear about what they expect from cooperating. Cooperation can result in both tangible and intangible collaborative benefits: tangible benefits include additional profits, access to a new market, increased market share, and competitive advantages; intangible benefits can be reaped through learning skills and competences, ways of cooperating effectively, and "how to learn from collaborations" (Simonin 1997, p. 1154). Cooperation also carries considerable disadvantages, however. Managers and scholars know that cooperating to achieve the expected benefits and objectives is a managerially challenging and costly endeavour (White and Siu-Yun Lui 2005).

In this chapter, we present the major motives and expectations of SMEs entering into cross-border cooperation and the potential barriers, risks, and challenges involved in this international venture.

3.1 Benefits of cooperation: Reasons to cooperate across borders

Firms join forces for various reasons, among them are the following (Kale and Singh 2009; Johansson and Ylinenpää 2006):

- to increase their market power;
- to obtain efficiency gains;
- to reduce risk (e.g., by sharing investments);
- to get access to key resources and capabilities;
- to enter new markets.

The last reason, gaining access to new markets, is particularly relevant for cross-border cooperation, in which one partner seeks to obtain the local experience, know-how, and relationships of the other(s).

As we have seen in Chapter 1, new market access is a salient motive for SMEs entering into cross-border cooperation (Spence et al. 2008). However, SMEs may collaborate across borders for other reasons also; these fall into one of the following four categories (Chen et al. 2008):

- *Strategy-oriented reasons*, with partners trying to achieve their own strategic goals, such as gaining market share.
- *Cost-oriented reasons*, with the goal of increasing efficiency and reducing the partners' cost base, for instance, by leveraging economies of scale or scope or through cooperative process optimisation (Johansson and Ylinenpää 2006).
- *Resource-oriented reasons*, focusing on key resources (such as capital or relationships) that partners try to obtain from cooperating.
- *Learning-oriented reasons*, with access to know-how and technology playing a key role in the decision to engage in a partnership.

The underlying rationale behind all these reasons to cooperate is gaining competitive advantage. Partners can use cooperation as a source of competitive advantage, for example, by exploiting synergies (in the form of economies of scale and scope), an increased awareness of the competition, a lower dependence on others, or an enhanced competitive capacity gained through the combination of key resources (Street and Cameron 2007).

By pooling their strengths, SMEs can (a) exploit market opportunities otherwise closed to them (Das and Teng 2000), (b) gain access to the resources their partners possess and that can be leveraged through joint use, (c) reduce costs through efficiency gains, and (d) reduce individual risks by sharing them. We call the first two categories of motivation for entering cooperation *seeking motives*, as companies either seek access to markets or to resources that would otherwise be unavailable to them or be very costly to obtain. The other two categories of motive can be termed *reduction motives*, as SMEs entering into cooperation try to reduce either costs or risks. An overview of the main reasons for cooperation is presented in Fig. 3.1.

As mentioned, one of the main motives for entering into cross-border cooperation is the intention to find new markets for one's product or services, subsumed in our framework under the term *market-seeking motives*. A study among UK companies found that the top five reasons for entering cross-border cooperation were all associated with market-seeking motives: gaining presence in a new market, faster market entry, facilitating international expansion, competing against a common competitor, and maintaining market position (Glaister and Buckley 1996); only the sixth and seventh were linked to other categories, such as gaining access to technology or achieving economies of scale. Market-seeking motives might be so salient because, while many SMEs have distinct advantages (in technology, for example), "small businesses often do not have the in-house resources to identify or go directly to foreign customers" (Rowden 2001).

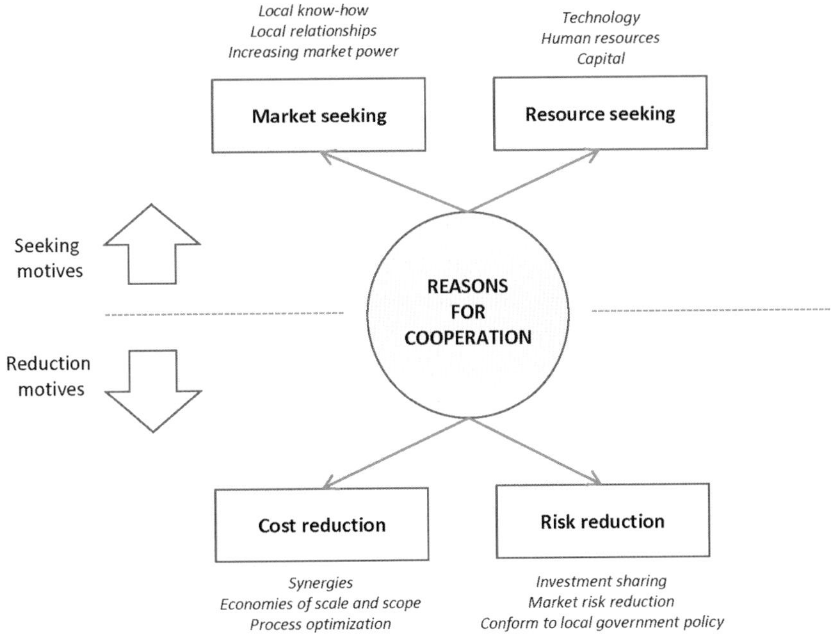

Fig. 3.1 Reasons for cooperation

Source: Author

Market-seeking motives are the main drivers of international marketing cooperation, which SMEs enter to expand sales channels, share experience and know-how, increase market share, promote sales, accelerate the rate of return on marketing investments, and enter overseas markets (Chen and Huang 2004). Firms need local know-how and, especially, local relationships in order to effectively sell their offers in foreign markets. Finding a local cooperation partner can considerably ease the process of forming relationships with customers and other key players in a target market abroad. Forming alliances with local partners can for example positively affect the profitability of joint ventures formed by SMEs, as they are a source of the local knowledge required to be successful in a different cultural and institutional environment (Lu and Beamish 2006).

Even SMEs with access to a market often lack the resources necessary to exploit it. In this case, *resource-seeking motives* are particularly relevant when deciding whether to enter into cross-border cooperation. Capital shortage is a particularly pressing problem for small companies but can be overcome through joint investment with cooperation partners. A partner can also bring technology to a partnership or the specific know-how of its employees.

Another category of reason for cooperating is *cost-reduction motives*. Cooperation allows SMEs to achieve collective efficiencies, by, for example, the joint use of resources, achieving economies of scale, or production efficiencies gained through the coordination of processes (Mesquita and Lazzarini 2008; Schmitz 1995). These collective efficiencies can also lead to cost reductions that enable the cooperation partners to access new foreign markets. Cost reductions are also possible if the comparative advantage of each partner is used, when, for example, partners with different production sites produce components at the site with the lowest production cost (Glaister and Buckley 1996).

Cooperation can also reduce risks for all partners involved. *Risk-reduction motives* include the opportunity to share investment risk, to diversify into new product/market combinations, to enjoy a faster market entry and thus a shorter payback period for the investment, and gain "cost subadditivity", in which the cost of the investment is lower for the partnership than if each partner had invested separately (Contractor and Lorange 1988). In addition, entering a foreign market can be less risky with a local partner with a good understanding of the market conditions. Close links with local companies might also be needed to conform to the host government's policies (Glaister and Buckley 1996). Cross-border alliances are therefore often formed to "transcend economic, legal, and cultural boundaries" (Dickson et al. 2006, p. 495).

Given the main drivers for cooperation, three forms of cooperation can be identified (García-Canal et al. 2002):

- *independent local alliances*, with the primary motive of combining the technology and/or products of a multinational company with the local market knowledge and resources of a firm in the target market;
- *multi-country (or global) alliances*, in which firms seek to coordinate their strategies and operations in several different target markets at the same time; and
- *competence-building alliances* to improve international competitiveness, through, for example, cost reduction, by blocking competitors or combining and exploiting key capabilities.

3.2 Barriers to cross-border cooperation

We have seen that the reasons for entering into cooperation are manifold. But alliances do not hold only advantages for the cooperation partners, but also involve considerable barriers and risks, which need to be considered before deciding to initiate cooperation across borders.

To give an overview of the common obstacles to SME cooperation, we present the main barriers in the table below, which is based on the findings of Estanyol Casals (2011), who has identified what the literature considers the internal and external barriers to SME cooperation. To address international alliances, we added the barriers specifically related to cross-border cooperation.

Table 3.1 Barriers to SME cooperation

Firm internal barriers	Firm external barriers
Problems finding the right cooperation partner	Eventual poor efficiency of cooperation
Lack of strategic diagnosis if cooperation is on the right track	Lack of efficient mechanism to monitor and evaluate cooperation
Scarcity of resources to offer	Competition with larger firms with more competences for cooperation
Objectives and type of cooperation are not clear at the beginning	Difficulty of managing and organising cooperation
Reluctance to share knowledge and know-how	Inability to overcome trust, credibility, and compromise problems
Lack of skilled personnel for cooperation	Lack of commitment of the cooperation partner
Inability to devise new business opportunities	Language and cultural differences
Disinclination to invest in cooperation	External conditions hindering cooperation (legal, political, economic, or institutional conditions)

Source: Adapted from Estanyol Casals (2011)

Let us consider the issue from an enterprise perspective. The European Commission (2003) carried out a study (the ENSR Enterprise Survey) among European SMEs that asked them to name the most significant barriers to cooperation (see Table 3.2).

Table 3.2 Barriers to cooperation from an enterprise perspective

Barriers to cooperation	SMEs EU-15
Wish to remain independent	39%
Lack of information on suitable partners	16%
Do not wish to disclose sensitive information	15%
Restriction imposed by taxation or legal regulation	15%
High risk involved	12%
Language and cultural barriers	3%

Source: ENSR Enterprise Survey (European Commission 2003)

The results of this study show that the most important barriers to cooperation are the wish to maintain independence, the lack of information about cooperation partners, the wish to withhold sensitive information from other SMEs, restrictions imposed by taxation or legal regulation, and the high risks involved. Language and cultural barriers play only a minor role, possibly explained by the fact that this study did not focus on international cooperation but rather cooperation largely occurring between national partners.

Looking at the specific perceived barriers to international cooperation, the results of a study of van Elk and van Lin (2005) carried out among SMEs from the Netherlands differ slightly from the results of the ENSR study. In this study, SMEs again see "taxes and legislation" and the "lack of information on partners" as important barriers, but "language and cultural barriers" are also mentioned as a main barrier to international cooperation, followed by the "wish to remain independent" and the wish to "protect information".

In the following section, we describe the main risks firms need to consider when deciding whether to enter into a partnership and the main challenges involved in cooperating across borders.

3.3 Potential risks and disadvantages of cross-border cooperation

Cooperating is generally a risky endeavour, as, in addition to performance risk, it also entails relational risk; the latter, a unique feature of collaborative strategies, refers to the possibility that the partner firms will act opportunistically or lack real commitment to the partnership (Das and Teng

1999). There are two basic kinds of potential disadvantages for firms deciding to enter into cooperation (Lei and Slocum Jr. 1991; Moen et al. 2010):

- First is the possibility of creating new competitors if the partner firms decide to act opportunistically. This is a particularly serious problem for SMEs partnering with large enterprises. Due to their superior resource endowments, larger firms can exploit a partnership to the detriment of the smaller partner.
- The other main disadvantage is the risk of becoming highly dependent on the partner, thus increasing the risk to the firm and reducing its strategic options. Once again, SMEs are particularly susceptible to this risk, as the likelihood that a smaller company will come to depend on a larger one is generally higher than vice versa. Powerful technological advantages or patents, however, can also place SMEs in a powerful position in this game of mutual dependence (Kelley and Rice 2002).

Elmuti and Kathawala (2001) have compiled another list of challenges and problems that partners may face in strategic cooperative endeavours and which are applicable to cross-border cooperation:

- Clashes of culture and personality between the alliance partners;
- A lack of clear alliance objectives and common strategy;
- A lack of coordination between the partners' management teams;
- Differences in diligence and attitude between the partners;
- The risk of a partner's opportunistic behaviour ("relational risk"); and
- Performance risk – the possibility that the alliance will fail despite the efforts of the partners.

One type of risk specific to cross-border cooperation is the risk of working with culturally different partners (Lee et al. 2008). Without prior experience with partners from a certain culture, it can be difficult to assess how they will react in different situations.

A further potential pitfall for SMEs lies in trying to establish committed relationships with many partners in several different foreign markets. In their research among SMEs in Greece and the Caribbean, Nakos and Brouthers (2008) found that those companies who concentrated on a few key markets and worked with only a few close partners outperformed companies with multiple partnerships across many different countries. These results could be explained by the limited resources that SMEs have for effectively managing their cooperation. Therefore, a focus on very few close cross-border relationships can be more effective for SMEs than trying to work with many different partners in many countries.

3.4 Challenges of cross-border cooperation

Beyond the risks associated with cross-border cooperation, there are also challenges that need to be addressed by the cooperating firms. From our perspective, the most important challenges are (1) finding the right cooperation partner and performing effective cooperation management, (2) reducing the cooperation's transaction costs and preventing the partners' opportunistic behaviour, (3) protecting the firm's key resources, and (4) managing conflicts in an intercultural setting.

Finding the right cooperation partner and performing effective cooperation management

Cooperation management can assist in overcoming most risks associated with cross-border cooperation. These risks include: (1) the risk of failing to select the right cooperation partner, (2) the risk that the partners will have non-complementary goals, (3) the risk of not creating a distinct value over pure market relationships, and (4) the risk that problems with the partnership will be recognised only when the cooperation fails. As regards correct *partner selection*, complementarity is a key to successful cooperation. In cross-border cooperation, complementarity comes in three different forms – resource complementarity (in which firms join their distinct resources), goal complementarity, and cultural complementarity. Potential partners should also be assessed for *prior cooperation experience*. In a six-country study, it was observed that, in SMEs with prior alliance experience, a higher satisfaction with the current performance of the firm positively correlated with the tendency to engage in new cooperation (Lohrke et al. 2006). These findings were supported by Lai et al. (2010), who found that cooperative experience is a critical factor in the success of international strategic alliances, suggesting that the lessons learnt from international alliances should be made explicit by writing them down and disseminating them within the organisation.

Cooperation makes sense only if it *supports the attainment of the strategic objectives of all partners involved*. Thus, complementary goals are a necessary prerequisite. Goals can be related in three forms – competitively, cooperatively, and independently (Wong et al. 2005). When goals are perceived as competitive, one can only win at the expense of the other. Cooperative goals, on the other hand, are complementary: their attainment is conducive to the success of all parties involved. Independent goals are not related to each other and thus do not have the potential to trigger any competitive or cooperative behaviour. Wong et al. (2005) observe a positive correlation in partnerships between competitive goals and opportunistic behaviour, the pursuit of one's self-interest at the expense of an exploited partner. When partners had cooperative goals, however, opportunistic behaviour tended to be considerably lower.

To be effective, cooperative partnerships also need to *produce a distinct value over pure market relationships* (Dyer and Singh 1998). According to Dyer and Singh's "relational view of competitive advantage", such value (or "relational rent") can be obtained by investing in assets specific to the partnership, pursuing joint learning via the exchange of knowledge, creating unique products or services through the combination of scarce and complementary resources and capabilities, or achieving transaction costs lower than other forms of exchange.

Moreover, it is necessary to introduce an *effective control and monitoring system* to identify problems or potential opportunistic behaviour early enough to allow adequate reactions and therefore preserve cooperation.

Reducing the transaction costs by preventing opportunistic behaviour and building trust

We have seen that cooperative agreements are often characterised by the inherent instability arising from uncertainty regarding the behaviour of the cooperation partner(s) and the absence of a higher authority that could help ensure compliance (Parkhe 1993). The cooperation partners need each other, but this need intersects with uncertainty and creates vulnerability to opportunistic behaviour (ibid). Opportunistic behaviour could include "shirking, appropriating the partner's resources, distorting information, harboring hidden agendas, and delivering unsatisfactory products or services" (Das and Teng 1999, p. 51). A partner firm's hidden agenda might consist of an intention to extract the other partner's know-how or take them over (Das and Teng 2001).

In analysing the challenge of opportunistic behaviour, research on alliance management suggests two managerial requirements – the need to control and the need to cooperate. Control is applied to minimise the likelihood of suffering from a partner's opportunistic behaviour; cooperation is meant to achieve the common or individual objectives of cooperation. Managing the control and cooperation aspects is not costless, as successful cooperation requires that the partners communicate, establish and maintain an inter-organisational interface, and make internal adjustments in response to the cooperation partners' actions or to changes in the external environment (White and Siu-Yun Lui 2005). These costs of negotiating, monitoring, and enforcing a contract to ensure against the possibility of opportunistic behaviour are called "transaction costs" (Hill 1990) and arise from the task-related coordination needs and social integration necessary for the combining of resources and integration of activities in the course of undertaking a joint task (White and Siu-Yun Lui 2005).

Parkhe (1993) argues that successful cooperation rests on two pillars: (1) the initiation of a mutually beneficial relationship between the cooperation partners with a commitment of some credible, non-recoverable investments on both sides; and (2) the fading of fear of opportunism as the partners start to work on a cooperative partnership and as mutual trust develops. This process later leads to reduced coordination efforts and costs.

Protecting the firm's key resources

From a resource perspective (Wernerfelt 1984), unique resources constitute the basis of a firm's competitive advantage. When resources are contributed towards a partnership, they are also put at risk. Protecting their key resources is therefore a priority issue for firms deciding whether to enter into cross-border cooperation. Das and Teng (1999) distinguish between two types of resources:

1. *Property resources*, to which a firm has a clear legal right, such as physical resources, financial resources, and patents, licenses, copyrights, or other contractually or legally protected rights.
2. *Knowledge resources*, both explicit and tacit knowledge regarding, for example, technology, management, organisation, or a specific target country market.

Although property resources can generally be protected by law, this is less straightforward in cross-border cooperation, as different legal and political systems tend to be involved. Resources that are well-protected in one country are not necessarily safe under the legal framework of another – as in the case of, for example, technology patented in only one country. Furthermore, financial resources can be subject to repatriation restrictions, thus potentially locked up in one country.

Knowledge resources, on the other hand, are generally less protected by law. It is important to distinguish between explicit and tacit knowledge in this context. Explicit knowledge can be clearly articulated, while tacit knowledge is not verbalised and is thus difficult to transfer (Simonin 1999). As explicit knowledge is easier to replicate and use, Becerra et al. (2008) suggest that the risk of its transfer to cooperation partners is perceived as higher than the risk of tacit knowledge transfer. Consequently, cooperation partners often concentrate on securing explicit knowledge, although it is often in the tacit knowledge that the real competitive advantages lie (ibid.).

The primary resource contribution of a cooperating company can also have an effect on the choice of adequate resource protection mechanisms when facing the risk of opportunistic behaviour. If a partner mainly contributes property resources, the potential misuse of property needs to be avoided through control mechanisms such as contractual control (the clear specification of how and by whom resources can be used), equity control (through majority ownership), or managerial control (e.g., having one's own managers in key positions within the cooperative venture) (Das and Teng 1999). When, on the other hand, the key contribution of a firm to alliance is knowledge, security rather than control will be the focus of attention, as the firm will try to protect its know-how (ibid.).

Managing conflicts in an intercultural setting

One of the main challenges of cooperating is having to deal with conflict situations. Child et al. (2005) distinguish between two different forms of conflict: (1) "hard" conflicts over resources and (2) "soft" conflicts of a more interpersonal nature. They propose that hard conflicts can be mitigated through better communication, information sharing, and documentation, as well as through clear rules and procedures established at the beginning of a partnership. Softer disputes, on the other hand, will need sensitivity from the partners, open discussions, and socialising efforts (ibid.). The main external reasons for conflicts are determined by (1) environmental factors like change of economic, legal or political conditions, changes in the competitive environment, or changes in consumer habits, or (2) firm-specific factors like changes in the legal position or management of the cooperation partners, and influences of share- and stake-holders (Osiecka 2006; Fontanari 1996). Reasons for intenal conflict might be goal formulation, different assessment of the cooperation process, the distribution of new tasks, different time horizons, incompatible organisational- and decision-making structures, cultural differences, lack of trust and underdeveloped relationships, imbalance of the staff involved, unclear rules and regulations and general disagreements between the cooperation partners (ibid).

Any type of cooperation brings different company cultures together, but particularly in cross-border cooperation, managing the cultural differences is a challenging endeavour. In these partnerships, the partners need to invest effort and time into mutual understanding and adjustment, as cultural insensitivity and inflexibility can destroy a relationship and end the partnership (Child et al. 2005). In cross-border cooperation, it is important that intercultural conflicts be managed adequately, as managing conflicts in an integrative, win-win-oriented way also fosters learning in cooperative partnerships, both directly and in building up relational capital (Kale et al. 2000).

There are two general approaches to managing conflict situations in alliances: a rights-based approach and an interest-based approach (Brett et al. 1990; Lumineau and Malhotra 2011). In a *rights-based approach*, the conflicting parties usually take a competitive or win-lose perspective, trying to defend their position as legitimate and claiming that the other's demands are not valid (Ury et al. 1988). In an *interest-based approach*, on the other hand, the parties first exchange perspectives in terms of the basic interests that lie behind their positions in order to find a solution that is integrative and solves the problem for both sides (ibid.). Interest-based negotiations aim to find win-win solutions, while, in a rights-based perspective, conflicts are generally seen as zero-sum games. The two approaches to dealing with conflict can also appear together as different tactics in the same dispute (ibid.). Lumineau and Malhotra (2011) point out that when cooperation partners too often refer to contract clauses, the rights-based approach prevails, causing the parties to dispute solely about who is right and who is wrong instead of adopting an interest-based approach more likely to yield mutually acceptable results to which both parties can commit. As conflicts between firms can become extremely costly, taking a solely rights-based approach carries risks. If conflicts reach a stalemate, it is often better to seek alternative solutions than to just refer to one's rights. Brett et al. (1996) found that alternative dispute resolution methods such as mediation are less costly than full confrontation through litigation. In addition to saving money, using dispute resolution can also increase the chances of further fruitful cooperation, chances that are, of course, close to zero if the former partners end up fighting each other in court.

3.5 The decision to cooperate across borders

To summarise, when deciding whether to cooperate with partners across borders, managers must be explicit about their goals and take into account the possible barriers, risks, and challenges involved in this international endeavour.

Companies should also be aware of the alternatives to cooperation. In addressing why so many partnerships fail to deliver value, Lambert and Knemeyer (2004) argue that "[o]ften it's because they shouldn't have existed in the first place" (p. 116). Instead of cooperating to obtain access to a particular market or specialised resource, for instance, a firm could set up a subsidiary or acquire a local firm. The advantage of cooperation lies in the combination of the positive effects of internalisation (e.g., the key know-how an alliance creates) and of exchange relationships (e.g., flexibility in resource commitments). Cooperation is especially preferable to acquiring a company when only parts of the resources of the potential partner firm are valuable, thus avoiding a mix of needed and undesired resources (Das and Teng 2000; Hennart and Reddy 1997).

However, although barriers, risks, and challenges can be seen to speak against cooperation, it should be kept in mind that most of them arise from inappropriate behaviour or incorrect cooperation formalisation rather than from the concept of cooperation itself (Estanyol Casals 2011). Overcoming the risks of cooperation is often a challenge for SMEs, but most relationship-based risks can be overcome through effective and jointly coordinated cooperation management. Meanwhile, performance risk also exists in non-alliances; it is the probability that an undertaking will fail to achieve its goals even if all partners are fully committed, because of, for example, unforeseen changes in the environment (Das and Teng 1999). Performance risks can be reduced through effective planning and coordination of the cooperative activities, by being aware of the influential economic, legal, political, and institutional conditions, and through effective cooperative management.

Therefore, it is crucial to exploit the opportunities in cross-border cooperation and overcome its barriers, manage its challenges, and avoid its risks. In the following Chapters, we will describe the success factors of cross-border cooperation, take a look at the external conditions influencing cooperation, especially in the European context, and then explain how most of the risks and challenges can be overcome through effective cooperation management.

Summary of the benefits and challenges influencing the decision to cooperate

In cross-border cooperation, at least two partners from different countries need to deliberately decide whether cooperation is the right path for them. In order to be able to make a thoroughly evaluated decision, it is important for managers to be clear about what they expect from cooperating (benefits) and what main risks and challenges need to be avoided or overcome.

1. Firms join in a partnership for a variety of reasons, such as to increase their market power, obtain efficiency gains, reduce risk, gain access to key resources and capabilities, and to enter new markets (particularly relevant to cross-border cooperation). Aside from entering a new market, SMEs collaborate across borders for strategic reasons, cost-oriented reasons, resource-oriented reasons, and learning-oriented reasons.
2. Cross-border cooperation involves considerable barriers, risks and challenges. From an entrepreneurial perspective, the restrictions imposed by taxation or legal regulation, the lack of information on partners, language, and cultural differences, and the desire to remain independent as well as to protect information and key resources are perceived as some of the main barriers to international cooperation.
3. Cooperation itself is a relatively risky endeavour. In addition to performance risk, the cooperation partners are also confronted with relational risk, a unique feature of collaborations. The disadvantages of cooperation can be grouped into two categories: (1) the possibility to create new competitors if the cooperation partner(s) decide to act in an opportunistic way and (2) the threat of becoming highly dependent on the partner, thereby increasing the firm's risk and reducing its strategic options.
4. In addition to the risks of cross-border cooperation, there are also other challenges that need to be addressed by the cooperation partners. The most important ones are (1) finding the right cooperation partner and performing an effective cooperation management, (2) reducing the transaction costs of cooperation and preventing opportunistic behaviour of the cooperation partners, (3) protecting the individual firm's key resources, and (4) managing conflicts in an intercultural setting.
5. When considering whether to cooperate, managers need to be clear about their reasons for and goals of cooperation, taking into account the possible barriers, risks, and challenges involved. Risks and challenges of coopera-

tion often arise from inappropriate behaviour or incorrect formalisation of the cooperation rather than from the concept of cooperation itself.

References

Becerra, M., Lunnan, R., and Huemer, L. (2008) Trustworthiness, risk, and the transfer of tacit and explicit knowledge between alliance partners. *Journal of Management Studies* 45(4), 691–713

Brett, J. M., Goldberg, S. B., and Ury, W. L. (1990) Designing systems for resolving disputes in organizations. *American Psychologist* 45(2), 162–170

Brett, J.M., Barsness, Z. I., and Goldberg, S.B. (1996) The effectiveness of mediation: An independent analysis of cases handled by four major service providers. *Negotiation Journal* 12(3), 259–269

Chen, H.-L. and Huang, Y. (2004) The establishment of global marketing strategic alliances by small and medium enterprises. *Small Business Economics* 22(5), 365–377

Chen, S.-H., Lee, H.-T., and Wu, Y.-F. (2008) Applying ANP approach to partner selection for strategic alliance. *Management Decision* 46(3), 449–465

Child, J., Faulkner, D., and Tallman, S. (2005) Cooperative strategy, 2nd edn. Oxford: Oxford University Press

Contractor, F. J. and Lorange, P. (1988) Why should firms co-operate? The strategy and economics basis for cooperative ventures. In: Contractor, F. J. and Lorange, P. (eds.) Co-operative strategies in international business. Lexington, MA: Lexington Books, 1–28

Das, T. K. and Teng, B.-S. (1999) Managing risks in strategic alliances. *Academy of Management Executive* 13(4), 50–62

Das, T. K. and Teng, B.-S. (2000) A resource-based theory of strategic alliances. *Journal of Management* 26(1), 31–62

Das, T. K. and Teng, B.-S. (2001) Trust, control, and risk in strategic alliances: An integrated framework. *Organization Studies* 22(2), 251–283

Dickson, P. H., Weaver, K. M., and Hoy, F. (2006) Opportunism in the RandD alliances of SMEs: The roles of the institutional environment and SME size. *Journal of Business Venturing* 21(4), 487–513

Dyer, J. H. and Singh, H. (1998) The relational view: Cooperative strategy and sources of interorganizational competitive advantage. *Academy of Management Review* 23 (4), 660–679

Elmuti, D. and Kathawala, Y. (2001) An overview of strategic alliances. *Management Decision* 39(3), 205–217

Estanyol Casals, F. (2011) *The SME co-operation framework: A multi-method secondary research approach to SME collaboration.* Paper presented at the 2010 International Conference on E-business, Management and Economics IPEDR Hong Kong

European Commission (2003) SMEs and cooperation. In: European Commission (ed.), *Observatory of European SMEs* (Vol. 5). http://ec.europa.eu/enterprise/policies/sme/files/analysis/doc/smes_observatory_2003_report5en.pdf (date accessed 1 July 2012)

García-Canal, E., López Duarte, C., Rialp Criado, J., and Valdés Llaneza, A. (2002) Accelerating international expansion through global alliances: A typology of cooperative strategies. *Journal of World Business* 37(1), 91–107

Glaister, K. W. and Buckley, P. J. (1996) Strategic motives for international alliance formation. *Journal of Management Studies* 33(3), 301–332

Hennart, J.-F. and Reddy, S. (1997) The choice between mergers/acquisitions and joint ventures: The case of Japanese investors in the United States. *Strategic Management Journal* 18(1), 1–12

Hill, C. W. L. (1990) Cooperation, opportunism, and the invisible hand: Implications for Transaction Cost Theory. *Academy of Management Journal* 15(3), 500–510

Johansson, J. and Ylinenpää, H. (2006) *SME alliance motives and knowledge modes.* Paper presented at the 14th Nordic Conference on Small Business Research, Stockholm, Sweden

Kale, P. and Singh, H. (2009) Managing strategic alliances: What do we know now, and where do we go from here? *Academy of Management Perspectives 23*(3), 45–62

Kale, P., Singh, H., and Perlmutter, H. (2000) Learning and protection of proprietary assets in strategic alliances: Building relational capital. *Strategic Management Journal* 21(3), 217–237

Kelley, D. J. and Rice, M. P. (2002) Leveraging the value of proprietary technologies. *Journal of Small Business Management* 40(1), 1–16

Lai, J.-H., Chang, S.-C., and Chen, S.-S. (2010) Is experience valuable in international strategic alliances? *Journal of International Management* 16(3), 247–261

Lambert, D. M. and Knemeyer, A. M. (2004) We're in this together. *Harvard Business Review* 82(12), 114–122

Lee, S.-H., Shenkar, O., and Li, J. (2008) Cultural distance, investment flow, and control in cross-border cooperation. *Strategic Management Journal* 29(10), 1117–1125

Lei, D. and Slocum Jr, J. W. (1991) Global strategic alliances: Payoffs and pitfalls. *Organizational Dynamics* 19(3), 44–62

Lohrke, F., Kreiser, P., and Weaver, K. M. (2006) The influence of current firm performance on future SME alliance formation intentions. *Journal of Business Research* 59(1), 19–27

Lu, J. W. and Beamish, P. W. (2006) Partnering strategies and performance of SMEs' international joint ventures. *Journal of Business Venturing* 21(4), 461–486

Lumineau, F. and Malhotra, D. (2011) Shadow of the contract: How contract structure shapes interim dispute resolution. *Strategic Management Journal* 32(5), 532–555

Mesquita, L. F. and Lazzarini, S. G. (2008) Horizontal and vertical relationships in developing economies: Implications for SMEs' access to global markets. *Academy of Management Journal* 51(2), 359–380

Moen, Ø., Båkas, O., Bolstad, A., and Pedersen, V. (2010) International market expansion strategies for high-tech firms: Partnership selection criteria for forming alliances. *International Journal of Business and Management* 5(1), 20–30

Nakos, G. and Brouthers, K. D. (2008) International alliance commitment and performance of small and medium-size enterprises: The mediating role of process control. *Journal of International Management* 14(2), 124–137

Osiecka, A. (2006) Grenzüberschreitende Unternehmenskoooperationen. Standortbezogene Analyse deutsch-polnischer Unternehmenspartnerschaften im Grenzgebiet. Wiesbaden: Deutscher Universitäts-Verlag

Parkhe, A. (1993) Strategic alliance structuring a game theoretic and transaction cost examination of interfirm cooperation. *Academy of Management Journal* 36(4), 794–829

Rowden, R. W. (2001) Research note: How a small business enters the international market. *Thunderbird International Business Review* 43(2), 257–268

Schmitz, H. (1995) Collective efficiency: Growth path for small scale industry. *Journal of Development Studies* 31(4), 529–566

Simonin, B. L. (1997) The importance of collaborative know-how: An empirical test of the learning organization. *Academy of Management Journal* 40(5), 1150–1174

Simonin, B. L. (1999) Transfer of marketing know-how in international strategic alliances: An empirical investigation in the role and antecedents of knowledge ambiguity. *Journal of International Business Studies* 30(3), 463–490

Spence, M. M., Manning, L. M., and Crick, D. (2008) An investigation into the use of collaborative ventures in the internationalization of high performing Canadian SMEs. *European Management Journal* 26(6), 412–428

Street, C. T. and Cameron, A.-F. (2007) External relationships and the small business: A review of small business alliance and network research. *Journal of Small Business Management* 45(2), 239–266

Ury, W. L., Brett, J. M., and Goldberg, S. B. (1988) Getting disputes resolved: Designing systems to cut the costs of conflict. San Francisco: Jossey-Bass

Van Elk, K. and van Lin, M. (2005) International co-operation. In: van Elk, K. and de Vries, J. (eds.), Entrepreneurship in the Netherlands. SMEs and international co-operation, pp. 9–30. EIM Business and Policy Research. http://www.ondernemerschap.nl/pdf-ez/A200505.pdf (date accessed 1 July 2012)

Wernerfelt, B. (1984) A resource-based view of the firm. *Strategic Management Journal* 5(2), 171–180

White, S. and Siu-Yun Lui, S. (2005) Distinguishing costs of cooperation and control in alliances. *Strategic Management Journal* 26(10), 913–932

Wong, A., Tjosvold, D., and Yu, Z.-Y. (2005) Organizational partnerships in China: Self-interest, goal interdependence, and opportunism. *Journal of Applied Psychology* 90(4), 782–791

4 Success factors for cross-border cooperation

One of the main concerns of SMEs that are planning to engage in cross-border cooperation is how to facilitate the success and avoid the failure of their partnership. Research confirms that numerous inter-firm partnerships and alliances fail or falter quickly. According to Das and Teng (2000) studies show, that less than 50 % of alliances perform satisfactorily. In light of this high rate, SMEs understandably often fear the high risks of cooperation despite the potential mutual benefits. Even when firms decide to cooperate, they often fail to maintain the partnership (Swoboda et al. 2011). Bearing in mind the many national and cultural partner contexts in which cross-border alliances operate, it is particularly important to identify the success factors for establishing and managing an effective cooperation (Smallbone et al. 2008).

The success of cooperation can be measured in several ways: using performance indicators (such as sales, cash flow, and profits), efficiency indicators (such as transaction costs), or through the subjective perceptions of the actors involved (such as the perceived degree to which the alliance's goals are achieved) (Hoffmann and Schlosser 2001; Lohrke et al. 2006; Swoboda et al. 2011). Marxt and Link (2002) suggest that the success of a partnership can manifest itself in four dimensions:

- achieving the cooperation's original objectives,
- obtaining joint revenues for the cooperation partners,
- gaining organisational learning through experience and know-how exchange, and
- experiencing subjective positive personal feelings.

The success of cooperation is influenced by multiple factors; however, although much research on SME alliances and collaborations has been conducted, no comprehensive theory regarding the key success factors for cross-border cooperation has emerged (Estanyol 2011; Hoffmann and Schlosser 2001).

Hoffmann and Schlosser (2001) identify several factors that positively influence the success of cooperation and classify them in a model of cooperation phases. The authors argue that most of the success factors they identified need to be considered early in the cooperation building process (Hoffmann and Schlosser 2001). A similar phase-based success factor framework has been suggested by Nielsen (2007) and he distinguishes between pre-alliance formation factors and post-alliance formation factors. Wittmann et al. (2009) have presented three explanations for the success of cooperation: (a) the *resource-based approach*, in which success is influenced by the resources each cooperation partner is willing to contribute to the alliance and the extent to which the alliance creates new resources; (b) the *competence approach*, in which alliance success is significantly influenced by the ability of the partners to identify, develop, and manage alliances; and (c) the *relational factors approach*, which involves factors such as trust, commitment, communication, and cooperation.

Furthermore, the concept of "fit" is often used to explain the success of international cooperation (Chi Cui et al. 2002; Douma 1997; Murray and Kotabe 2005; Nielsen 2010; Swoboda et al. 2011). This approach suggests that success is directly determined by the configurational fit (strategic, structural, and cultural) among the cooperation partners (Swoboda et al. 2011).

Numerous studies have been conducted on the specific success factors of international alliances and cross-border cooperation, such as *geographic distance* (Huber 2003; Teixeira et al. 2008), *trust* and *commitment* (Chaturvedi and Gaur 2009; Cullen et al. 2000; Fink et al. 2008; Fink and Kessler, 2010; Fink and Kraus, 2007), effective *contractual agreements* (Faems et al. 2008; García-Canal 1996; Kelly and Mui-Siang Tan 2010; Luo 2002; Malhotra and Murningham 2002), *cooperation experience* (Lai et al. 2010), the *resources and capabilities* of the cooperation partners (Anand and Khanna 2000; Das and Teng 1998b; De Mattos et al., 2009; Hitt et al. 2006; Wittmann et al. 2009), and *managerial, organisational, structural, and strategic fit* (Chi Cui et al. 2002; Douma, 1997; Murray and Kotabe 2005; Nielsen 2010; Swoboda et al. 2011).

In this chapter, following a review of previous studies on cooperation, strategic alliances, and joint ventures, we present the key factors influencing the success of *cross-border* cooperation. We also integrate them into one conceptual model, thereby shedding light on the complex structure of the factors affecting cooperation success in the cross-border context. The model includes a combination of strategic, structural, organisational, and relationship-based factors directly related to cooperation, as well as the firm-specific and environmental conditions that influence the ability of partnering firms to cooperate effectively and successfully (see Fig. 4.1).

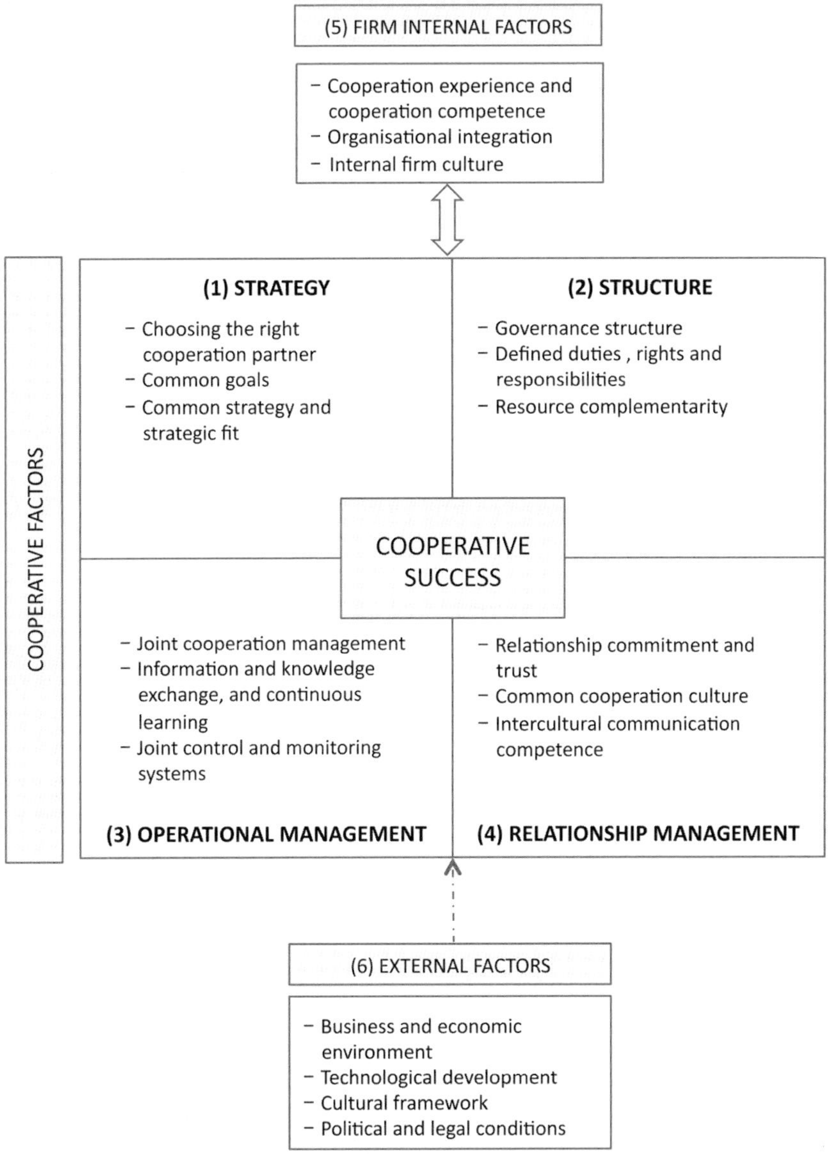

Fig. 4.1 Success factors for cross-border cooperation

Source: Author

4.1 Cooperative success factors

We define *cooperative success factors* as those factors that can be directly influenced and managed by the cooperation partners. We divide them into four categories: (a) strategic success factors, (b) structural success factors, (c) operational success factors, and (d) relationship-based success factors.

Strategy-related success factors

Fig. 4.2 Strategy-related success factors

Source: Author

Strategic cooperation management comprises the analyses, decisions, and actions undertaken by the management of the partner firms to create and sustain competitive advantage through cooperation. Choosing the right partners, defining common goals, and identifying the right strategy to achieve these goals can strongly influence the overall cooperative success.

Choosing the right cooperation partner

The success of a partnership largely depends on finding the right cooperation partner(s). Although a formalised partner selection process is not common for SMEs, adopting a systematic approach to identify the right partner can improve the quality of the selection, thereby increasing the chances of success.

In practice, many SME alliances are not formed through an extensive partner search and selection process but by capitalising on existing personal relationships and informal contacts among managers. In such cases there is usually a less formal approach to negotiating the terms of cooperation. Although good relations among partners may indeed provide a good starting point, this should not be the sole basis of cooperation (Douma 1997), as other partner combinations could, for example, yield stronger results through a better capabilities fit. Empirical studies have shown that an effective partner selection process can significantly impact the performance of cross-border alliances, as the choice of partner largely determines the skill sets and resources that will be available to the partnership (Geringer 1991). Therefore, it is crucial to define the specific criteria the potential partner(s) must or should fulfil.

Partner selection criteria can be *partner-related* (e.g., based on the national and organisational cultures of the firm, prior cooperation experience, the mutual trust between the management teams, or firm size and structure) and/or *task-related* (focused on the resources and capabilities the partner could contribute to the cooperation) (Geringer 1991). Shah and Swaminathan (2008) and Wood et al. (2009) emphasise that good cooperation partners should have both strategic congruence and tactical congruence, implying that the partner firms need to share a fit regarding common business opportunities and cultural factors while also being able to coordinate the partnership on a daily basis. Kale and Singh (2009) and Shah and Swaminathan (2008) suggest that firms should take the following four criteria into account when attempting to identify the appropriate cooperation partner: (1) partner complementarity, (2) commitment of the partner, (3) compatibility of the partners, and (4) the potential financial payoff of cooperation of both market access and cost reduction.

Common goals

After appropriate partners have been found, it is important to define realistic and achievable goals for the alliance. This is a crucial step in guaranteeing that the partnership stays on the right path. The common objectives of an alliance should derive from the partner firms' individual corporate- and business-level strategies (Hoffmann and Schlosser 2001), and should be defined jointly by all partners. Strategic agreement on the overall goals of cooperation can help build a strong basis for a supportive collaborative environment (Koza and Lewin 2000), as "where parties share goals [...] they can be expected to act instinctively for the benefit of one another" (Gundlach et al. 1995, p. 80).

Cooperation agreements will usually include both short- and long-term goals, with short-term goals having the advantage of usually being more swiftly controlled and monitored. In strategic alliances, partners often prefer a high degree of goal formalisation, which allows easier control of the outcome (Das and Teng 1998a).

Common goals have a strong guiding function and are therefore instrumental in achieving effective cooperation. The goal-setting process itself can also be seen as a useful social control mechanism. Joint decision-making regarding the outcomes and goals of a partnership helps the cooperation partners gain a better understanding of each other's objectives, interests, and styles and can foster the development of collective norms and values (Das and Teng 1998a). According to Fink et al. (2008), determining common objectives can also help to avoid conflicts.

As mentioned before, the success of partnership is often measured by the extent to which its goals have been attained. Therefore it is necessary not only to be clear about common goals but furthermore also to identify indicators and determine measurement criteria (both quantitative and qualitative) to operationalise the objectives and be able to determine the success of cooperation.

Joint strategy and strategic fit

One of the main preconditions for a long-lasting and successful cooperation is the strategic fit among the partner firms (Swoboda et al. 2011). Wood et al. (2009) argue that strategic congruence requires the identification of common business opportunities, along with compatible missions, values, and goals. Goal and strategy compatibility is also necessary for avoiding conflict (Estanyol 2011).

According to Douma (1997), "[t]here is strategic fit if the partners' strategies and objectives are mutually dependent and compatible, and the alliance is of strategic importance to the partners' competitive position" (p. 51). He further suggests that having both compatible cooperative and firm-specific strategies is a good starting point for cooperation. Therefore, partners should consider abandoning a partnership if their objectives are no longer compatible, unless they are willing to adjust their strategies. During the cooperation negotiations, partners with conflicting strategic objectives need to determine whether they are prepared to make concessions or allow differences in strategic direction, weighing individual interests against the anticipated advantages of cooperation (Douma 1997).

The results of Hoffmann and Schlosser (2001) reveal that the absence not only of a common cooperation strategy but also of clear individual strategic positions can strongly influence the likelihood of cooperation failure. Douma (1997) concludes that a lack of sufficient strategic fit significantly reduces the chances of cooperative success.

Structure-related success factors

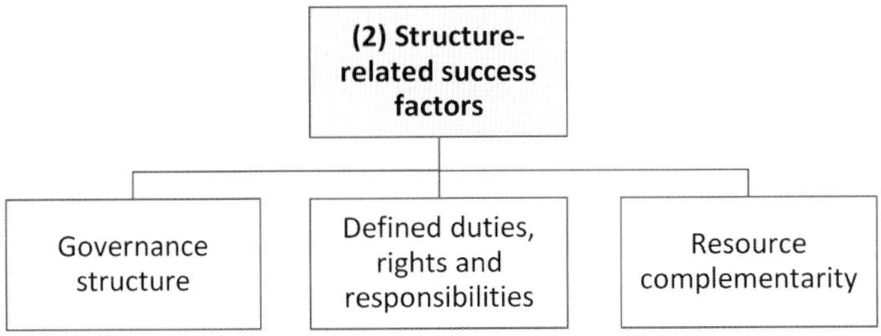

Fig. 4.3 Structure-related success factors

Source: Author

The structural success factors of cooperation include its governance system, the cooperation partners' duties, rights, and responsibilities, and the resources and capabilities dedicated to cooperation.

Governance structure

Forming cooperation requires deciding on a suitable governance structure (see also the corresponding chapter in this book). Grundlach et al. (1995) argue that successful cooperation requires the development and introduction of a governance structure that helps to prevent uncertainty, conflict, and the opportunism of market transactions, while avoiding bureaucracy and the inefficiencies of enforced cooperation by using hierarchy or third-party governance. Cooperation partners need to jointly decide on a governance structure on the basis of the purpose of their cooperation.

Kale and Singh (2009) distinguish among three basic forms of governance for cross-border cooperation: (a) *equity-based governance structures* such as joint ventures, (b) *contract-based governance structures* with relatively formalised interactions, and (c) *relationship-based governance structures*, which are based on mutual trust without the inclusion of any equity exchange or contractual arrangements. When partners are choosing the most suitable governance form for their cross-border cooperation, they need to consider several internal and external factors, such as the type of assets contributing to the partnership (Hoetker and Mellewigt 2009), their national cultural differences (Tallman and Shenkar 1994), their alliance management experience, and the internationality of the cooperation partners (Teng and Das 2008).

Clearly defined duties, rights, and responsibilities

An effective cooperation governance system should also include the partners' administrative responsibilities, division of the cooperative activities' outcomes, general arrangements for daily collaborative work, and legal and social control mechanisms for coordinating and safeguarding the alliance partners' resource contributions (de Man and Roijakkers 2009). Hoffmann and Schlosser (2001) argues that disputes over cooperation inputs (the partners' duties) and the sharing of cooperation outputs (the partners' rights) frequently result in costly conflict resolution procedures and prevent the partnership from fully reaping its potential benefits. Therefore, it is essential to establish precise definitions of the tasks and duties of each partner, clarify expectations and responsibilities, and clearly and formally determine how the cooperation outcomes will be shared. Within the overall alliance governance system, this requires adequate coordination, control, monitoring, and incentive (motivation) mechanisms (Albers 2010; Jensen 1983). Coordination mechanisms such as direct supervision, mutual adjustment, and standardisation are necessary to achieve the defined goals through a coordinated integration of the many tasks and activities performed by the cooperation partners. Monitoring mechanisms (e.g., using key performance indicators or standardised reports) lower the risk of opportunistic partner behaviour. Incentive mechanisms, such as rules for sharing the positive outcomes of the partnership, are necessary for encouraging partners to act in the best interests of the partnership rather than in just their own (Albers 2010).

Resource complementarity

In order to ensure effective performance, the cooperative venture needs a resource endowment that is adequate for its goals (Fink and Kessler 2010). The availability of resources influences the success of cooperation in two ways: (1) having the right resources is a prerequisite for finding a suitable cooperation partner; and (2) the output of cooperation is highly dependent on the combined resources committed by the partner firms. Hoffmann and Schlosser (2001) found that "[e]stablishing required resources" and "[c]ontributing specific strengths and looking for complementary resources" were among the most significant factors influencing the success of a strategic alliance (p. 368).

A firm with sufficient financial resources and technological know-how (Bar-Nir and Smith 2002), a good market position, positive reputation, unique human resources, or significant competitive advantage is usually considered a "good" partner for cooperation. Existing networks are also considered important cooperation assets. We agree with Ahuja's (2000) argument that "[t]he greater a firm's stock of resources, the greater the firm's attractiveness to partners, and the greater the firm's collaboration opportunities" (p. 319). In this respect, SMEs are at a disadvantage, as they usually have fewer resources at their disposal than their larger counterparts. In many cases, however, it is not the quantity of the resources that is of consequence but their quality and appropriateness.

In successful cooperation, firms both give and take. While one firm has something to offer its potential partner, it is also seeking complementary or similar resources to use through transfer or pooling (Ahuja 2000). Resource complementarity is a necessary condition for effective alliance performance (Dyer and Singh 1998; Harrison et al. 2001). In successful cooperation, each firm contributes resources to help overcome the corresponding resource weaknesses of the partner(s); thus, the cooperative output highly depends on the quantity and quality of the resources dedicated to it (Hoffmann and Schlosser 2001). In addition to resources, partners also share complementary capabilities and competences, such as marketing expertise, production know-how, technology, cooperation experience, and market access (Spence et al. 2008). If cooperating firms identify and use the synergetic potential of combining resources and capabilities, the performance of all the partners can improve (Fink and Kessler 2010).

Success factors related to operational cooperation management

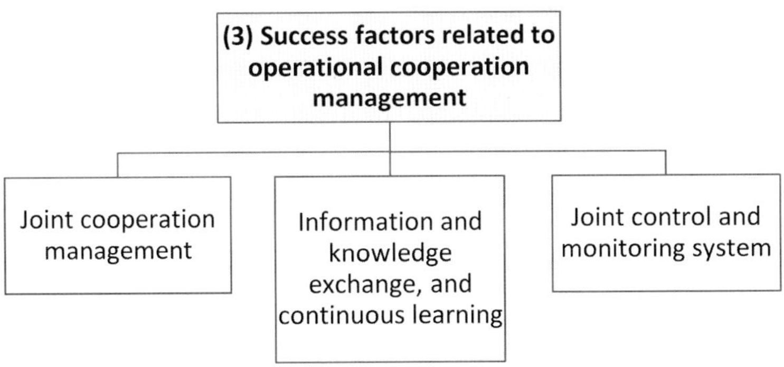

Fig. 4.4 Success factors related to operational cooperation management

Source: Author

After the successful establishment of cooperation, it is necessary to create a joint operational management structure in charge of maintaining the partnership and achieving results. The operational management success factors of cooperation include joint management, the coordinated and organised exchange of information and knowledge, and an integrated control and monitoring system.

Joint cooperation management

We have highlighted the importance of joint cooperation strategies as a key success factor in cross-border partnerships. However, strategic fit alone is not enough for alliances to perform effectively. The quality of the operative cooperation management greatly contributes to its capacity to realise its full potential (Douma 1997). Although the management of a partnership is somewhat comparable to the management of a firm, cooperation has several characteristics that add to the complexity of the management task. For example, cooperation managers need to consider the different backgrounds of the partner firms, interdependence of their activities, constant need to align conflicting interests, and occasionally temporary nature of cooperation (Douma 1997). Whether cooperation partners are able to overcome these managerial challenges depends on the governance structure, existence of clearly defined tasks and responsibilities, capabilities of the management team, and personal relationships among the managers. To be effective, the management team of the partnership requires diversity, with members contributing different (functional and cultural) knowledge, skills, and perspectives. Furthermore, the management team needs leaders who are able to navigate the cooperation through the challenges of new and unfamiliar territory (Kemeny and Yanowitz 2000). Effective cooperation management teams should include both individuals with the necessary decision-making authority and those with more tactical skills and hands-on mentalities. The integration of new team members needs to be carefully planned as they need to understand that the goals and operating norms of a joint team are frequently different from those of their home organisation (Kemeny and Yanowitz 2000).

Information and knowledge exchange, and continuous learning

Several authors suggest that the creation, transfer, and application of knowledge contribute significantly to alliance survival and the organisational performance of the partnership (Kale et al. 2000; Meier 2011). Cooperation partners must realise and accept that collaboration unavoidably leads to knowledge transfer (Douma 1997) and that managing this knowledge transfer is a major cooperation task. Knowledge management has two dimensions

(Grant and Baden-Fuller 2004): the first dimension includes activities that increase an organisation's stock of knowledge; the second dimension refers to activities that deploy existing knowledge to create value. Understanding the distinction between knowledge generation and knowledge application is a necessary precondition for managing knowledge in a cooperative environment.

According to Smallbone et al. (2007), the following points need to be considered when managing knowledge in a cross-border cooperation:

- A certain degree of fit among the cooperation partners is necessary for a mutual transfer of knowledge. Partners need to be open and trust each other.
- Firms' learning processes are affected by the availability of resources (capital, time, and human resources) and their managerial competence. Therefore, allocating resources appropriately is crucial for knowledge transfer and learning.
- Willingness and learning competence in a cross-border context are influenced by previous collaboration experience.
- A firm's commitment, learning orientation, trust, and cross-cultural competences affect its learning process.
- Although difficult, sharing tacit knowledge is one of the most important resources for achieving positive learning results.
- Barriers among partners like language and cultural differences, different opinions, beliefs, educational backgrounds, and attitudes to learning can negatively influence the ability to learn through cooperation.
- The formal and informal institutional framework conditions in the border region and its different economic and socio-cultural norms can constitute barriers to cooperation and learning.
- As firms often fear the potential for opportunistic partner behaviour when sharing knowledge, introducing an adequate risk management system is advisable.

Joint control and monitoring systems

Inter-firm alliances fail for many reasons, but one of the main ones is inadequate control and management of cooperation risks (Chua and Mahama 2007). Two important forms of cooperation-related control are (a) *performance risk control*, focusing on how well the joint cooperation goals have been achieved under all the partners' full cooperation and (b) *relational risk control*, focusing on detecting opportunistic partner behaviour (Coletti et al. 2005). The implementation of systems and mechanisms for the continuous monitoring of partner contributions can help lower the risk of partners' performance below their capabilities (Estanyol 2011).

Cooperation control also involves significant challenges for the partners involved. Control instruments such as monitoring and sanctioning systems can be beneficial to cooperation by reducing the incentives for opportunistic behaviour, but such control may cause the cooperation partners to view the collaborative setting as non-cooperative and the partners as untrustworthy (Coletti et al. 2005; Tenbrunsel and Messick 1999). Therefore, cooperation partners should strive to achieve an adequate balance between control and trust.

It is challenging to identify the appropriate control level while taking into consideration the impact of such control on interpersonal trust (Coletti et al. 2005). Some studies have found that control can negatively affect interfirm trust (Malhotra and Murningham 2002; Tenbrunsel and Messick 1999). However, according to Colleti et al. (2005), these studies have failed to fully acknowledge the positive effects of control systems, such as providing economic incentives and feedback to cooperation partners regarding their contributions. They have also found evidence that control can induce cooperation, which in turn has a positive impact on trust. The results of this study reveal that "the effect of control on cooperation is reinforced by the trust that it engenders" (Coletti et al. 2005, p. 496) and that "[t]he earlier a strong control system is put into place, the larger are the ultimate trust and cooperation levels achieved" (p. 497). This is also supported by Nicolaou et al. (2011), who found that, particularly in cooperation based on mutual understanding and gains for all partners, the level of trust remains high even when information drawn from integrated systems is used for control purposes.

Jointly developed and applied key performance indicators can be used to coordinate, plan, and control cooperative activities and foster cooperation success (Balke and Küpper 2003). As alliances are often not organised hierarchically, traditional forms of direct control are not always effective (Chua and Mahama 2007). Given the lack of hierarchical relationships, some forms of control need to rely on firms' voluntary adoption of control instruments and related measurement criteria. Moreover the intercultural nature of cross-border cooperation means that certain control systems are not socially legitimate or acceptable in some cultures.

Despite certain drawbacks maintaining a control and monitoring system within the partnership is necessary for the effective performance of cooperation. This is particularly valid for SME cooperation. Because of their limited resource bases, SMEs will only be willing to commit resources and capabilities when the risk of opportunistic partner behaviour is perceived to be low and the probability of attaining common goals is perceived to be high.

Relationship-oriented success factors

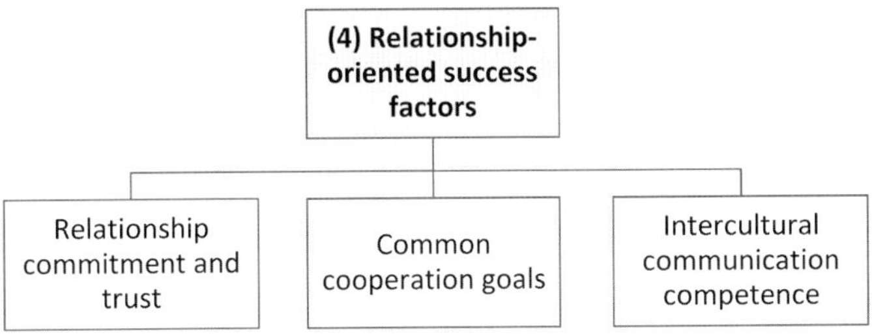

Fig. 4.5 Relationship-oriented success factors

Source: Author

Despite the importance of the success criteria frequently referred to as "hard factors", considering only the strategic, structural, and operational elements of cooperation is insufficient. The "softer" factors that can influence cooperation performance include the development and management of relationship capital (Cullen et al. 2000); commitment and trust; the creation of a common cooperation culture; and intercultural communication competence, particularly in a cross-border setting. According to Cullen et al. (2000), building relationship capital requires that the cooperation partners are willing to invest time. Good working relationships among the managers of the partner firms represent an important precondition for successful cooperation. According to Child et al. (2005), successful cooperation strongly depends on the partners' positive attitudes towards it, manifested in a strong commitment on the part of both the top and middle managements of the partner firms, mutual trust, and – importantly for cross-border cooperation – a sensitivity to cultural differences.

Relationship commitment and trust

Trust and commitment are central to cross-border cooperation, as "no contract or other agreement, no matter how complete or detailed, can account for every issue or every contingency that might arise" (Cullen et al. 2000, p. 226). The importance of commitment and trust is also emphasised by

Child and his colleagues, who find that in cooperation, "[n]o amount of energy and clear direction will compensate for their absence" (2005, p. 7).

Partner commitment, one of the essential ingredients of a functioning long-term partnership (Gundlach et al. 1995), can be described as "the willingness of partner firms to maintain a stable relationship and the degree to which an alliance partner expects the alliance to continue into the future" (Nakos and Brouthers, 2008, p. 125). Commitment reduces opportunistic behaviour and transaction costs and can therefore enhance the overall performance of the partnership (Ren et al. 2009). Cullen et al. (2000) describe two forms of commitment:

- *Calculative commitment* focuses on the rational and economic side of cooperation. The firm must see a potential for return, and each partner's cost-benefit analysis must be positive.
- *Attitudinal commitment* emphasises the emotional side of cooperation. It occurs when partners internalise the alliance, identify themselves with the partnership and its goals, and are therefore willing to work beyond mere contractual obligations.

Trust has been identified as one of the main prerequisites of a successful cooperation or partnership. Fink et al. argue (2008) that "trust builds the basis for self-commitment" (p. 430). Chaturvedi and Gaur (2009) have combined various definitions of trust found in the literature to argue that trust is "the *belief* of the partners involved about the degree to which the other party will behave with goodwill, in a manner that would be in the best interest of both the parties involved, and that they would not take actions generated by self-interest, which may result in loss, financial or otherwise, for the other party" (p. 177). Fink et al. (2008) also distinguish between two types of trust in cooperation – (a) an extrinsically motivated *(instrumental)* trust and (b) an intrinsically motivated *(maxim-based)* trust. In instrumental trust, cooperation partners trust each other through control and sanctions, whereas maxim-based trust is a self-imposed commitment to cooperative behaviour.

The benefits of trust in cooperation include (a) lower transaction costs, (b) a greater likelihood of desirable partner behaviour, and (c) a reduced need for formal contracts and dispute resolution mechanisms (Das and Teng 1998a). Trust is also a source of confidence in cooperation, as it is usually not possible to monitor every detail of a partnership. Fink and Kraus (2007) also show that establishing cooperation with foreign partners based on trust positively affects the success of the participating companies.

Therefore, we can argue that although commitment can exist without trust and trust can theoretically play a role in cooperative efforts without special commitments from the partner firms, both factors are necessary prerequisites for a long and stable cooperation (Child et al. 2005).

Common cooperation culture

Much literature exists on the role of culture and the cultural differences among partners in cross-border business ventures, particularly in joint ventures and mergers and acquisitions. Most of the work has focused on the role of national and organisational cultures in cooperation performance, while comparatively little research has been conducted on the formation and development of a common culture emerging from these cooperative activities.

For example, Barger (2007), in describing international joint ventures, refers to the fact that they involve at least three organisational cultures, as two organisational cultures come together to form a third. This can be said of all joint business collaborations: either the characteristics of one of the organisational cultures are adopted (usually the dominant culture prevails), or a new, unique culture is formed that contains elements of both. Salk and Shenkar (2001) indicate that "IJVs reside at the confluence of different cultures, including national, corporate and occupations" (p. 163).

In any cross-border cooperation, the numerous individuals with differing organisational, professional, national, and personal values working together create a breeding ground for conflicts over communication (and language), use of time, management styles, and ways of working. These elements should be considered in the negotiation of a common working culture within the newly formed cooperation. The stage of cooperation determines whether the potential for cultural conflict is sufficiently large to require a decision on whether to proceed or, if already operational, whether a plan is required to manage the working culture of the cooperative partnership with a view to reducing the possibility of friction and enhancing the chances of success.

Managing a common cooperation culture requires that all partners know their organisations' "cultural map" (Hofstede 2005) and possible subcultures (such as their professional, administrative, and customer interfaces). These elements must be taken into consideration when deciding on a partner or partners, agreeing on common objectives, or choosing a joint management and governance structure. A crucial factor in any form of change process is the degree of the company's awareness of both its culture and operational environment. Cultural changes such as those involved in cross-border cooperation often also require a combination of structural, process, and/or personnel changes. The companies must harmonise to a certain extent, a process often affected by the key human and cultural factor: the people working together. Cooperation is a complex evolutionary process because of the inevitable changes in the cultures involved. The same can be said of the formation and management of the cooperation culture.

Intercultural communication competence

The best way to deal with the interpersonal challenges inherent in cross-cultural cooperation is to develop intercultural communication competence. Key to understanding and developing this competence is recognising that it requires a combination of knowledge, attitude, and behaviour (Bennett and Bennett 2004; Bennett 2001; Ting-Toomey 1999). Occasionally, this is referred to as an interaction among the head, the heart, and the hands: "Intercultural competence is the ability to communicate effectively in cross-cultural situations and to relate appropriately in a variety of cultural contexts" (Bennett and Bennett 2004, p. 149) Developing this kind of competence is crucial to any kind of diverse organisation or team.

Bennett and Bennett (2004) emphasise the need for an intercultural mindset and skillset as a link between behaviour and the emotions and thoughts underlying that behaviour, for effective and appropriate intercultural communication. Mindset is defined as "one's awareness of operating in a cultural context" (ibid., p. 149), requiring cultural self-awareness, frameworks facilitating cultural contrasts – including both communication styles and cultural values – and the ability to use cultural generalisations accurately without overgeneralising or stereotyping. An intercultural mindset embodies attitudes of openness, curiosity, and tolerance. For example, useful cultural generalisation implies an awareness of the predominant behavioural tendencies of groups of people and the cultural values underlying these tendencies without using them to label individuals. Having an intercultural skillset implies having a set of behavioural skills, including "the ability to analyse interaction, predict misunderstanding, and fashion adaptive behaviour" (Bennett and Bennett 2004, p. 149).

One means of dealing with the challenges an SME may face when cooperating across cultural boundaries is to consider the different stages that may arise while working in the intercultural environment. Here, it is perhaps useful to refer to the Milton Bennett Developmental Model of Intercultural Sensitivity (DMIS), widely considered a helpful means of reflecting on how we experience difference in intercultural situations. The model's key premise is that "as one's experience of cultural difference becomes more sophisticated, one's competence in intercultural relations increases" (Bennett and Bennett 2004, p. 152). The ability to learn about and value cultural differences and then reconcile these differences can be invaluable within a diverse environment. Bennett's model identifies how people and organisations move from an ethnocentric to an ethnorelative experience of difference. In progressing through these stages, greater intercultural sensitivity is generated, as is the potential for more intercultural competence. Those working in intercultural environments are highly likely to experience the stages depicted in Bennett's model.

It is important to be aware of how we experience cultural differences. In the first stage, "*denial*", cultural differences are not recognised or are not considered of interest (Bennett and Bennett 2004; Dancourt-Cavanagh 2010). At this stage, an organisation is ignorant of cultural issues and fails to use cultural diversity as a resource (ibid.). In the second stage, "*defence*", some differences are recognised but tend to be evaluated negatively (ibid.). In this stage, other cultures are experienced as inferior to ours. From an organisational perspective, experiencing difference this way may damage valuable cross-cultural partnerships, as partners may come across as arrogant, and cultural diversity is not perceived as a potential resource to be leveraged (Bennett and Bennett 2004). In the "*minimisation*" stage differences are minimised and individuals tend to remain unaware of their own culture and do not recognise how elements of their own cultural values are projected onto other cultures; while perhaps well-intentioned, this may not be so perceived by others (Bennett and Bennett 2004; Dancourt-Cavanagh 2010). Bennett and Bennett (2004) categorise these first three stages as "*ethnocentric*" because people are using their own cultural frames of reference to determine what is they consider as normal behaviour. They suggest that these stages can be considered ways of avoiding cultural differences (Bennett and Bennett 2004, p. 153). As our experiences of cultural differences help us move towards a more "ethnorelative" position, we develop an awareness of different frames of reference and come to see them as equally valid. Thus these stages represent ways of seeking cultural difference.

The first ethnorelative stage is the "*acceptance*" stage. Here, an awareness of our culture as only one of a number emerges, as does the recognition that behaviour can have different meanings in different cultures (Bennett and Bennett 2004; Dancourt-Cavanagh 2010). The next progression occurs at the "*adaption*" stage, where individuals begin to evaluate the behaviour of others from their cultural frames of reference, thus displaying empathy with other cultures (ibid.). This is the point at which cultural awareness is coupled with intercultural competence and where cultural differences are perceived as a resource. The *"integration"* of difference, Bennett's last stage, is a stage that few people enter. In this stage, people move between different frames of reference. This stage is not associated with an improvement of intercultural skills as such, but it represents the point at which people move between different cultural worldviews. At this stage, intercultural competence is strongly embedded within the organisation (Bennett and Bennett 2004). Philippe Rosinski, a renowned expert in executive coaching, has built on this model to incorporate a seventh stage, which he calls *"leveraging"* (see Dancourt-Cavanagh 2010). Rosinski argues that being able to use different frames of reference allows one to make the most of and reconcile cultural differences.

It is generally held that most people who consider themselves as being in one of the ethnorelative stages are really in one of the last two ethnocentric stages. Progressing to the ethnorelative stages often requires some form of intercultural coaching or training. Individuals usually need help reaching a DMIS stage where they can not only recognise and show respect for cultural differences but also work through these differences and make the most of them.

4.2 Firm-specific success factors

Fig. 4.6 Firm-specific success factors

Source: Author

Despite the crucial importance of the success factors directly related to cooperation, partner firms' backgrounds may also have a considerable impact on performance. Factors such as the size and age of the firm, its business field, and the profile of its employees can influence the partnership (Estanyol

2011). For SMEs, these factors are often difficult or even impossible to influence or change, particularly in the short term. However, other firm-internal factors can be influenced by management, such as the ability to learn from cooperation experience, integrating cooperation within the home organisation, and developing a firm-internal cooperation culture. These factors are discussed in greater detail in the next part of this chapter.

Cooperation experience and cooperation competence

Research results suggest that one of the most important factors in the success of a partnership is the partners' previous cooperation experience (Anand and Khanna 2000). Enterprises can develop the capacity to handle complex relationships by gaining experience in relevant cooperative settings (Fink and Kessler 2010). This accords with the evolutionary theory argument that a firm's competences evolve over time through a process of incremental adaptation and continuous learning (Kale et al. 2002).

Cooperation experience is determined not only by the extent and frequency of a firm's cooperation with others but also by the intensity, longevity, and types of cooperation involved (Simonin 1997). According to Huber (2003), firms with previous cooperation experience are more likely to enter into new cooperative relationships. Simonin (1997) demonstrated that firms learn from past collaborations, thereby developing skills that help them benefit more from subsequent cooperation. In addition to experience, collaborative know-how can also be developed through non-experiential methods such as congenital learning, imitation, and searching (Huber 1991).

Cooperation know-how is required in four phases of a collaboration (Simonin 1997). First, in the selection and identification of potential cooperation partners (when firms need to understand the strategic implications of choosing one firm over another); second, when negotiating the terms and structure of a collaborative agreement (when firms need an ability to evaluate the various implications of different forms and structures); third, when monitoring and managing an ongoing cooperation (when firms require skills in staffing, trust building, resolving conflicts, transferring resources, and renegotiating agreements); and finally, when terminating the partnership (when firms need to know when and how to exit cooperation).

However, previous experience is valuable only if the knowledge gained from the experience was absorbed and internalised and then converted into specific know-how by the firm. Thereafter, SMEs can apply the lessons learned from the success or failure of cooperation to new collaborative ventures. In this manner, having partner firms with more cooperation experience can have a considerable influence on the effectiveness of the partnership.

Cooperation experience has a positive influence not only on later collaborations but also on an SME's strategic decision-making competence in an international environment. According to Nielsen (2007), "[a]lliances are often viewed [...] as vehicles to acquire knowledge and learn new skills, and the experience gained from prior international collaboration may influence subsequent international strategic decisions" (p. 343).

Organisational integration

For successful cooperation, partners need to have individual organisational and daily operating structures that allow them to react flexibly to the opportunities and challenges emerging during cooperation and that enable them to quickly respond to changing market demands and unanticipated competitive moves (Wood et al. 2009). The partnership must have the full support of the partner firms' top management teams; this is a key factor for the success of cooperation. People with the suitable competences need to be dedicated to managing and implementing cooperation. This is particularly important, as the diversity of the characteristics of team members can influence the success of cooperation (Agarwal et al. 2010). However, this can pose a problem, particularly for smaller businesses with limited human resources.

The following competences have particular relevance in cooperative settings (Agarwal et al. 2010):

(1) Complementary project-relevant skills and knowledge of the involved staff.
(2) Collaboration skills (the ability to cooperate effectively), often based on prior cooperation experience.
(3) The appropriate attitude and motivation towards cooperation, with trust in the partner(s) being most important.

The partner firms also need to consider that the staff members involved in the cooperation activities are usually not independent but have strong and occasionally overriding allegiances to their home organisations (Douma 1997); moreover, employees not directly involved in cooperation often have little or no knowledge of the alliances goals and strategy. Therefore, the personnel in the partner firms may not always have the cooperative goals in mind when planning and executing their jobs. Occasionally, they may inadvertently take actions that work against the efforts of the alliance team (ibid). A misalignment between existing organisational goals and alliance activities will create barriers even for staff who support the alliance objectives. Thus, it is crucially important that, during the joint goal definition process, attention is paid to how the partnership meshes with existing operational goals (ibid). A planned and coordinated integration of cooperation into the daily business routines of the home organisation is highly important for ensuring long-term cooperative success.

Internal firm culture

In our context, internal firm culture can be understood as organisational culture. Hofstede, building on his well-known definition of "culture" as "the collective programming of the mind that distinguishes the members of one group or category of people from another", describes organisational culture as "the collective programming of the mind that distinguishes the members of one organisation from another" (Hofstede and Hofstede 2005, p. 282f).

Hofstede and Hofstede (2005) identify the following six main dimensions of organisational cultures (p. 292f):

- Process-oriented versus results-oriented (relating to goals);
- Employee-oriented versus job-oriented (relating to the importance attached to either concern for people or concern for getting the job done);
- Parochial versus professional (referring to employees' dependence on either their organisation or their type of job for their identity);
- Open system versus closed system (referring to the communication climate within the organisation);
- Loose versus tight control (referring to the internal structure of the firm and the employees' attitudes to elements like cost reduction, efficiency, and punctuality);
- Normative versus pragmatic (referring to the differences between an organisation that is rule- and procedure-oriented and one that is customer-oriented).

These six dimensions reflect the managerial tendencies of an organisation and have a major impact on the daily work of its employees. The dimensions are widely accepted as providing valuable insight into the organisational culture of firms. As such, other authors have used them to study the differences among organisations and their practices (Pothukuchi et al. 2002).

In studying the impact of cultural differences on international joint venture performance, Pothukuchi et al. (2002) found that differences in organisational practices and routines can result in incompatible organisational processes, thereby suggesting that the more different the organisational cultures are, the more time and resources are needed to develop common management practices and routines. Process and result-orientation differences within a newly formed cross-border alliance, for example, can lead to disagreement within the partnership over goals, roles, and practices. Differences between open and closed systems orientations and between loose and tight control orientations may affect the communication among partners, while employee- versus job-oriented differences may negatively impact the communication among hierarchical levels within the partnership; differences between normative and pragmatic orientations may cause conflict over managerial practices.

Therefore, before entering into cross-border cooperation, it is important for firms to be aware of their own internal firm culture. Cultural issues, whether national, organisational or a combination of both, are all too often only taken into consideration only after problems have already emerged.

4.3 External success factors

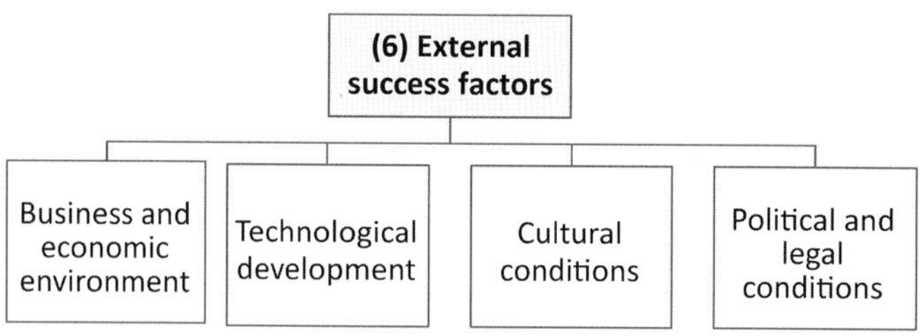

Fig. 4.7 External success factors

Source: Author

In addition to the aforementioned success factors, the development of cooperative endeavours is influenced by external conditions not under the partners' direct control. These external framework conditions, whether economic, technology, legal, policy, or funding related, can either facilitate or constrain cooperation. Empirical findings show that the stability and success of cooperation depend highly on external framework conditions, which cannot be influenced by the cooperation partners themselves (Holtbrügge 2003).

This book considers framework conditions to be the laws, rules, policies, and regulations defining the boundaries of and conditions for SME cooperation, technological development, partners' cultural backgrounds, and all other characteristics of the market and the business environment influencing the development of business cooperation.

Market size, trends, the number of competitors, and the type of industry are *economic factors* affecting the success of a cooperative venture. In industries with high growth rates, many competitors, and a constant flow of new market entries, cooperation has a higher likelihood of success than in sectors experiencing stagnation or negative growth (Holtbrügge 2003). From a *technological perspective*, new information and communication technologies facilitate international cooperation by opening up a broader range of collaborative possibilities across borders. Each cross-border cooperation is also exposed to *intercultural influences*, as the expansion of business activities beyond national borders typically requires collaborative interaction with people of other cultural backgrounds. In this context, language is often mentioned as either an enabling or a hindering factor in the establishment of cross border cooperation. The inability to understand mentality or language differences can lead to a misinterpretation of information, consequently complicating communication and information exchange (Osiecka 2006). Cooperation among SMEs is also affected by the wider *European institutional framework conditions*, including the policies, legal instruments, and institutional support the EU has put in place to improve and regulate the business environment for collaboration across borders.

In the following chapter and in part 2 of this book, we therefore specifically focus on the external framework conditions influencing the development and success of SME cooperation in Europe, beginning with an overview of the external conditions influencing cooperation and then concentrating on the political, institutional, and legal framework conditions the European Union has established.

Summary of the main factors influencing the success of SME cross-border cooperation

The success of cross-border cooperation is influenced by multiple factors, including a combination of strategic, structural, organisational, and relationship-based factors directly relating to cooperation, and the firm-specific and environmental conditions indirectly influencing SMEs' ability to cooperate effectively.

1. *Strategy-related success factors*: the success of cooperation largely depends on finding the right cooperation partner; after appropriate partners are identified, it is important to define realistic and achievable cooperation goals. Furthermore, working on a joint strategy and having a good strategic fit between the partners are crucial.
2. *Structure-related success factors*: it is essential to develop and introduce a governance structure can help prevent uncertainty, conflict, and the opportunism of market transactions. An effective governance system should include the partners' administrative responsibilities, the division of outcomes, general arrangements for daily cooperative work, and legal and social control mechanisms. An effective cooperative venture also needs a resource endowment adequate for achieving its goals.
3. *Success factors related to operational management*: strategic fit alone is not enough for effective alliance performance, as the quality of operative management contributes strongly to the capacity to reach the joint goals. Cooperation partners must also realise that collaboration unavoidably leads to knowledge transfer and that managing this knowledge transfer is a major cooperation task. It must also be understood that cooperation often fails because of inadequate management and control of cooperation risks.
4. *Relationship-oriented success factors*: considering only the strategic, structural, and operational elements of cooperation is not enough. The softer factors, including developing and managing relationship capital, commitment and trust, creating a common cooperation culture, and (especially in cross-border cooperation) intercultural communication competence, have a significant influence on the success of the cooperative endeavour.
5. Despite the crucial importance of the success factors directly related to the partnership, the *firms' backgrounds* also have a considerable impact on the performance of cross-border cooperation. The ability to learn from cooperation experience, integrating cooperation within the home organisation, and being aware of the internal firm culture are essential. In addition to these factors, cooperation development is also influenced by *external conditions* not directly controlled by the cooperation partners, including the economic environment, technological development, cultural framework conditions, and political and legal conditions.

References

Agarwal, R., Croson, R., and Mahoney, J. T. (2010) The role of incentives and communication in strategic alliances: An experimental investigation. *Strategic Management Journal* 31(4), 413–437

Ahuja, G. (2000) The duality of collaboration: Inducements and opportunities in the formation of interfirm linkages. *Strategic Management Journal* 21(3), 317–343

Albers, S. (2010) Configurations of alliance governance systems. *Schmalenbach Business Review* 62(3), 204–233

Anand, B. N. and Khanna, T. (2000) Do firms learn to create value? The case of alliances. *Strategic Management Journal* 21(3), 295–315

Balke, N. and Küpper, H.-U. (2003) Controlling in Netzwerken: Struktur und Systeme. In: J. Zentes, J., Swoboda, B., and Morschett, D. (eds.) Kooperationen, Allianzen, Netzwerke. Wiesbaden: Gabler, 941–964

Barger, B. B. (2007) Culture an overused term and international joint ventures: a review of the literature and a case study. *Journal of Organizational Culture, Communications and Conflict* 11(2), 1–14

BarNir, A. and Smith, K. A. (2002) Interfirm alliances in the small business: The role of social networks. *Journal of Small Business Management* 40(3), 219–232

Bennett, M. J. (2001) Developing intercultural competence for global leadership. In: Reineke, R-D. and Fussinger, C. (eds.) Interkulturelles Management: Konzeption – Beratung – Training. Wiesbaden: Gabler

Bennett, J. M. and Bennett, M. J. (2004) Developing intercultural sensitivity: An integrative approach to global and domestic diversity. In: D. Landis, J. M. Bennett and M. J. Bennett (eds.), Handbook of Intercultural Training, 3rd edn. Thousand Oaks, CA: Sage, 147–165

Chaturvedi, S. and Gaur, A. S. (2009) A dynamic model of trust and commitment development in strategic alliances. *IIMB Management Review (Indian Institute of Management Bangalore)* 21(3), 173–188

Chi Cui, C., Ball, D. F., and Coyne, J. (2002) Working effectively in strategic alliances through managerial fit between partners: Some evidence from Sino–British joint ventures and the implications for RandD professionals. *RandD Management* 32(4), 343–357

Child, J., Faulkner, D., and Tallman, S. (2005) Cooperative strategy, 2nd edn. Oxford: Oxford University Press

Chua, W. F. and Mahama, H. (2007) The effect of network ties on accounting controls in a supply alliance: Field study evidence. *Contemporary Accounting Research* 24(1), 47–86

Coletti, A. L., Sedatole, K. L., and Towry, K. L. (2005) The effect of control systems on trust and cooperation in collaborative environments. *Accounting Review* 80(2), 477–500

Cullen, J. B., Johnson, J. L., and Sakano, T. (2000) Success through commitment and trust: The soft side of strategic alliance management. *Journal of World Business* 35(3), 223

Dancourt-Cavanagh, M., comp. (2010) The Intercultural Dimension in European Projects: How Does it Add Value. Les Cahiers de L'Institut Européen pour la Coopération Territoriale. Région Nord-Pas Calais

Das, T. K. and Teng, B.-S. (1998a) Between trust and control: Developing confidence in partner cooperation in alliances. *Academy of Management Review* 23(3), 491–512.

Das, T. K. and Teng, B.-S. (1998b) Resource and risk management in the strategic alliance making process. *Journal of Management* 24(1), 21–42

Das, T. K. and Teng, B.-S. (2000) Instabilities of strategic alliances: An internal tensions perspective. *Organization Science* 11(1), 77–101

De Man, A.-P. and Roijakkers, N. (2009) Alliance governance: Balancing control and trust in dealing with risk. *Long Range Planning* 42(1), 75–95

De Mattos, C., Salciuviene, L., Auruskeviciene, V., and Thomas, S. (2009) Investigating the importance of matching expectations of contributions to SME's international strategic alliance formation. *Economics and Management* 14, 375–380

Douma, M. U. (1997) *Strategic alliances. Fit or failure.* Doctoral thesis, University of Twente, Enschede. Retrieved from http://doc.utwente.nl/58679/1/thesis_Douma.pdf (date accessed 17. Juli 2012)

Dyer, J. H. and Singh, H. (1998) The relational view: Cooperative strategy and sources of interorganizational competitive advantage. *Academy of Management Review* 23 (4), 660–679

Estanyol C. F. (2011) The SME co-operation framework: A multi-method secondary research approach to SME collaboration. Paper presented at the 2010 International Conference on E-business, Management and Economics, IPEDR Hong Kong

Faems, D., Janssens, M., Madhok, A., and Van Looy, B. (2008) Toward an integrative perspective on alliance governance: Connecting contract design, trust dynamics, and contract application. *Academy of Management Journal* 51(6) 1053–1078

Fink, M., Harms, R., and Kraus, S. (2008) Cooperative internationalization of SMEs: Self-commitment as a success factor for international entrepreneurship. *European Management Journal* 26(6), 429–440

Fink, M. and Kessler, A. (2010) Cooperation, trust and performance – Empirical results from three countries. *British Journal of Management* 21(2), 469–483

Fink, M. and Kraus, S. (2007) Mutual trust as a key to internationalization of SMEs. *Management Research News* 30(9), 674–688

García-Canal, E. (1996) Contractual form in domestic and international strategic alliances. *Organization Studies* 17(5), 773–794

Geringer, J. M. (1991) Strategic determinants of partner selection criteria in International Joint Ventures. *Journal of International Business Studies* 22(1), 41–62

Grant, R. M. and Baden-Fuller, C. (2004) A knowledge accessing theory of strategic alliances. *Journal of Management Studies* 41(1), 61–84

Gundlach, G. T., Achrol, R. S., and Mentzer, J. T. (1995) The structure of commitment in exchange. *Journal of Marketing* 59(1), 78–92

Harrison, J. S., Hitt, M. A., Hoskisson, R. E., and Ireland, R. D. (2001) Resource complementarity in business combinations: Extending the logic to organizational alliances. *Journal of Management* 27(6), 679–690

Hitt, M. A., Biermann, L., Uhlenbruck, K., and Shimizu, K. (2006) The importance of resources in the internationalization of professional service firms: The good, the bad, and the ugly. *The Academy of Management Journal* 49(6), 1137–1157

Hoetker, G. and Mellewigt, T. (2009) Choice and performance of governance mechanisms: Matching alliance governance to asset type. *Strategic Management Journal* 30(10), 1025–1044

Hofstede, G. and Hofstede, G. J. (2005) Cultures and organizations: Software of the mind, 2nd edn. New York: McGraw-Hill

Hoffmann, W. and Schlosser, R. (2001) Success factors of strategic alliances in small and medium-sized enterprises – An empirical survey. *Long Range Planning* 34(3), 357–381

Holtbrügge, D. (2003) Management internationaler strategischer Allianzen. In: Zentes, J., Swoboda, B. and Morschett, D. (eds.) Kooperationen, Allianzen und Netzwerke. Grundlagen – Ansätze – Perspektiven, 2nd edn. Wiesbaden: Gabler, 1182–1201

Huber, G. P. (1991) Organizational learning: The contribution processes and the literature. *Organization Science* 2(1), 88–115

Huber, P. (2003) On the determinants of cross-border cooperation of Austrian firms with Central and Eastern European partners. *Regional Studies* 37(9), 947–955

Jensen, M. C. (1983) Organization theory and methodology. *Accounting Review* 58(2), 319–339

Kale, P., Dyer, J. H., and Singh, H. (2002) Alliance capability, stock market response, and long-term alliance success: The role of the alliance function. *Strategic Management Journal* 23(8), 747–767

Kale, P. and Singh, H. (2009) Managing strategic alliances: What do we know now, and where do we go from here? *Academy of Management Perspectives* 23(3), 45–62

Kale, P., Singh, H., and Perlmutter, H. (2000) Learning and protection of proprietary assets in strategic alliances: Building relational capital. *Strategic Management Journal* 21(3), 217–237

Kelly, K. and Mui-Siang Tan, P. (2010) The effects of profit-sharing contract and feedback on the sustainability of cooperation. *Journal of Management Accounting Research* 22, 251–269

Kemeny, J. M. and Yanowitz, J. (2000) Strategic alliances: Finding the hidden leverage for success. *Reflections* 1(3), 62–71

Koza, M. and Lewin, A. (2000) Managing partnerships and strategic alliances: Raising the odds of success. *European Management Journal* 18(2), 146–151

Lai, J.-H., Chang, S.-C., and Chen, S.-S. (2010) Is experience valuable in international strategic alliances? *Journal of International Management* 16(3), 247–261

Lohrke, F., Kreiser, P., and Weaver, K. M. (2006) The influence of current firm performance on future SME alliance formation intentions. *Journal of Business Research* 59(1), 19–27

Luo, Y. (2002) Contract, cooperation, and performance in international joint ventures. *Strategic Management Journal* 23(10), 903–919

Malhotra, D. and Murningham, J. K. (2002) The effects of contracts on interpersonal trust. *Administrative Science Quarterly* 47(3), 534–559

Marxt, C. and Link, P. (2002) Success factors for cooperative ventures in innovation and production systems. *International Journal of Production Economics* 77(3), 219–229

Meier, M. (2011) Knowledge management in strategic alliances: A review of empirical evidence. *International Journal of Management Reviews* 13(1), 1–23

Murray, J. Y. and Kotabe, M. (2005) Performance implications of strategic fit between alliance attributes and alliance forms. *Journal of Business Research* 58(11), 1525–1533

Nakos, G. and Brouthers, K. D. (2008) International alliance commitment and performance of small and medium-size enterprises: The mediating role of process control. *Journal of International Management* 14(2), 124–137

Nicolaou, A. I., Sedatole, K. L., and Lankton, N. K. (2011) Integrated information systems and alliance partner trust. *Contemporary Accounting Research* 28(3), 1018–1045

Nielsen, B. B. (2007) Determining international strategic alliance performance: A multi-dimensional approach. *International Business Review* 16(3), 337–361

Nielsen, B. B. (2010) Strategic fit, contractual, and procedural governance in alliances. *Journal of Business Research* 63, 682–689

Osiecka, A. (2006) Grenzüberschreitende Unternehmenskooperationen. Standortbezogene Analyse deutsch-polnischer Unternehmenspartnerschaften im Grenzgebiet. Wiesbaden: Deuscher Universitäts-Verlag

Pothukuchi, V., Damanpour, F., Choi, J., Chen, C.C., and Park, S.H. (2002) National and organizational culture differences and international joint venture performance. *Journal of International Business Studies* 33(2), 243–265

Ren, H., Gray, B., and Kim, K. (2009) Performance of international joint ventures: What factors really make a difference and how? *Journal of Management* 35(3), 805–832

Salk, J. E. and Shenkar, O. (2001) Social identities in an international joint venture: An exploratory case study. *Organization Science* 12(2), 161–178

Shah, R. H. and Swaminathan, V. (2008) Factors influencing partner selection in strategic alliances: The moderating role of alliance context. *Strategic Management Journal* 29(5), 471–494

Simonin, B. L. (1997) The importance of collaborative know-how: An empirical test of the learning organization. *Academy of Management Journal* 40(5), 1150–1174

Smallbone, D., Labrianidis, L., Venesaar, U., Welter, F., and Zashev, P. (2007) Challenges and prospects of cross border cooperation in the context of EU enlargement. Deliverable 7: State of the art literature review, http://www.crossbordercoop.net/Publications/Integrated_lit_review.pdf (date accessed 15. February 2012)

Spence, M. M., Manning, L. M., and Crick, D. (2008) An investigation into the use of collaborative ventures in the internationalization of high performing Canadian SMEs. *European Management Journal* 26(6), 412–428

Swoboda, B., Meierer, M., Foscht, T., and Morschett, D. (2011) International SME alliances: The impact of alliance building and configurational fit on success. *Long Range Planning* 44(4), 271–288.

Tallman, S. B. and Shenkar, O. (1994) A managerial decision model of international cooperative venture formation. *Journal of International Business Studies* 25(1), 91–113

Teixeira, A. A. C., Santos, P., and Oliveira Brochado, A. (2008) International RandD cooperation between low-tech SMEs: The role of cultural and geographical proximity. *European Planning Studies* 16(6), 785–810

Tenbrunsel, A. E. and Messick, D. M. (1999) Sanctioning systems, decision frames, and cooperation. *Administrative Science Quarterly* 44(4), 684–707

Teng, B.-S. and Das, T. K. (2008) Governance structure choice in strategic alliance. *Management Decision* 46(5), 725–742

Ting-Toomey, S. (1999) Communicating Across Cultures. New York and London: The Guilford Press

Ting-Toomey, S. and Chung, L. C. (2005) Understanding Intercultural Communication. Los Angeles: Roxbury

Wittmann, C. M., Hunt, S. D., and Arnett, D. B. (2009) Explaining alliance success: Competences, resources, relational factors, and resource-advantage theory. *Industrial Marketing Management* 38(7), 743–756

Wood, V. R., Pitta, D. A., and Franzak, F. J. (2009) Successful strategic alliances with international partners: Key issues for small- to medium-sized enterprises. *Journal of Business Innovation and Research* 3(3), 232–251

5 External framework conditions

As outlined in the previous chapter cross-border partnerships are not only influenced by factors directly controlled by the cooperation partners, but the external environment also impacts on the development, success and stability of the cooperative endeavour. Especially in a cross-border setting the formation of cooperation is strongly influenced by both general economic conditions and the institutional frameworks in the countries of operation.

In literature, we find different external factors that influence the founding, and subsequently the success of a partnership. When considering environmental conditions, it is apparent that these frameworks, with the exception of the cultural framework conditions, mainly influence the process of forming and building up a partnership, whereas their influence on the cooperation itself is only marginal. Balling (1998) describes the factors that influence the number of partnerships being established by SMEs as follows:

- The intensification of competition.
- Technological development.
- The increased growth of large companies that leads to increasing ambitions of SMEs to compensate this growth.
- The growing internationalisation and search for new markets.
- The opening of new markets such as the European internal market or the European eastern enlargement.

Furthermore, especially in the context of cross-border cooperation, differences in cultural backgrounds and languages deeply influence the forming, and subsequently the functioning, of intercultural partnerships. The policies and legal conditions set on national as well as European levels also have a considerable impact on cooperation formation.

Therefore, we describe the main factors influencing the development of cooperative endeavours by focusing on (1) the economic factors affecting cooperation building, (2) technological development as a facilitator of international cooperation by opening up a broader range of cooperation opportunities, and (3) differences in culture and language as an underlying condition of cross-border cooperation. We further present the policies and legal instruments that aim to improve the framework conditions for cooperation across borders in this chapter.

5.1 Business and economic environment

Globalisation is a major driver of the internationalisation of SMEs and impacts on almost every business. Globalisation can be understood as "major increases in worldwide trade and exchanges in an increasingly open, integrated, and borderless international economy" (Intriligator 2003, p. 2). Intriligator (2003) describes the following points as the main facilitators of globalisation: (1) technological advances, as it lowers transportation and communication costs, as well as data processing and information storage, (2) all forms of economic liberalisation that help to reduce trade protection and enable the liberalisation of the world trading system, (3) change in institutions due to technological changes and of attitude towards internationalisation at the management level, (4) existence of a global agreement on ideology, which describes the convergence of beliefs in the value of a market economy and a free trading system, and (5) the movement towards a globalised and homogenised internationalisation of media, arts, and popular culture as well as the widespread use of the English language for global communication purposes. In particular, technological development has significantly reduced transaction costs for operating across borders and has made the internationalisation of SMEs much easier. Globalisation can affect SMEs in two main ways: (1) they can either perceive globalisation as an opening for new opportunities for market expansion and/or growth, or (2) they can see themselves confronted with competitive challenges and threats because of competitive forces from outside their domestic markets. Therefore, SMEs need to decide whether they regard increasing competition as an opportunity or a threat.

According to Zentes and Schramm-Klein (2003), the increasing competition within certain industries and the entry of new competitors in the market are the main drivers of inter-firm cooperation. Globalisation leads to an increasing number of competitors in the market and because of this ever-growing competitive pressure on the home market, SMEs try to improve their positions in the market, increase their competiveness, and to access new markets through different forms of cooperation. Competition among enterprises within the same industry leads to horizontal, vertical, and lateral alliances, as companies seek to overcome their own lack of resources and try to reach the right size to compete successfully in the global marketplace. Furthermore, Zentes and Schramm-Klein (2003) see the increasing negotiation power of the consumers and suppliers as factors that increase pressure on companies to cooperate.

The specifics of certain industries also strongly influence SME cooperation, because the intensity of industry competition and the social organisation of specific product or service markets have strong impacts on the decision if (1) activities are internalised to compete for greater market shares, (2) the firms seek new foreign markets, or (3) cooperation with other firms might bring particular strategic advantages (Todeva and Knoke 2005). Cooperation is widespread across industry sectors and appears both in production and service-oriented sectors; however, the tendency of firms to join forces with others depends somewhat on the industry sector that they are operating in. Cooperation is more likely in the business service or transport and communication sectors, and less likely in the retail sector (European Commission 2003). Non-formal cooperation is more common in the business service, transport and communication, and manufacturing sectors, whereas the construction sector has a relatively high level of formal cooperation (ibid.).

One reason to cooperate is to lower uncertainty and lower the risks; but environmental uncertainty has an effect not only on the forming of a partnership but also on a firms' satisfaction with cooperation. Weaver and Dickson (2006), for example, show that the type of industry an SME is involved in plays a major role in how the partnership is perceived. According to them it can be assumed "that the more attractive the perceived future of the industry the more likely firm leaders are to express satisfaction with their alliance relationships" (p. 13). Uncertainty can be caused by the fear of market shifts, changing trade barriers, changing economies of scale, as well as growing concerns regarding technological development and complexity, and the fear of technological obsolescence (ibid). Therefore, Weaver and Dickson assume that the higher the perceived uncertainty of the market, the lower the likelihood that SMEs are pleased with their cooperation.

5.2 Technological development

The trend to cooperate has been intensified by the latest developments in information and communication technology. Specifically the Internet has a major impact as it enables easy information exchange between cooperation partners which are geographically distant. Picot et al. (1996), referring to the transaction cost theory, explain the increase in the amount of formed cooperation with the developments in the information and communication technology field as these developments reduce the transaction costs of cooperation. This reduction allows for a more efficient coordination of the partnership, leading to the fading of the traditional boundaries of a firm (ibid). Cooperation as a means of communicating and working together across organisational and national boundaries needs technical support to overcome the high transaction costs associated with acting across borders. Therefore, reducing communication and control problems, costs, and gaining easier access to information are very important, especially in cross-border cooperation (Osiecka 2006). Information and communication technology provides opportunities for cooperation partners situated in geographically dispersed locations to communicate, share, and collaborate on tasks and help them achieve their cooperation goals.

The reduction of transaction costs by improved information technology can be observed in every step of the cooperation process. The partner searching process, for example, can be simplified through use of online databases, partner searching platforms and other tools. During cooperation, new communication tools can help to lower transactions costs, for example, by reducing the travel costs of direct meetings (Osiecka 2006). It is also easier to control the output of cooperation using jointly used technology-based key performance indicator systems.

5.3 Cultural framework

Language differences

Language is often represented in literature as constituting either an enabling or a hindering factor in establishing cross border cooperation. In 2005, the Council of Europe's Committee of Ministers recognised the fact that linguistic diversity can be considered an obstacle to cross-border cooperation. As a result, they recommended that in border regions, member states promote the teaching of neighbouring languages (Bohner 2011). In the same year, a study, *ELAN: Effects on the European Economy of Shortages of Foreign Language Skills in Enterprise*, was initiated by the European Commission to investigate the use of language skills by SMEs and their impact on business performance (European Commission 2006). Data was collected among some 2000 exporting SMEs across 29 European countries (EU, EEA, and candidate countries) on approaches to usage of language skills and language strategies, intercultural competence, and loss of business due to a lack of language skills. The study found that "[a] significant percentage of SMEs across the EU and the wider Europe are losing export business through lack of language skills and, to a lesser degree, lack of intercultural skills" (European Commission 2006, p. 57). 11% of respondents lost an actual or potential export contract as a direct result of a lack of language skills. At least 10 businesses lost contracts worth over € 1 million (ibid.).

A more recent European Commission report based on a 2009 survey on the internationalisation of SMEs shows language as a perceived internal barrier for internationalisation to be much higher among SMEs planning to become internationally active than those already operating internationally (European Commission 2010). On a scale of 1 (not important) to 5 (very important), firms actively involved in international activities ranked language at 2.2, while those firms planning to internationalise ranked language as a perceived internal barrier to internationalisation at 2.9 (ibid). A further study initiated by the European Commission, *Collaborative work: Globalisation and New Collaborative Working Environments – New Global. Final Report*, was conducted among 1,015 globally active European SMEs from Belgium, Denmark, Finland, Germany, Portugal, Sweden, the Netherlands, and the UK (Stanoevska-Slabeva et al. 2009). This study revealed that, from a list of potential difficulties related to global collaboration, the largest numbers of respondents (47%) confirmed encountering problems caused by language or other cultural barriers (ibid). Lack of cultural understanding and language fluency was identified as having a negative impact on both the effectiveness and efficiency of the collaboration.

Language can have a key influence on the successful intercultural interaction within a partnership, having an effect on:

- Informal and formal relationships within the partnership;
- Possible misunderstandings and conflict;
- The choice of individuals from a company to be involved in the partnership (which may be the case in smaller enterprises with limited human resources, but it is not the best criteria for choosing the appropriate individuals to work within cooperation).

Language and communication are inextricably linked. In a business context, language plays a crucial role as a means of exchanging and transferring knowledge, values, and business goals. Just as working styles and approaches vary from culture to culture and from cooperation to cooperation, so too will the choice of communication style, including the decision on language use. Very often, from a European context, the choice of a *lingua franca* for cooperation is English. In many cases, English represents a second language or first foreign language for cooperation partners. Regardless of the language chosen as the *lingua franca*, it is important to remember that individuals will often automatically transfer their own culture-specific form of communication, including the style, topic choice etc. to the foreign language. Having exceptional command of the *lingua franca* is no guarantee that communication will be effective. Some authors (see Glaser 2010) suggest that having near native fluency of the foreign language can actually increase the risk of misinterpreting the underlying cultural meaning of certain terms or expressions in the common language. This can eventually lead to barriers to communication. The assumption that a common language will solve all difficulties is a falsehood. The ability to speak the same language does not automatically guarantee mutual understanding. In business interactions, a subject specific language may be considered adequate in doing business, in which case grammar and syntax (sentence construction) take a secondary role. Glaser (2010), referring to work by Luhmann (2000), suggests, "simplifying language in this particular domain can reduce the complexity of human communication and enhance trust between (business) partners from different cultures" (p. 70). However, use of a common cooperation language among partners from different linguistic backgrounds can also prove problematic when the partners have different understandings of the same terminology. Ensuring language clarity is crucial. It is imperative to recognise that there is a deeper context to words and communication, including aspects such as cultural values. Linguistic imbalance within cooperation can be detrimental to the proper functioning of the cooperation.

In addition to language, a further element of communication worth mentioning is the diverse styles of communication. Hall (1976) differentiates between what he terms as "low-context" and "high-context" communication (the characteristics of high-context and low-context communication are presented in Fig. 12.2 in Chapter 12). In cultures that are inclined to use low-context communication, this communication is characterised by a direct style where the words convey their meaning (see Ting-Toomey and Chung 2005; Glaser 2010). The message is expressed through words that allow the receiver to explicitly understand them without interpretation. Cultures that use low-context communication are often characterised by linear and logical thinking and have individualistic values (ibid). In a European context, examples include Germanic and some western Scandinavian cultures (ibid). While countries such as China, Japan, and South Korea are often associated with high-context communication, the countries of southern Europe also gravitate more towards high-context communication usage (Glaser 2010). This form of communication involves the receiver interpreting the message and reading between the lines to decode the message's intended meaning. The message may not be explicitly formulated. It can be multi-layered, relying on different contexts such as social norms, status, roles, and relationships between the speakers (ibid). At all stages in SME cross-border cooperation, it is crucial for members of the cooperation team to be familiar with both the cultural characteristics and communication styles of other members in the partnership in order to avoid possible miscommunication or conflict.

If competency in a common language does not exist, the cooperation partners may need to rely on translators and interpreters. Consequently, trust also needs to be established with the translator or interpreter (or cultural mediator), as the individuals are not always in a position to know if the message has been conveyed as intended. In business cooperation, sometimes individuals who do speak the language of their partners will nonetheless choose to make use of translators and interpreters. In the interest of building trust, it is advisable to speak the language of the partner, at least in an informal context, in order to establish a good business relationship. In general, any demonstration of an ability to speak the partner's language is welcomed and considered as a sign of respect for or interest in the partner's culture.

Translators and interpreters ideally should be able to translate the message in a way that conveys the message of the original language as closely as possible. If an interpreter is interpreting between culturally-distant cooperation partners, then it is also important that cultural norms are taken into consideration. For example, an interpreter working with a "goal-oriented" culture and a "relationship-oriented" culture might reduce the directness of the statements from the goal-oriented culture with a view that maintains the relationship between the partners (see Glaser 2010). If the language is translated directly, the danger is that the business interaction will fail. Glaser (2010) suggests that it is more difficult to find a common cognitive basis when translating or interpreting when the "cultural, psychological, economic, technological, and political distance" is strong (p. 72).

Language and communication differences clearly have a key influence on the intercultural interaction within cross-border SME cooperation. Hence, it is important to take both into consideration from the beginning of the cooperation and not wait until the first signs of conflict emerge among the cooperation partners.

Psychic distance and cultural background

Psychic distance is essentially a construct used to capture the broad concept of cultural distance between national cultures. The term was originally coined by Beckerman (1956) and was explained simply as "fewer language differences, and so on" (p. 38). Later, the term became popular through the work of the Uppsala School (Johanson and Wiederheim-Paul 1975; Johanson and Vahlne 1977) in relation to internationalisation. They identified a broader concept of psychic distance to incorporate differences in language, culture, political systems, education, and industrial development etc. as "factors preventing or disturbing the flows of information between firm and market" (Johanson and Wiederheim-Paul 1975, p. 308). Psychic distance, in its broadest context, can be understood as limitations of knowledge about or the ability to understand a foreign environment (both factually and cognitively). In this sense, we can refer to perceived or interpreted remoteness of a "foreign" environment. While the usefulness of this construct has been debated in the past, in recent years it has been considered worthy of some revival (see Child et al. 2009).

Cultural backgrounds can impinge on people at a number of levels including interpersonal, societal, professional, and organizational. Cultural differences have a very practical influence on how we act and how we do business. Within a work and professional context, differences in culture can affect crucial activities such as communication, goal setting, planning (timing, perception of deadlines etc.), decision-making, and conflict handling. As we all have different assumptions, beliefs, and expectations, these impact on how we act and interact. While some aspects of culture are clearly visible and can be identified relatively easily, such as language, dress codes, and behaviour, there is a complex and intricate web of cultural dimensions that are much more difficult to identify. These are the norms, values, and assumptions that shape our cultural identity and determine our sense of the world, our behaviour, and actions. In order to look beyond the visible surface culture of someone else and to understand their mode of thinking, it is necessary to look outside of our own cultural framework. The analogy of the pair of sunglasses is often used in this context to explain the fact that each of us sees the world through our own particular lens that we use to view, analyse, and most often, judge those we meet. One needs to be aware of cultural differences in order to leverage their potential within cooperation and avoid their hindering the joint working process. Häkli (2004) provides evidence that a common identity and language are useful in successful cooperation across national borders.

Any cross-border cooperation, regardless of the type or specific field of the cooperation, has at least one common aspect: a cultural dimension. Expansion of business activities beyond national borders typically requires collaborative interaction or use of networks at a regional, national, or international level. Diversity of cultural background is evident in this type of cooperation. The European Commission report (2010a) on the internationalisation of SMEs, based on a survey of 9,480 SMEs in 33 European countries conducted in 2009, shows that 23% of the surveyed firms perceive cultural differences (including business culture) to be an important external barrier to internationalisation on EU-EEA markets, while 29% consider culture and cultural differences as an important barrier in non EU-EEA markets. In this particular study, internationalisation referred to all activities that place SMEs into a meaningful business relationship with a foreign partner (exports, imports, foreign direct investment, international subcontracting, and international technical cooperation). According to Leick (2010), differences in culture, language, and mentality as well as in leadership style are considered as barriers to internationalisation between CEE and Western European markets. These can represent the psychic distance between actors from different cultural backgrounds discussed above. Leick (2010) also points out that the transaction costs of cross-border collaboration increase as a consequence of physic distance for enterprises looking to undertake activities in foreign markets with strong differences: leaving certain markets less attractive compared to others. Krätke (1999) and Zander et. al (2008) also identify socio-economic barriers such as cultural and mentality differences as obstacles to cooperation for both German and CEE enterprises.

There is widespread acceptance that a significant number of alliances face problems due to culture. According to research, "40 to 55% of alliances (and similarly for mergers-acquisitions) fail to deliver the value that was expected due to the human factor and in particular the cultural factor" (Dancourt-Cavanagh 2010, pp. 56–57). The culture factor need not, however, have negative implications on cross-border cooperation activities, as a number of further studies show. A study of 800 cross-border acquisitions over the period 1991–2004 shows that, contrary to popular belief, cross-border acquisitions actually perform better in the long run if the acquirer and target come from culturally disparate countries (Chakrabarti et al. 2009). Results also show that while cultural differences may lead to challenges during post-merger integration, mergers between firms from culturally disparate countries may in fact provide the acquirer with higher synergies, and organisational strengths are likely to emerge (ibid). This can perhaps be explained by the fact that some managers of cross-border mergers and acquisitions are more sensitive to cultural issues, have more international and intercultural experience, or may be the result of specific strategies chosen to incorporate cultural differences.

Differences in language and culture, lack of knowledge of attitudes, and behavioural patterns of the other partner can contribute to a lack of trust between potential partners and hamper cross-border cooperation (Smallbone

2007). The cooperation is often made up of individuals from different professional fields, organisations, and national cultures. Depending on the specifics of the cooperative context, the people involved often hardly know each other, and because of the nature of cross-border cooperation, often have to work together from a distance. This distance, or the virtual element to cooperation, can prove especially challenging. While this is a key dimension in any cross-border cooperation activity, it is often given inadequate attention. In today's increasingly complex and dynamic business environment, entering a cooperative agreement with a partner or partners from different cultures can be a daunting process. Without adequate preparation, it is likely to lead to frustration, slower cooperation, and negative impacts on the overall success of the cooperation activity, costing time and money.

Like any other dimension of cooperation, the cultural aspect of cooperation can be seen from two points of view: as a problem that makes communication difficult, leads to frustration and slows down the partnership in achieving goals – hence a possible barrier to successful cooperation; or, it is seen as an opportunity to enhance innovation and provide added value when appropriately managed, enriching the cooperation experience for both the individuals and the SME involved. This is true for any collaborative activity involving different cultures regardless of the geographical or psychological proximity to the counterpart. If approached properly, cooperation can broaden the frames of reference of those involved in the interaction, promoting mutual learning, understanding, and intercultural dialogue, resulting in an increase in innovation and creativity.

5.4 Policy framework and legal conditions

The legal conditions

The legal framework is one important dimension of the rules of conduct for businesses as it limits the forms of SME cooperation and the actions they can take (European Commission 2003). First it is necessary to highlight that in most European countries there are no specific laws or regulations that focus on SME cooperation, but some regulations can influence SMEs willingness to cooperate and determine how the partnership is arranged. That legal conditions sometimes have an indirect influence on cooperation building is evident from the fact that SMEs often mention legal conditions as a main barrier to cooperation (ibid.). This can be explained by the fact that although in most

European countries there are no legal barriers to cooperation as such, other than the European and national competition regulations, unintended barriers can nonetheless sometimes occur. Furthermore SMEs are weary of the legal burden of cooperating across borders, remaining apprehensive of the different legal systems in other countries.

The European Commission (2003) describes four different parts of the legal framework that may potentially have an impact on cooperation among SMEs: (1) the competition regulations at the EU and national level, (3) available legal forms to facilitate cross-border cooperation, the *European Economic Interest Grouping* (EEIG) for example, (3) taxation laws at a national level, and (4) liability laws at a national level. National taxation laws may influence the economic benefits derived from the cooperative venture and national liability laws may have an influence on the risk SMEs associate with cooperation; however, there is no evidence that taxation and liability laws have a practical influence on SME cooperation in Europe (ibid). Therefore, in the following section, we will focus on the competition regulations and the available legal forms for SME cooperation within the European Union.

Competition regulations

Europe's competition law condemns anticompetitive behaviour and aims to ensure that competition in the common market is not distorted. It comes into effect when there is a risk of trade between member states being negatively affected by anticompetitive behaviour.

European competition regulations comprise four main areas (European Commission Competition 2012):

1. *Antitrust and cartels regulations* aiming to eliminate agreements that artificially restrict competition (such as price-fixing agreements or cartels between competitors) and are abused by firms holding a dominant position in the market;
2. *Merger control* by reviewing if firms create an enlarged business that would later dominate the market;
3. *Market liberalisation* in former monopolistic industries; and
4. *State aid control* which refers to the control of state aid measures of national governments to ensure that they do not distort competition in the Single Market.

Only in exceptional cases will SME cooperation result in monopolistic control over a large part of the European market; thus, SME cooperation is usually unaffected by the European competition regulations. However, national competition laws might include regulations directly or indirectly influencing SME cooperation; thus, SMEs must be aware of the national laws.

Legal forms

If firms wish to place the partnership with their cooperation partners on a formal footing, they can choose between a range of legal forms which are set out in different national laws (Commission of the European Communities 1998). In choosing the right legal form for cooperation, it is necessary to understand what the requirements and advantages of the different legal forms are, and in a cross-border context, this becomes much more difficult due to national differences. The cooperation partners need to agree on the use of one national law, which sometimes leaves one of the partner enterprises feeling left at a disadvantage. A further problem is that SMEs are sometimes not aware that a formal legal form of cooperation can emerge even without a written contract, as is the case, for example, with the German civil law partnership (§§ 705–740 BGB). If two or more organisations combine their activities or resources for their common benefit and act together in the market, they constitute a partnership under civil law even without signing a formal contract. There is no written form prescribed for the conclusion of this partnership agreement, and, as there are no formal provisions, the partnership has at the very latest been formed when it makes its first public appearance, which is the point at which it participates in the market. This indicates the need for cooperation partners to be aware of the legal consequences (e.g., concerning the question of liability) of their cooperative activities. It is, therefore, advisable to choose the legal instrument that best corresponds with the economic activity the cooperation partners wish to undertake, but only after seeking the advice of experts, such as lawyers or consultants.

There are currently three legal forms which make it possible for companies to work together across borders with companies from other member states of the European Union.

- The *European Economic Interest Grouping* (EEIG), Regulation (EC) of 1985 (Council Regulation 1985).
- The *European Company* (formally known under the term "Societas Europaea"), Regulation (EC) of 2001 (Council Regulation 2001).
- The *European Cooperative Society*, Regulation (EC) of 2003 (Council Regulation 2003).

All three forms were established to encourage the development of the internal market by facilitating the activity of these types of companies at the European level.

The *European Economic Interest Grouping* (EEIG) (see Council Regulation 1985; Commission of the European Communities 1998) is a transnational legal instrument for cooperation between entrepreneurs in Europe, and aims to facilitate and develop the economic activities of the cooperation partners and to improve or increase the results of the cooperative activities. The activities of this grouping should be related to the economic activities of its members rather than the making profits for itself. It should also be mentioned that the cooperation members have unlimited joint liability for the debts of the EEIG. EEIGs are taxed according to the national law of the individual cooperation member. The profit should be divided between the partners, or can be reinvested or turned into reserves. The EC regulation for EEIGs reduces rules to a minimum and provides members of this type of grouping with considerable freedom for their contractual relationships and control over the internal organisation of the partnership. The founding agreement provides regulations only for fundamental points; all other decisions should be made by the members (Zahorka 2001).

Reasons for choosing an EEIG are as follows (Commission of the European Communities 1998):

- It is a legal form for cooperation, which is largely independent of the various national legal systems. Therefore, all EEIG members are on an equal footing, which enables members to overcome the fear that the partners will be in a more favourable position, as they are working in a more familiar legal environment.
- EEIGs can be formed by different types of organisations, ranging from SMEs to multinationals and other legal bodies such as local authorities, chambers of commerce, and research centres. Therefore, it is also possible to combine the skills and resources of different types of partners to get a highly complementary package.
- The groupings can be adapted very flexibly to changing economic circumstances because the formalities of an EEIG are very simple. EEIGs are also very flexible concerning their financing, as no start-up capital is required for their foundation, and the members can make all forms of contributions, for example, in cash, in material assets, or even in skills. Members are also free to decide how to share their profits and losses.
- Despite its flexibility, this legal form of cooperation also provides the enterprises with a certain degree of stability. EEIGs have full and autonomous

legal capacity, which differentiates them from purely contractual forms of cooperations.

- The EEIG has an ancillary nature, which maintains the autonomy of the cooperation members. The activities of the grouping must be related to the economic activities of its members; however, they must not replace them. Therefore, the EEIG members always retain a certain degree of legal and economic autonomy.

But firms using this legal form of cooperation should be aware of the types of problems that can arise, such as internal communication and its costs, linguistic problems, taxation, distribution of profits and losses, and the lack of confidence in the other members (Zahorka 2001).

The *European Company* (see Council Regulation 2001, Council Directive 2001) has its own legislative framework and allows companies incorporated in different member states to merge or form a holding company. The legal and practical constraints arising from the existence of different national legal systems can, therefore, be avoided. The European Company can be formed in four ways: (1) merger, (2) formation of a holding company, (3) formation of a joint subsidiary, or (4) conversion of a public limited company previously formed under national law.

The advantages of becoming a *European Company* lies in the reduction of administrative and legal costs, as this legal form allows firms which are established in more than one country to merge or form a holding company or joint subsidiary, to adopt a single set of rules and a unified management and reporting system, and to possibly avoid the legal and practical constraints arising from the existence of 28 different legal systems (Enterprise Europe Network London 2006). Furthermore, companies are able to expand and restructure their cross-border activities without setting up a network of subsidiaries governed by different national laws (ibid.). This legal form is predominantly used by large companies as it does not meet the needs of SMEs. The public form, the high share capital of at least EUR 120,000, the requirement to create it out of several companies incorporated in different member states, and the complicated regulations including both national and EU law discourage SMEs from using this legal form (Katuoka and Česnulevičiute 2012).

The *European Cooperative Society* (see Council Regulation 2003, Council Directive 2003) is a legal entity that allows its members to carry out certain activities together, while preserving their independence. With this legal form, the European Union facilitates cooperatives wishing to engage in cross-border business by making legislative provisions which take into account their specific features. It allows the creation of new cooperative enterprises of natural or legal persons at the European level and ensures the rights of information, consultation, and participation of employees in a European cooperative society. It was created to remove the need for cooperatives to establish a subsidiary in each Member State in which they operate. It also allows them to move their registered office freely from one Member State to another, keeping their legal identity. The objective is to provide cooperatives with adequate legal instruments to facilitate their cross-border and transnational activities. The idea is to provide an ideal legal instrument for companies who want to group together for their common benefit, i.e. to access a new market, achieve economies of scale, or undertake research. A European Cooperative Society can be created (1) as a completely new business with five or more people, by two or more legal entities, or by a combination of the two from at least two member states, or (2) by merging two or more existing cooperatives from at least two member states by way of conversion of a cooperative that has had a subsidiary in another member state for at least two years. The European Commission (Commission of European Communities 2004) wants to promote the creation of cooperatives for three main reasons: (1) the cooperatives support the building or the increasing of economic power of SMEs in the market; (2) the cooperatives provide high-quality services to people that would otherwise not be able to access them because supplying such services is not attractive to profit-driven companies; and (3) the cooperatives help to build a knowledge-based society. Cooperatives should act as schools of entrepreneurship and management for those who might not otherwise have access to positions of responsibility (Commission of European Communities 2004). Members of this legal form can include clients, employees, or suppliers, and thus the European Cooperative Society does not directly create a form to conduct business, but rather one to satisfy the needs of its members through economy of scale (Katuoka and Česnulevičiute 2012).

The European Union is, furthermore, currently working on a *European Private Company* statute to improve access for SMEs to the Single Market and to promote their development in the EU with the aim to enable small and medium sized companies to be set up across the Community, under simplified conditions (Commission of the European Communities 2008).

Further legal conditions

Beyond competition regulations and available legal forms for cooperation, other legal conditions can influence cooperation building. For example, as previously mentioned, SMEs often do not consider cooperation a strategic option for fear of sharing knowledge with partners who could make use of it opportunistically. Therefore, intellectual property rights legislation can influence cooperation formation. The currently fragmented patents system is a good example: it stifles innovation and knowledge exchange, as it fails to properly protect a firm's inventions (European Commission 2010b); it thus also has a negative impact on cross-border cooperation building. In order to protect their innovations, every company must go through a separate patent validation system in each member state, which involves high costs and makes it difficult for SMEs to protect their innovations properly. The European Union is currently working on a European patent, but it will take until 2014 to enact it (ibid.).

Furthermore, the contract, employment, and commercial laws, accounting standards, and export regulations of each country need to be considered when cooperating across borders. In this context, firms need to realise that, despite the common market, rules and regulations widely differ across countries and need to be coordinated between the cooperation partners (Bundesministerium für Wirtschaft und Arbeit 2003). The different fiscal policies concerning tax and duties, capital controls, and investment protection also need to be taken into account before considering cooperation abroad (see also Chapter 9).

Policy framework

Firms planning to cooperate with partners abroad are often confronted with different political conditions in the target country. Therefore, it is necessary to be informed about the current economic situation and political climate of the foreign country and to keep the potential difficulties in mind from the beginning. But not only the current political conditions but also the policy measures introduced to support cross-border cooperation have a direct impact on SME cooperation.

Almost all European countries have witnessed an increase of SME cooperation in their national policy programmes (European Commission 2003). Most of the introduced policy measures do not focus on a specific industry. Usually, the objective of the policy measures is not to directly encourage SMEs to cooperate. Cooperation is rather seen as a vehicle to stimulate SMEs to improve specific business areas (ibid.). Most policy measures that encourage SMEs to cooperate have an objective to stimulate SMEs to (1) improve the technological and innovation output in research networks, (2) foster internationalisation, (3) encourage innovation and entrepreneurship, and (4) handle human resource management (ibid.).

Policies that affect the nature and extent of cross-border cooperation can be divided into two groups (Smallbone 2007): (1) policies concerned with the encouragement and facilitation of cross-border cooperation between institutions, and (2) policies specifically fostering cross-border cooperation of enterprises. Both groups are linked to each other, as institutionally based collaboration often includes measures to encourage and support cooperation at the enterprise level. Cooperation at the institutional level is an important mechanism for laying the basis for SME cross-border cooperation as it provides a framework to facilitate contacts and provide businesses with instruments, helping them to identify potential partners, and to access resources (ibid.). Policies that are designed to encourage and enable SMEs to cooperate across borders should aim to facilitate the development of mutually beneficial cooperative arrangements, which are appropriate for the needs of the participating firms as well as the cross-border region (ibid.).

On the national level, most support programmes focus on the following main instruments (European Commission 2003):

- Subsidies that help to reduce the costs of achieving the objectives of the programmes.
- Counselling with the aim of directly supporting enterprises planning to cooperate by offering advice and transferring knowledge and cooperation competence to the enterprises.
- Providing meeting places and venues that can be used by SMEs to meet potential cooperation partners.
- Providing localities where SMEs can start to operatively work on their cooperation, often combined with a meeting place and counselling.

Smallbone et al. (2008) identified measures that specifically aim at encouraging, promoting, and facilitating cross-border cooperation of SMEs:

- Measures that raise awareness regarding the opportunities presented by the different forms of cross-border cooperation on both sides of the border.
- Establishment of cross-border partner search facilities through technological platforms and other partner searching tools.
- Measures to foster business-to-business contacts through trade missions or other joint events.
- Introduction of funding possibilities to finance cross-border cooperation among public authorities, firms, and associations in border regions.
- Increasing the international networking capacity and cooperation between national business associations, chambers of commerce, and agencies.

- Introduction of cross-border partnership programmes which offer, for example, cross-border training to help SMEs get the most out of their cooperation.
- Cross-border cooperation can also be promoted by the availability of experts and specialists in cooperation to provide enterprises with information and tips on how to find cooperation partners and how to maintain a successful cooperation.

Moreover, the Bundesministerium für Wirtschaft und Arbeit (2003) sees the following measures as necessary to minimize the risk and maximize trust in partnerships:

- The organisation of information events in each partners' home country as well as information and match-making events organised in foreign countries.
- The exchange of experience with enterprises, which already have experience in cross-border cooperation. Often these contacts can be established by national business associations or chambers of commerce.
- The elaboration and distribution of material for enterprises to give them background information on the market where potential cooperation partners are situated.
- The organisation of joint business missions for enterprises.
- The provision of training to facilitate the inter-cultural and language competencies of the potential cooperation partners.
- The provision of professional external support in conflict situations.

Firms planning to cooperate should also consider the relative importance cooperation enjoys in the foreign target country. Countries often request foreign investment cooperation with domestic firms and fund these forms of cooperation. It is sometimes not possible to invest in a foreign market without having domestic cooperation partners.

Thus, external conditions directly or indirectly influence cross-border collaborations, and can be either a hindering or a facilitating factor in SME cooperation. Focusing on SME cross-border cooperation in Europe, and considering the major influences of the measures introduced by the European Union, we – in Part II of this book – discuss the role of European institutions, initiatives, regulations and programmes promoting and facilitating cross-border cooperation in Europe; thus aiming to achieve a more comprehensive understanding of European framework conditions that influence SME cross-border cooperation.

Summary of external conditions influencing cross-border cooperation

The founding, success and stability of cooperation among SMEs are influenced by external framework conditions. Globalisation and as a consequence the intensified competition, the technological development, differences in cultural background and language, as well as the policies and legal conditions set at national as well as European level can either facilitate or hinder cross-border cooperation.

1. Globalisation is a major cooperation driver. Globalisation increases the number of competitors in the market; therefore, SMEs, through different cooperation forms, try to increase their competitiveness and gain access to new markets. Industry specifics also influence SME cooperation, as the intensity of the industry competition and social organisation of the markets has a significant impact on whether cooperation is seen as beneficial for SMEs.
2. The increase in established cross-border partnerships can also be explained by the developments in information and communication technology. These developments have reduced the transaction costs of cooperation through more efficient communication, information exchange, and coordination of activities. The new technologies provide new opportunities, especially for cooperation partners situated in geographically dispersed locations.
3. Furthermore, cultural framework conditions deeply influence the success of cross-border cooperation. Language diversity can be seen as a major obstacle for SME cross-border cooperation. Language is crucial as a means of exchanging and transferring knowledge, values, and business goals; lack of language fluency can negatively impact both the effectiveness and efficiency of cooperation. Therefore, SMEs need to take both language and communication differences into account from the beginning of their cooperation and must not wait until the first signs of conflict emerge.
4. Every cross-border partnership, regardless of type or field, has a cultural dimension. Cultural differences have considerable influence on the behaviour and conduct of SMEs. They can affect crucial cooperative activities, such as communication, goal setting, planning, decision making, and conflict handling within the partnership. Thus, SMEs need to be aware of cultural differences in order to leverage their potential within cooperation and avoid impediments to the joint working process.

5. Although no specific laws or regulations focus on SME cross-border cooperation, the national and European legal frameworks influence the formation and management of cooperation. The European and national competition regulations and the possible legal cooperation forms have an effect on the formation of cross-border cooperation. Furthermore, the contract, employment, and commercial laws, and the export regulations in the concerned countries need to be considered when deciding to cooperate across borders. Moreover, most European countries have included the improvement and increase of SME cooperation in their policy programmes. Therefore, SMEs should exploit the national and European policy measures aimed at encouraging, promoting, and facilitating SME cross-border cooperation.

References

Balling, R. (1998) Kooperation: Strategische Allianzen, Netzwerke, Joint-Ventures und andere Organisationsformen zwischenbetrieblicher Zusammenarbeit in Theorie und Praxis. Frankfurt am Main: Lang

Beckerman, W. (1956) Distance and the pattern of intra-European trade. *Review of Economics and Statistics* 28(1), 31–40

Bohner, U. (2011) The European dimension of cross-border cooperation: Opening Speech. In: Wassenberg, B. and Beck, J. (eds.) Living and researching cross-border cooperation, Vol. 3: The European dimension. Stuttgart: Franz Steiner Verlag, 21–28

Bundesministerium für Wirtschaft und Arbeit (2003) Gemeinsam stärker. Kooperationen planen und durchführen. Ein Leitfaden für kleine und mittlere Unternehmen. http://www.competence-research-centres.eu/fileadmin/compera-daten/BMWA_20Brosch_C3 _BCre_20Kooperationen_20planen_20und_20durchf_C3_BChren.pdf (date accessed 1 July 2012)

Chakrabarti, R., Jayaraman, N., and Mukherjee, S. (2009) Mars-Venus marriages: Culture and cross-border MandA. *Journal of International Business Studies* 40(2), 216–237

Child, J., Rodrigues, S. B., and Frynas, J. G. (2009) Psychic distance, its impact and coping modes: Interpretations of SME decision makers. *Management International Review* 49(2), 199–224

Cohen, S.G. and Mankin, D. (1999) Collaboration in the virtual organization, In: Cooper, C. L., and Rousseau, D. M. (eds.) Trends in organizational behavior: The virtual organization. Chichester: Wiley

Commission of the European Communities (1998) The EEIG: an instrument for transnational cooperation. A practical handbook for SMEs, 2nd edn., http://ec.europa.eu/employment_social/equal/products/sup/pro-122-hb.pdf (date accessed 1 July 2012)

Commission of the European Communities (2004) Communication form the commission to the council and the European parliament, the European economic and social committee and the committee of regions on the promotion of co-operative societies in Europe. http://eur-lex.europa.eu/LexUriServ/LexUriServ.do?uri=COM:2004:0018:FIN:EN:PDF (date accessed 1 July 2012)

Commission of the European Communities (2008) Proposal for a Council Regulation on the Statute for a European private company. http://eur-lex.europa.eu/LexUriServ/LexUriServ.do?uri=COM:2008:0396:FIN:EN:PDF (date accessed 1 July 2012)

Council Directive 2001/86/EC of 8 October 2001 supplementing the Statute for a European company with regards to the involvement of employees, L 294/22, p. 1–11

Council Directive 2003/72/EC of 22 July 2003 supplementing the Statute for a European Cooperative Society with regard to the involvement of employees L 207/25

Council Regulation (EEC) No 2137/85 of 25 July 1985 on the European Economic Interest Grouping (EEIG). [1985] OJ L 199, p. 1–9

Council Regulation (EC) no 2157/2001 of 8 October 2001 on the statute for a European company (SE). [2001] OJ L 294, p. 1–21

Council Regulation (EC) No 1435/2003 of 22 July 2003 on the statute for a European Cooperative Society (SCE). [2003] OJ L 207, p. 1–24

Dancourt-Cavanagh, M., comp. (2010) The intercultural dimension in European projects: How does it add value. Les Cahiers de L'Institut Européen pour la Coopération Territoriale. Région Nord-Pas Calais

Enterprise Europe Network London (2006) The European company statute. http://www.londonchamber.co.uk/docimages/7034.pdf (date accessed 1 July 2012)

European Commission (2003) SMEs and cooperation. In: European Commission (ed.), Observatory of European SMEs (Vol. 5). http://ec.europa.eu/enterprise/policies/sme/files/analysis/doc/smes_observatory_2003_report5_en.pdf (date accessed 1 July 2012)

European Commission (2006) ELAN: Effects on the European economy of shortages of foreign language skills in enterprise. http://ec.europa.eu/languages/documents/doc421_en.pdf (date accessed 16 May 2012)

European Commission (2010a) Internationalisation of SMEs. http://ec.europa.eu/enterprise/policies/sme/marketaccess/files/internationalisation_of_european_smes_final_en.pdf (date accessed 16 May 2012)

European Commission (2010b) Single market act booklet. Luxembourg: Publications office of the European Union. http://ec.europa.eu/internal_market/smact/docs/brochure-web_en.pdf (date accessed 1 July 2012)

European Commission (2012) Competition, http://ec.europa.eu/competition/index_en.html (date accessed 1 July 2012)
Glaser, E. (2010) Foreign language competence in intercultural cooperation. In: Thomas, A., Kinast, E., and Schroll-Machl (eds.) Handbook of intercultural cooperation: Basics and areas of application. Göttingen: Vandenhoeck & Ruprecht, 65–82
Häkli, J. (2004) Governing the mountains: Cross-border regionalization in Catalonia. In: Kramsch, O. and Hooper, B. (eds.). Cross-Border governance in the European Union. London: Routledge, 56–69
Hall, E. T. (1976) Beyond culture. New York: Anchor Books
Intriligator, M. D. (2003) Globalization of the world economy: Potential benefits and costs and a net assessment. Milken Institute Policy brief Number 33. http://www.milkeninstitute.org/pdf/globalization_pb.pdf (date accessed 1 July 2012)
Johanson, J. and Vahlne, J. E. (1977) The internationalization of the firms: A model of knowledge development and increasing foreign market commitment. *Journal of International Business Studies* 8(1), 23–32
Johanson, J. and Wiedersheim-Paul, F. (1975) The internationalisation process of the firms: Four Swedish case studies. *Journal of Management Studies* 12(3), 305–322
Katuoka, S. and Česnulevičiutė, V. (2012): European private company: Perspectives of legal regulation. *Jurisprudence* 19(1), 159–178
Krätke, S. (1999) Regional integration or fragmentation? The German-Polish border region in a new Europe. *Regional Studies* 33(7), 631–641
Leick, B. (2010) What determines the co-operative potential for firms in western European and CEE border regions? A Comparative micro-level analysis. *Economic and Business Review* 12(2), 109–128
Luhmann, N. (2000) Vertrauen. Ein Mechanismus der Reduktion sozialer Kompetenz. Stuttgart: UTB
OECD (1997) Globalisation and small and medium enterprises (SMEs). Vol. I – Synthesis report. Paris: OECD Publishing
Osiecka, A. (2006) Grenzüberschreitende Unternehmenskooperationen. Standortbezogene Analyse deutsch-polnischer Unternehmenspartnerschaften im Grenzgebiet. Wiesbaden: Deutscher Universitäts-Verlag
Picot, A., Ripperger, T., and Wolff, B. (1996) The fading boundaries of the firm: The role of information and communication technology. *Journal of Institutional and Theoretical Economics* 152(1), 65–79
Smallbone, D., Labrianidis, L., Venesaar, U., Welter, F., and Zashev, P. (2007) Challenges and prospects of cross border cooperation in the context of EU enlargement. Deliverable 7: State of the art literature review. http://www.crossbordercoop.net/Publications/Integrated_lit_review.pdf (date accessed 16 May 2012)
Stanoevska-Slabeva, K., Blijsma, M., Gareis, K., Vartiainen, M., and Verburg, R. (2009) Collaborative work: Globalisation and new collaborative working environments – New global. Final Report. http://www.empirica.com/aktuelles/documents/Final%20Report_Final%20Version.pdf (date accessed 16 May 2012)

Ting-Toomey, S. and Chung, L. C. (2005) Understanding intercultural communication. Los Angeles, CA: Roxbury Publishing Company

Todeva, E. and Knoke, D. (2005) Strategic alliances and models of collaboration. *Management Decision* 43(1), 123–148

Weaver, K. M. and Dickson, P. H. (2006) Current use, unique challenges, outcomes, and success attributes for SME-based alliances: Towards a future research agenda. Paper presented at the USASBE National Conference, Tucson, Arizona

Zahorka, H.-J. (2001) EEIG European economic interest grouping. The only transnational in-strument for co-operation between entrepreneurs in Europe. http://www.europarkinson.net/download/EEIG_basic_info.pdf (date accessed 1 July 2012)

Zander, I. (2004) The micro foundations of cluster stickiness – walking in the shoes of the entrepreneur. *Journal of International Management* 10(2), 151–175

Zentes, J. and Schramm-Klein, H. (2003) Exogene und endogene Einflussfaktoren der Kooperation. In: Zentes, J., Swoboda, B., and Morschett, D. (eds.) Kooperationen, Allianzen und Netzwerke. Grundlagen – Ansätze – Perspektiven. Wiesbaden: Gabler, 257–276

Part II:
A European institutional perspective on cross-border cooperation

Eithne Knappitsch

6 History of cross-border cooperation in Europe

A range of terminology is used in discussions of European cross-border cooperation, particularly from the institutional perspective, and definitions are imprecise. The expression "cross-border cooperation" might well, for example, be substituted by "transborder cooperation", although this formulation is used neither by the EU nor the Council of Europe (Odendahl 2011). Odendahl also notes that the Council of Europe uses "transfrontier cooperation" and, more recently, "interterritorial cooperation" in its documents and that the EU Commission once commonly used "cross-border cooperation", which has largely been replaced by "European territorial cooperation". In the use of "territorial cooperation", differentiation is made among "cross-border cooperation", "interregional cooperation", and "transnational cooperation": cross-border cooperation is considered to take place across neighbouring borders, interregional cooperation is any form of cooperation among non-contiguous regions, and transnational cooperation refers to any cooperation that occurs across the greater European space (Lambertz 2011). Regardless of the choice of expression or its use in a Council of Europe or EU context, the overall concept can be understood to denote any form of cooperation across national borders (usually at the local or regional as opposed to the national level) to deal with common problems, use potential synergies, or contribute to sustainable development. In order to highlight its relevance for SME cooperation across national borders, it should be observed that "problems" can refer to economic, administrative, political, environmental, spatial, infrastructural, security, cultural, or labour market issues. Bearing this in mind, a broader discussion of cross-border cooperation from a European perspective is directly relevant to the potential cooperation among small and medium-sized enterprises (SMEs) across national borders. The general framework conditions, whether socio-cultural, legal, policy, or funding-related, can either facilitate cooperative arrangements or hinder them.

6.1 The evolution of cross-border cooperation in Europe

Cross-border cooperation in Europe has evolved for two obvious reasons. One, often cited, relates to the desire to heal the scars of war marring the landscape of Europe. In the early 1970s, Alfred Mozer referred to the idea of "overcoming borders as the scars of history" (Wassenberg 2011, p. 29). While the scars have faded, a new mesh of relationships and networks has emerged across Europe, erasing the marks left by often violent confrontation. The second reason flows from the ever popular desire for a "Europe without frontiers", the much strived-for aim of either a borderless Europe or, at the very least, a Europe of permeable borders and a large single market where persons, goods, services, and capital may move freely. This concept, one of the most popular features of European Union (EU) rhetoric, aims to communicate the idea of a borderless Europe in which cohesion, harmony, a "Europe of regions", and uniformity in diversity can thrive. The Council of Europe (1949) and the European Coal and Steel Community, precursor to the European Economic Community (1957), were founded on the basis of interstate cooperation. Initiatives began at the regional level, perhaps with the Council of European Municipalities and Regions in 1951: twenty years later, the Association of European Border Regions (AEBR) was established. The importance of cross-border cooperation as both a contribution to the creation of a united Europe and a means of promoting economic and social development has grown considerably since the 1950s (Sadowski 2005).

Before embarking on any further discussion of the evolution of European cross-border cooperation, it is perhaps necessary to first clearly identify cross-border cooperation as an element within the larger territorial cooperation context mentioned above. Territorial cooperation has evolved from the town- and city-twinning of the post-World War Two era, through the establishment of regional associations (such as the Committee of the Regions), to witness the emergence of sub-national initiatives incorporating cross-border, interregional, and transnational activities (e.g., the Interreg programme, Eurodistricts, Euroregions) as well as supranational initiatives (e.g., the Council of Europe and the EU) and interstate initiatives. Research on the general development of territorial cooperation, particularly cross-border territorial cooperation, has largely been neglected, with some exceptions (Perkmann 2003; 2005). However, it is currently receiving more attention.

The end of the Second World War and the development of Franco-German relations marked not only the beginning of a long and sustained European integration but also the institutionalisation of European cross-border cooperation. This process was to prove successful despite the post-war emergence of two distinctive ideological and political blocks in Europe. From the 1950s, differences across territories in terms of power and administrative structures and the level of responsibility of territorial authorities have affected cross-border cooperation. Further factors that cannot be underestimated are the levels of political, financial and legal support available at the local/regional, national, and supranational levels. The availability of these factors has affected the degree to which cross-border cooperation has been fostered or impeded across Europe. Early efforts to get cross-border cooperation up and running did not run smoothly. Cooperation was initially based mainly on informal agreements "with varying degrees of formality and mostly relied on good will" (Perkmann 2003, p. 155). One of the institutional starting points of cross-border cooperation in Europe was the founding of the Conference of Local Authorities (CLA) by the Council of Europe in 1957 to examine neighbourhood issues at both the local and regional levels (Wassenberg 2011; Congress of Regional and Local Authorities 2012). Subsequently, cross-border regions became integrated into the regional policy of the European Economic Community, particularly following the introduction of the Interreg Programmes in 1991. These developments are considered crucial, as they essentially linked the local and regional authorities on the ground with the decision-makers in Brussels and Strasbourg. Since the 1990s, alongside the emerging concept of a "Europe of regions", there has been a clear link between the regional level, the process of European integration, and the EU institutions. A further developmental stage can be traced to 2005 and 2006, when the multilevel governance theories of European integration began to take centre stage (Wassenberg 2011; Durà-Guimerà and Oliveras González 2010). These periods in the development of cross-border cooperation in Europe will be outlined below.

6.2 Different periods in the development of cross-border cooperation

In analysing the growth of cross-border initiatives and the development of supporting instruments, Durà-Guimerà and Oliveras González (2010) identify three historical periods since the 1950s using three variables – the number of cross-border initiatives, spatial distribution, and the instruments of international support. Following Durà-Guimerà and Oliveras González, we can identify an initial period of European cross-border cooperation spanning from 1950 to 1979. The end of the war was a sort of catalyst in the creation of new forms of territorial cooperation. This phase saw the emergence of partnerships among towns in various European states, particularly Germany and France. Informal contacts developed around issues perceived as common. Durà-Guimerà and Oliveras González (2010) suggest that cooperation initiatives occurred in this period "almost exclusively at the borders between Germany, the Netherlands, Belgium, Luxembourg, France and Switzerland, and Scandinavia" (p. 4), perhaps too narrowly circumscribed, as informal cooperation initiatives were undoubtedly occurring elsewhere in Europe but on a smaller scale. As mentioned, cooperation was initially based on loosely defined agreements, and relied on the participants' goodwill, a factor that remains crucial in all forms of cross-border cooperation, SME or otherwise. In this period, neither regional nor local authorities were able to offer much financial or technical support for cross-border cooperation initiatives. Until the 1970s, intergovernmental committees were responsible for most cross-border issues. Throughout the 1970s, a series of transnational and interregional initiatives were consolidated; particularly notable were the Working Communities promoted by the Council of Europe. According to many experts (Perkmann 2003; Beck 2011), the territorial distribution of cooperation was again concentrated in Western Europe, particularly around Germany, throughout this period.

Durà-Guimerà and Oliveras González (2010) define the second period in the evolution of cross-border cooperation in Europe as that between 1980 and 1989, which is distinct because the first instruments for legal cooperation support were made available at that time; the European Outline Convention on Transfrontier Co-operation between Territorial Communities or Authorities (later the Madrid Convention of 1980) and the European Charter of Local Self-Government of 1985 are worth mentioning here. In this period, legal instruments for cross-border cooperation were not based on strict legal criteria. Instead, the basis for future legal structures emerged as a series of guidelines or principles underpinning future legal structures (Council of Europe 2006). These instruments are detailed in the following chapter, which focuses on the institutional dimension of cross-border cooperation. The Madrid Convention and Charter resulted in a large number of European countries signing bilateral treaties and adopting bilateral agreements. AEBR's European Charter for Border and Cross-Border Regions (1981) had no legal basis but contributed nonetheless to strengthening the commitment to the application of the Madrid Convention. Despite the presence of the Communist bloc, a number of initiatives included countries in Southern and Eastern Europe (for example, the Alps-Adriatic Working Community; see Knappitsch et al. 2011), some of which played a crucial role in the reintegration of former Communist states following the fall of the iron curtain.

The third period of cooperation identified by Durà-Guimerà and Oliveras González (2010) spans the 1980s to the present, during which a significant increase in both the financial support available for cross-border activities and the expansion of those activities can be observed. Following the two protocols of the Madrid Convention there has been a clear link between the regional level, the process of European integration, and EU institutions. Conventions were signed in 1995 and 1998, the first recognising the right of territorial communities to adopt cross-border agreements (valid in domestic law) and their legal personalities and the second establishing authorities' rights to conclude twinning agreements and outlining the necessary legal framework (Bohner 2011). State-level agreements and treaties were signed, such as the Agreement of Rome between France and Italy in 1993 and the Treaty of Bayonne between France and Spain in 1995 (Durà-Guimerà and Oliveras González 2010). Another milestone was reached with the development of the European Regional Policy, stimulating cross-border cooperation via a set of Community Initiatives using the Structural Funds and providing a set of financial programs (including Interreg) to support cross-border activities. The EU also developed a set of programs for border regions with non-EU states and the Mediterranean basin (PHARE, TACIS, CARDS, and MEDA). In 1995, the Council of Europe developed a program to promote cross-border cooperation in Eastern Europe. Some of these initiatives demonstrated that cross-border cooperation could be used as a sort of tool for preparing countries for EU accession (Durà-Guimerà and Oliveras González 2010). These developments functioned as a catalyst for the emergence of many Euroregions and other bodies with the aim of managing (and attracting) projects financed by Interreg or the Council of Europe.

Durà-Guimerà and Oliveras González (2010) suggest that a fourth period of cross-border cooperation in Europe may have begun around 2006, a "turning point in the evolution of cross-border cooperation in Europe" (p. 6). They note that, while some dynamics remain unchanged from those of the third period, there has been a change in institutional support (including both legal and financial elements). Durà-Guimerà and Oliveras González believe this period to be characterised by fewer new initiatives, particularly those creating formal legal cooperation structures. The EU and the Council of Europe have placed a new emphasis on promoting the formation of cooperation initiatives with and among local and regional authorities from third countries, such as future EU accession states and, for example, countries in Northern Africa or the Middle East. The Union for the Mediterranean (UfM) was established in 2009 and the Euro-Mediterranean Assembly of Local and Regional Authorities in the following year; this support is essentially financial. Older initiatives have been revamped or replaced by new ones, such as the Instrument for Pre-

Accession assistance (IPA), which replaces programmes such as PHARE and CARDS, and the European Neighbourhood and Partnership Instrument (ENPI), which merges the former MEDA and the European part of TACIS. The latter focuses on states with no clear prospects of joining the EU, while the former pertains to either candidates or potential candidates for accession. Such initiatives can be considered instruments of a broader European Enlargement process and complements to the overall European integration process. As the interconnection between cross-border cooperation and EU enlargement deserves a separate discussion, it is the focus of the next section.

6.3 European enlargement and SME cross-border cooperation

All the cross-border cooperation aspects mentioned above impact the SME sector. The transformation of local, regional, national, and EU contexts through various policies and processes of regionalisation and integration have direct implications for SMEs: the economic, political, administrative, and socio-cultural conditions underpinning European developments also shape the entrepreneurship and business climate.

Cross-border cooperation has long complemented European integration and has clearly retained this function. The introduction of the Single Market, EU enlargement, and the introduction of a single currency changed the business environment both within and outside the EU. Entrepreneurs across the European landscape experienced new challenges and opportunities, for example in their access to new markets, the increased competition after the removal of import duties, quantity restrictions, and physical barriers. Smallbone et al. (2007) observe the "global tendency for firms to use cross-border alliances to strengthen and maintain their position in the market place" (p. 16). Cross-border alliances are perceived as a means to expand and grow. The closer the proximity of markets, the higher the likelihood of lower transportation costs, resource sharing, and the joint delivery of public services, all adding to the attractiveness of cross-border entrepreneurship.

The 2004 and 2007 enlargements suggest that the EU's centre of gravity has shifted eastwards. Some argue that regional disparities have since increased (see for example Cassin and Zolin 2008), which is certainly true in terms of income levels. Trading patterns have also changed: the EU's trade volume has increased significantly. For SMEs, the elimination of trade barriers offers the opportunity to expand across borders and gain access to a wide and diversified body of consumers. A larger market may have stronger impacts on certain sectors, thereby resulting in logistics being redesigned around these sectors, producing positive externalities across the entire cross-border region (see Niebuhr and Stiller 2004 and Hijzen et. al. 2006, qtd. in Smallbone et al. 2007). The lure of low or lower purchasing power may encourage enterprises to look abroad for new opportunities. However, the other side of the coin is that SMEs face increased competition and uncertainty, and the standards imposed by the EU can be considered an added deterrent to expanding the export market (SMEs may need to invest in, for example, emissions, waste management, product safety, and working conditions, depending on their industry). Added costs and compliance requirements impose serious burdens on SMEs in certain regions.

Substantial political developments across Central and Eastern Europe, such as the collapse of communism and the emergence of democratic political systems, and the on-going integration within the framework of the EU have significantly impacted the development of cross-border cooperation (Sadowski 2005). Eastern European enlargement has been cited by a number of authors as a factor driving the internationalisation of European enterprises (see Leick 2010). Enlargement has had, and will continue to have, many consequences for regional economic development throughout Europe. Integration is influenced not only by economic factors but also by political, cultural, social, and historical ones. Formerly external EU borders are now internal borders. New external borders begin a new relationship with their non-EU neighbours. Enlargement has brought a different set of opportunities and threats to the "old" and "new" member states. For example, internal border regions are expected to experience economic growth in the medium and long terms due to their favourable locations within the enlarged market (close to new member states) and the increased cross-border interaction (Smallbone et al. 2007). Differences across economic and social systems must not be underestimated, particularly differences between the former communist and non-communist blocs. The economic and social systems emerging from former communist states are fundamentally different. The roles of the central and local authorities in former Soviet bloc countries are dramatically different from those in the older EU member states, with central authority holding a much more powerful position and local authorities performing a somewhat smaller range of activities. This creates a very specific set of problems for cross-border cooperation, as different levels of government have different sets of functions (see, for example, Knappitsch et al. 2011). Another obvious characteristic of the former communist bloc is that entrepreneurism was minimal (Turnock 2005). This, too, impacted the business environments in its countries. With the predominance of centralisation, border areas were often assigned a specific role that marked their peripheral status, particularly their separating role. As the economic systems were oriented to the interior of the countries, border regions were often characterised by poor development. For example, Bufon and Markelj (2010) argue that the unfavourable situation in Eastern Europe's border areas was magnified by communist regimes after World War II "by encouraging or causing the emigration of autochthonous populations and hindering the social and economic development of border areas in general" (p. 21). Cross-border communication was actively discouraged and kept to a minimum. Infrastructure and industry in border regions were neglected. The newly independent accession states have had to work to reverse this legacy in order to integrate into the EU and, more generally, to adapt to the international system (Kennard 2004).

The new member states and, to some extent, the neighbouring states have seen increased investments, higher productivity, growth, and more efficient resource allocation. Another important aspect of enlargement has been the increased technological and financial transfers from the EU (see also Chapter 10 on EU initiatives supporting SME cross-border cooperation for further information on Cohesion and Structural Funds). The enlargement effects on SMEs have been the subject of study in existing research (Smallbone and Rogut 2005). These studies suggest that the specific characteristics of SMEs, such as size, affect their ability to "identify, cope with and respond to new sources of threat and opportunity" (Smallbone et al. 2007, p. 14). Moreover, SMEs have less control than their larger counterparts over external factors and their resources are more limited. Their threats include increased international competition (for products, services, and labour markets) and the cost of complying with EU standards and regulations. Smallbone at al. (2007) point out that "EU enlargement has been accompanied by a continuing process of integration, which has undoubtedly affected regional production structures, the level of competition, as well as social conditions" (p. 7). Trade flows, FDI, cross-border purchase flows, more commuters, migration, and structural changes are all examples of the "regional effects" of EU enlargement. It can be argued that the main barriers to the movement of goods, services, and people are now administrative and institutional disparities, technical regulations, problems with cross-border infrastructure, and cultural and linguistic differences (Smallbone et al. 2007).

Regional spatial variations also affect SMEs' business environments. Opportunities for and constraints on the general development of entrepreneurship and cooperation may rely on the market conditions in and economic well-being of the neighbouring states. The common problems and resources shared across a region comprising different jurisdictions may also impact the general conditions for cooperation across borders. Krätke (1998) points out that a lack of trust among cooperation partners can result from, among other things, differences in economic systems, economic development, and social systems across borders.

European Enlargement has been particularly important to SMEs wishing to internationalise within Europe, including those wishing to undertake some form of cross-border cooperation. A study conducted in South Eastern Europe reveals that "border firms tend to develop more intense cross-border trade relations than the national average" and finds that "this level of interaction and trade would have been significantly higher if current constraints in cooperation were absent" (Dimitrov et al. 2003, p. 16). The barriers to cooperation perceived by the border firms investigated in the study include the general conditions prevailing in a country, the lack of assistance in developing cross-border ties, and the financial conditions of the countries concerned. The countries involved in the study (Albania, Bulgaria, Greece, and the Former Yugoslavian Republic of Macedonia) did not consider the lack of a common language across borders to be of major importance (Dimitrov et al. 2003). This might be explained by the fact that, despite differences in language, their psychic distances are small because of their long history of interaction. An important study finding in light of EU regional policy is that the development of regional economies and economic conditions was considered the best cross-border cooperation policy (ibid.). Despite the clearly positive impacts of an integrated borderless Europe, formal borders are evidently not the only obstacles to cross-border cooperation. While the economic potential of cross-border entrepreneurship is clear, the heterogeneity of border regions, economic development levels, institutional structures, languages, and ethnicities continue to influence economic processes after formal borders are removed (Dimitrov et al. 2003; Perkmann 2003; 2005). Some of these issues will be addressed in the subsequent chapters of this part of the book.

A summary of the history of European cross-border cooperation

1. Two factors largely explain the development of cross-border cooperation in Europe: the first is the wish to heal the scars on the European landscape

left by decades of war; the second is the promotion of the economic and social integration of Europe and the establishment of the Single Market.
2. Cross-border cooperation in Europe has progressed from the goodwill town- and city-twinning projects of the post-war period to an integrated and legally supported set of activities within the broader territorial cooperation context of the EU.
3. The introduction of the Single Market, EU enlargement, and a single European currency have all significantly impacted the business environments both within and outside the EU.
4. The changing European business environment presents SMEs in different regions with different challenges and opportunities.
5. The potential for cross-border SME cooperation in Europe should be considered high given the developments towards an integrated Europe of social and economic cohesion. However, one must recognise that there are borders other than formal ones impeding cooperation.

References

Beck, J. (2011) Patterns of cross-border cooperation in Europe. Presentation at the European Cross-Border Symposium, 2 March 2011, Villach, Austria

Bohner, U. (2011) The European dimension of cross-border cooperation: Opening speech. In: Wassenberg, B. and Beck, J. (eds.) Living and researching cross-border cooperation, Vol. 3: The European dimension. Stuttgart: Franz Steiner Verlag, 51–58

Bufon, M. and Markelj, V. (2010) Regional policies and cross-border cooperation: new challenges and new development models in central Europe. *Revista Român de Geografie Politic* 1(May), 18–28

Cassin, M. and Zolin, M. B. (2008) Territorial cooperation and regional economic development: A case study. Department of Economics Working Paper No. 09/WP/2008, Ca Foscari University of Venice

Congress of Regional and Local Authorities (2012) The Congress of Regional and Local Authorities' website. http://www.coe.int/t/congress/default_en.asp (date accessed 15 May 2012)

Council of Europe (2006) Report on the current state of the administrative and legal framework of transfrontier co-operation in Europe. Strasbourg: Council of Europe

Dimitrov, M., Petrakos, G., Totev, S., and Tsiapa, M. (2003) Cross-border cooperation in Southeastern Europe: The enterprises' point of view. *Eastern European Economics* 41(6), 5–25

Durà-Guimerà, A. and Oliveras González, X. (2010) Recent dynamics in European cross-border cooperation: Towards a new period? Paper presented at the Regional Studies Association Annual International Conference 2010, 24–26 May, Pécs, Hungary

European Charter for Local Self Government (1985) http://conventions.coe.int/Treaty/EN/Treaties/Html/122.htm (date accessed 15 May 2012)

European Outline Convention on Transfrontier Co-operation between Territorial Communities or Authorities (1980) http://conventions.coe.int/treaty/en/treaties/html/106.htm (date accessed 15 May 2012)

Hijzen, A., Gorg, H., and Manchin, M. (2006) Cross border mergers and acquisitions and the role of trade costs. European Economy. Economic Papers, No. 242

Kennard, A. (2004) Cross-border governance at the future eastern edges of the EU: A regeneration project? In: Kramsch, O. and Hooper, B. (eds.) Cross-border governance in the European Union. London and New York: Routledge, 107–120

Knappitsch, E., Mundschütz, C., Petkovšek, V., and Setnikar-Cankar, S. (2011) Beyond needs analysis in the Alps-Adriatic region. ISMA Discussion Paper Series, No. 08-2011. http://isma.fh-kaernten.at/publikationen/discussion-papers.html (date accessed 15 May 2012)

Krätke, S. (1998) Problems of cross-border regional integration: The case of the German-Polish border region. *European Urban and Regional Studies* 5(3), 249–262

Lambertz, K-H. (2011) L'état de la coopération transfrontalière en Europe. In: Wassenberg, B. and Beck, J. (eds.) Living and researching cross-border cooperation, Vol. 3: The European dimension. Stuttgart: Franz Steiner Verlag, 59–66

Leick, B. (2010) What determines the co-operative potential for firms in western European and CEE border regions? A Comparative micro-level analysis. *Economic and Business Review* 12(2), 109–128

Niebuhr, A. and Stiller, S. (2004) Integration effects in border regions: A survey of economic theory and empirical studies. *Review of Regional Research* 24, 3–21

Odendahl, K. (2011) Legal instruments of transborder cooperation in Europe. In: Wassenberg, B. and Beck, J. (eds.) Living and researching cross-border cooperation, Vol. 3: The European dimension. Stuttgart: Franz Steiner Verlag, 89–104

Perkmann, M. (2003) Cross border regions in Europe: Significance and drivers of regional cross border cooperation. *European Urban and Regional Planning Studies* 10(2), 153–171

Perkmann, M. (2005) Cross-border co-operation as policy entrepreneurship: Explaining the variable success of European cross-border regions. CSGR Working Paper No. 166/05, Warwick

Sadowski, R. (2005) Similarities and differences of instruments and policies of the Council of Europe and the European Union in the field of transfrontier co-operation. Strasbourg: Council of Europe

Smallbone, D., Labrianidis, L., Venesaar, U., Welter, F., and Zashev, P. (2007) Challenges and prospects of cross border cooperation in the context of EU enlargement. Deliverable 7: State of the art literature review. http://www.crossbordercoop.net/Publications/Integrated_lit_review.pdf (date accessed 15 May 2012)

Smallbone, D. and Rogut, A. (2005) The challenge facing SMEs in the EU's new member states. *International Entrepreneurship and Management Journal* 1(2), 219–240

Turnock, D. (2005) Regional development with particular reference to cohesion in cross-border regions. In: Turnock, D. (eds.) Foreign direct investment and regional development in East-Central Europe and the Former Soviet Union. Aldershot: Ashgate Publishing, 141–182

Wassenberg, B. (2011) Le voisinage de proximité. Les eurorégions entre l'Ouest et l'Est. In: Wassenberg, B. and Beck, J. (eds.) Living and researching cross-border cooperation, Vol. 3: The European dimension. Stuttgart: Franz Steiner Verlag, 67–88

7 The European institutional dimension

When discussing the European dimension of cross-border cooperation, one must not neglect its institutional aspect. The convergence of Europe's political transformation and continuing integration has contributed much to the growth in significance of cross-border cooperation, which has become a priority for the two major European institutions – the Council of Europe and the EU. While different in scope and nature, both institutions "serve to promote balanced regional and local development and to reduce the barriers resulting from the existence of international borders" (Sadowski 2005, p. 5). The Council of Europe and the EU both strongly influence the development of cross-border cooperation throughout Europe, seen in the wider perspective of Europe's incorporation of the Council of Europe (with its 47 member states) and the progression among the 6, 9, 15, 24, and now 27 member states of the EU. The two supranational bodies have played an important role in improving the conditions in which non-central governments cooperate across borders. This chapter on the institutional dimension of cross-border cooperation will focus on the Council of Europe and the EU, examining their involvement in the institutionalisation of cross-border cooperation and exploring the development of the legal instruments and conventions underpinning that cooperation.

7.1 The Council of Europe

Since 1949, the Council of Europe (hereafter the "Council") has been working to help Europe overcome its dividing lines. The Council, working on the basis of intergovernmental cooperation, has played a major part in promoting neighbourhood relations between local and regional authorities on either side of the borders. The work of the Council has concentrated on "promoting cross-border cooperation and on finding ways to overcome the obstacles to successful cross-border partnerships" (Bohner 2011, p. 52). These obstacles – repeatedly cited and specifically with reference to SME cross-border cooperation – are the administrative, political, legal, and socio-cultural barriers predominating across the European landscape. They are, of course, much less problematic today than when the Council of Europe was founded but remain relevant. The Council was already involved in the establishment of a Conference of Local Authorities, the forerunner of the Congress of Local and

Regional Authorities, as early as the 1950s. The function of this body was to deal with neighbourhood issues at both the local and regional levels throughout its member states (Wassenberg 2011). The Congress would subsequently prove instrumental in developing and establishing a framework within which local and regional authorities could work together on their practical problems (see Congress of Local and Regional Authorities 2012).

The Council of Europe's encouragement of European cross-border cooperation is given in a number of ways, including promoting the very idea of cross-border cooperation, drafting international legislation, and setting cross-border cooperation standards. Three instruments considered particularly valuable in the development of cross-border cooperation are (1) political declarations, (2) recommendations, and (3) drafting of conventions. The latter can be considered the most important as once the recommendations have been drafted by the Council's Committee of Ministers, they are then signed and subsequently ratified by Council members. In addition to these specific instruments, the Council has a number of other tools at its disposal, which, although not legally important, deserve mention. The Council is an important forum for the exchange of ideas regarding and experiences in cross-border cooperation at the local and regional levels. This encompasses the organisation of conferences, seminars, and workshops on issues related to cross-border cooperation (Sadowski 2005). A further Council priority is its advisory and training role in the development of cross-border cooperation, such as providing legal advice to the Ukraine on its draft law on cross-border cooperation and assisting the establishment of various Euroregions such as the Eurobalkans and the Prespa/Ohrid Euroregion (ibid.). The Council's Parliamentary Assembly formulates recommendations and presents them to the Committee of Ministers, which can take internal decisions on transfrontier cooperation issues (Odendahl 2011). Decisions of the Parliamentary Assembly and advisory or other committees or commissions (considered subsidiary Council bodies) have no direct impact on member states, but may nonetheless be considered important in promoting and generating awareness of cross-border affairs (ibid.). Examples of relevant subsidiary bodies include the Congress of Local and Regional Authorities of the Council of Europe, the Committee of Advisors for the development of transfrontier cooperation in Central and Eastern Europe, and the Committee of Experts on local and regional government institutions and cooperation (Odendahl 2011; Sadowski 2005).

The Council has been a major driving force behind the development of cross-border cooperation in Europe, particularly in the initial years. It is occasionally argued that the Council has always shown a genuine interest in building Europe from the bottom up (Guerra 2011), its establishment of the European Conference on Local Authorities (CLA) serving as a good example. This was one of the first organisations to attempt a legal cross-border cooperation framework. By bringing together local representatives, the Conference of Local Authorities of Europe provided a crucial platform for the discussion of issues relevant to cross-border cooperation at the local and regional levels, where cooperation across territories is most likely to be implemented and where cooperation is executed mainly through local and regional authorities, semi-state bodies, local businesses, and NGOs. This type of cooperation greatly contributes to regional economic performance and the development of European border regions in a variety of ways, such as by transferring knowledge and innovation, promoting cluster development, and fostering joint research. The importance of cooperation between local and regional authorities across borders, particularly in the SME sector, should not be underestimated. The CLA is known for its role in getting the 1980 Madrid Outline Convention off the ground, drafting several recommendations and resolutions on cross-border issues, and co-organising two symposia on border regions in 1972 and 1975 with the Consultative Committee of the Council (Guerra 2011).

The Madrid Convention, marking the beginning of Durà-Guimerà and Oliveras González's (2010) second period in the development of cross-border cooperation in Europe, is widely considered a crucial cross-border cooperation milestone. Its official name is the European Outline Convention on Transfrontier Cooperation between Territorial Communities or Authorities. The signatories of the Convention undertake "to facilitate and foster transfrontier co-operation between territorial communities or authorities [...] [and] shall endeavour to promote the conclusion of any agreements and arrangements that may prove necessary for this purpose with due regard to the different constitutional provisions of each Party" (European Outline Convention on Transfrontier Cooperation between Territorial Communities or Authorities 1980, Article 1). The purpose of the Convention as highlighted in its Explanatory Report is to "outline the general, legal and common bases on which bilateral co-operation could be founded, in the framework of the national sovereignty of each country" (Explanatory Report 2009). Here, the idea of adaptation of co-operation to the specific conditions of each country and region is crucial. Signed in 1980 by 20 countries (Perkmann 2003), and subsequently updated with three additional protocols, the convention provides a common legal framework for binational and multinational public law agreements between regions and local authorities on different sides of the border (Kiefer 2011). Regarded as a "normative framework which has to be filled with substance by bi- or multilateral agreements defining the concrete shape and legal nature of transfrontier cooperation" (Kiefer 2011, p. 107), it becomes legally effective in the national state only following ratification. Treaties emerging from the premises of the Madrid Convention include the Benelux Cross-border Convention of 1989 and the German-Dutch cross-border treaty of 1991 (Perkmann 2003). Agreements such as these between local or regional authorities produced cross-national public bodies, whose decisions are binding only on the public authorities within the cross-border area. This clearly marked the involvement of local and regional authorities in an arena previously dominated by central state actors. However, some form of formalised agreement was necessary for effective cooperation, which is where the Madrid Convention played a crucial role. The 1985 European Charter of Local Self-Government is also worth mentioning here. Its main aim is to strengthen local authorities, particularly also in their competence to cooperate with partners from other countries (European Charter of Local Self-Government 1985).

The Council of Europe grew following developments across Europe and the collapse of communism in the late 1990s. These developments, coupled with the remaining obstacles to the practical application of the Outline Convention, prompted the introduction and adoption of a new Protocol to the Convention in 1995. Arguably the most important development of this new Protocol was the right of territorial communities or authorities to establish cross-border cooperation bodies with their own legal personalities in keeping with the domestic laws of the territories concerned. A further development was the 1998 introduction of a second protocol expanding the framework of the Convention to include "interterritorial cooperation", cooperation among territorial communities and authorities that are non-neighbouring but have common interests.

While the Council of Europe's conventions are seen to provide the legal framework for cross-border projects between contracting states, recommendations serve to reinforce this framework by providing a set of guidelines that are legally non-binding but important in encouraging measures to further cross-border cooperation. Recommendations encompass a broad spectrum of areas ranging from culture and languages, through good cooperation practices, to cooperation in South Eastern Europe (see Odendahl 2011).

Political declarations are the third type of instrument employed by the Council. These express the Council's political will regarding cross-border cooperation issues and urge Council of Europe bodies such as the Committee of Ministers, the Conferences of European Ministers, and the member states to adopt initiatives. Occasionally, political declarations can act as stepping-stones to concrete measures (Odendahl 2011), either relating directly to transfrontier cooperation issues or dealing with other policy issues while emphasising the role of transfrontier cooperation. For example, the Helsinki and Vienna Declarations give local authorities increased power in their conduct of cross-border activities. The Vienna Declaration of 9 October 1993 declares that "[t]he creation of a tolerant and prosperous Europe does not depend only on co-operation between States. It also requires transfrontier co-operation between local and regional authorities, without prejudice to the constitution and the territorial integrity of each State. We urge the Organisation to pursue its work in this field and to extend it to co-operation between non-adjacent regions" (Vienna Declaration 1993). This demand has since been realised. Examples of political declarations relating specifically to cross-border cooperation include the 1989 Declaration on Transfrontier Europe, the 2002 Vilnius Declaration on Regional Cooperation and the Consolidation of Democratic Stability in Greater Europe, and the 2003 Chişinău Political Declaration on Transfrontier and Interterritorial Co-operation between States in South-Eastern Europe (Odendahl 2011).

A third protocol to the European Outline Convention on Transfrontier Co-operation between Territorial Communities or Authorities was drawn up by the European Committee for Local and Regional Democracy (CDLR) of the Council of Europe and was opened to signature on 16 November 2009 (see Explanatory Report 2009). This protocol should further reduce the obstacles to cross-border cooperation, in particular, those emerging from differences in national legal systems. Four main principles were included in the protocol: a new legal instrument should provide for a standard legal arrangement in the form of Euroregional Cooperation Groupings (ECGs) for all local and regional authorities and all Euroregions; it should accord with the fundamental principles of member states' legislation; it should establish uniform rules with legal force in each nation state; and it should not require existing cross-border bodies to transform into this new type of Euroregion (Kiefer 2011). Hence, the third protocol to the Convention provides for the legal status, establishment, and operation of ECGs with the aim of harmonising the various national rules for transfrontier groupings. These can be considered similar to the EU's European Grouping of Territorial Cooperation (EGTC), as will be discussed subsequently in the chapter.

The Council of Europe has devoted considerable attention to updating the regulatory framework for cross-border cooperation. On the other hand, the EU has traditionally devoted financial resources to promoting and sustaining cooperation among European border regions and, more recently, with neighbouring countries.

7.2 The European Union

The role of the European Union in cross-border cooperation has gone from being that of financial and technical support provider to being the largest funder of cross-border cooperation projects in Europe and finally becoming the formulator of the legal frameworks of cross-border cooperation (Sadowski 2005). The EU considers cross-border cooperation as an important means of promoting European integration and guaranteeing a more balanced development of European territory. This is best reflected in the design of the policies on peripheral and marginalised areas, often border areas, meant to alleviate economic and social problems. However, as member states have exclusive competence in matters of internal organisation, the Union cannot directly intervene in regional matters. Article 4 of the Treaty of European Union states "[t]he Union shall respect the equality of Member States before the Treaties as well as their national identities, inherent in their fundamental structures, political and constitutional, inclusive of regional and local self-government" (Consolidated Version of the Treaty on European Union 2010).

The EU (or European Community) has been supporting cross-border cooperation since the 1975 establishment of the European Regional Development Fund (ERDF), which marked the beginning of the European Community's regional policy, as will be elaborated in the subsequent chapter on Europe's regional dimension. However, it is worth noting here that the formal involvement of regional and local authorities in the institutional framework of the Union was embodied in the creation of a Committee of Regions in 1992 (Treaty of Maastricht), allowing the subnational level to play a more decisive role in shaping and implementing the EU's regional policy.

The key EU instruments supporting cross-border cooperation are financed through EU structural funds, the most important of which include Interreg (now the Territorial Cooperation Programme), PHARE, TACIS, and CARDS (now IPA and ENPI). These will be outlined in Chapter 10. Interreg, one of the most significant funding programmes for cross-border cooperation, was introduced in 1990 as the Community Initiative Programme for Cross-border

Cooperation. Towards the end of the 1980s, the EU introduced some 14 projects as part of a pilot project aimed at granting support for territorial cooperation (Odendahl 2011). On the back of their success, the European Commission then introduced the Interreg Community Initiative, providing operational programmes across the EU's border landscape. This was followed by three Interreg programming periods: Interreg I from 1990 to 1993, Interreg II from 1994 to 1999, and Interreg III from 2000 to 2006 (see Sadowski 2005). The first two focussed on the economically and socially underdeveloped border regions of the EU. In 1996, financial support was also offered to transnational cooperation projects, moving away from the strictly neighbouring border element of the first programming period. By 2006, the EU's financial contribution to cross-border initiatives represented some 5 to 10% of European Regional Development Funds (Sadowski 2005, p. 23). Since then, funding has steadily increased.

After 2004's EU enlargement, its internal borders shifted dramatically and the diversity of its economic development again increased. This prompted the need for an appropriate EU response, which inspired a policy reform. The EU's structural funds were reformed, and a new legal framework for transnational cooperation was introduced in 2006 (EGTC). The aims of this new regulation were to enhance the EU's economic cohesion and regional cooperation in light of the enlargement and to more effectively implement EU-funded programmes, particularly in the new member states (Regulation [EC] No. 1082/2006). The three new ERDF objectives were identified as convergence, regional competitiveness and employment, and European territorial cooperation. The new Interreg programme (for the 2007–2013 programming period) was renamed "Territorial Cooperation Programme" and represented the third objective of the EU Cohesion Policy; it comprised three strands: Strand A focused on the funding of cross-border cooperation projects between authorities of neighbouring states; Strand B prioritised transnational cooperation among large groups of European regions; and Strand C was a new initiative for funding projects among regions or cities across different member states (Odendahl 2011, Sadowski 2005). This marked an important development: cross-border cooperation had been elevated into an official ERDF objective. In addition to an improved legal basis "providing more specific regulations and enhancing the support of cross-cutting themes linked to economic innovation and to the environment" (Odendahl 2011, p. 98), maritime borders were included as elements of cross-border cooperation, and the overall budget was increased.

EU programmes on transborder cooperation with third states focus on candidate, neighbouring, and partnership countries. This is relevant to the

SME sector, particularly to SMEs interested in cooperating with partner firms located in these countries. Until 2006, these programmes included PHARE, TACIS, and CARDS; these became the Instrument for Pre-Accession Assistance (IPA) and the European Neighbourhood and Partnership Instrument (ENPI) in 2007.

7.3 Similarities and differences between the Council of Europe and EU approaches to cross-border cooperation

With regard to the similarities and differences between the EU's and Council's roles in promoting cross-border cooperation, it can be said that both institutions – in aiming to achieve an integrated and stable Europe – strongly emphasise the subnational level of cross-border cooperation and the role of regional and local actors in implementing joint initiatives (Sadowski 2005). Therefore, the emphasis is on the bottom-up approach, while helping to coordinate interaction among the national, regional, and local levels. National law is clearly recognised by both institutions as being crucial to the overall development of cross-border cooperation. Hence, both institutions follow the principle that cross-border cooperation should be in keeping with the domestic laws of the countries involved. It is also important to bear in mind that "the legal instruments of the EC are supranational in character while the Council of Europe's tools are rooted in classic public international law and are, therefore, 'softer' towards national sovereignty" (Odendahl 2011, p. 101). While the instruments of neither institution are legally binding, their provisions become obligatory for the signatory states once they are signed and ratified (Sadowski 2005). In recent years, both institutions have provided new legal frameworks to accommodate the establishment of transborder legal bodies with the aim of harmonising territorial cooperation through groupings. The EU created the EGTCs in 2006, and the ECGs of the Council of Europe were officially established in 2009. While both are concerned with the establishment of legal personalities and the need to conform to international law, neither aims to replace existing forms of cooperation. Both EGTCs and ECGs function in accordance with the principle of subsidiarity. There are also a number of differences between the two types of groupings. The Council of Europe's ECGs – in addition to regional and local authorities, member states, and public law bodies – can also incorporate private non-profit law bodies such as chambers of commerce or trade unions (Kiefer 2011). This can be considered an important distinction given the key role economic actors play in cooperation (Kiefer 2011, p. 123). The membership and tasks of ECGs are less restrictive than those of the EGTCs. It is also worth noting that EGTCs are essentially foreseen in the implementation of territorial cooperation programmes co-financed by the EU.

The EU, while traditionally mainly providing financial assistance, has clearly moved into the sphere of legal instruments, as is evident in its EGTCs. Another important distinction between these institutions is that the Council's instruments can be said to have a broader range, encompassing all European countries, while EU programmes, applying often to specific regions or countries with a particular EU status, may have a broader financial capacity scope. While both institutions initially focussed on neighbouring countries, both have extended their foci to move beyond the strictly neighbourhood cross-border approach. Despite the differences in the two institutions' potential influence, their complementarity on cross-border cooperation issues is highly important.

7.4 Association of European Border Regions (AEBR)

The Association of European Border Regions is another transnational association widely considered important in representing cross-border regions at the European level. The concept of establishing a "union for the Border regions" was elaborated at the International Regional Planning Conference in 1965 (AEBR 2006). Six years later, the Association of European Border Regions was established at the Standing Conference of European Border regions. Initially, 10 border regions were involved; today, some 100 European border regions and cross-border regions are involved (AEBR 2012). AEBR's experience in the theoretical and practical aspects of cross-border cooperation is linked not only to cooperation across directly neighbouring borders but also to inter-regional and transnational cooperation (AEBR 2012).

AEBR, represented by a General Assembly, an Executive Committee, and a Secretary General, is located in Gronau at the joint secretariat of the EUREGIO, the first Euroregion (AEBR 2012). In 1981, the AEBR adopted the European Charter for Border and Cross-Border Regions (European Charter for Border and Cross-Border Regions 1981). This charter defines cross-border cooperation as the aim "to remove the obstacles and divisive factors found in these regions, and ultimately to transcend the border or reduce its importance to that of a mere administrative demarcation" (European Charter for Border and Cross-Border Regions 1981, p. 4). AEBR sees itself as a "forum for cross-border cooperation and makes the voice of the border and cross-border regions heard at the European level" (AEBR 2012). It essentially represents the interests of the border and cross-border regions within the EU, the Council, and its member states. Thus, AEBR is in constant contact with a vast range of institutions and bodies functioning at the European level, including the European Parliament (particularly the Committee on Regional Development), the European Commission (including a number of Directorate Generals), the Committee of the Regions, the Council of Europe, the Congress of Local and Regional Authorities, the Assembly of European Regions (AER), the Conference of European Municipalities and Regions, and the Association of European Regions with Legislative Powers (see Guillermo Ramirez, 2011). AEBR's work is multifaceted, ranging from organising cross-border events and issues, conducting programmes and projects, applying for and administering funding, and working closely with the EU and Council of Europe on cross-border cooperation matters. It also writes position papers and studies on various issues relating to cross-border cooperation. In the 1970s, AEBR was the first body to call for the introduction of legal instruments to facilitate cross-border cooperation similar to those of today's EGTC and ECG (Guillermo Ramirez 2011), now considered essential for long-term strategic cross-border cooperation throughout Europe.

Summary of the European institutional dimension of cross-border cooperation

1. The work of both the Council of Europe and the EU has been instrumental in the development of cross-border cooperation across Europe, with both institutions promoting cross-border cooperation as a means of achieving an integrated and stable Europe.
2. Both the Council and the EU emphasise the importance of the subnational level of cross-border cooperation, paying particular attention to the involvement of local and regional actors in the development of cross-border initiatives.
3. In the traditional role division between the two institutions, the Council helped establish the instruments necessary for facilitating the creation of a legal framework underpinning cross-border cooperation, while the EU was seen as the main financial assistance provider for cross-border cooperation initiatives.

4. This traditional role division changed significantly, with the European Commission now also responsible for introducing legal mechanisms accommodating the establishment of cross-border bodies recognised under Community law.
5. The Association of European Border Regions (AEBR) acts as a forum for the exchange of information and knowledge on cross-border cooperation and represents the interests of European border and cross-border regions within the EU, the Council of Europe, and its member states.

References

AEBR (2006) White paper on European border regions: Final version. Gronau: AEBR. http://www.espaces-transfrontaliers.org/document/doc_white_paper_AEBR_EN.pdf (date accessed 12 May 2012)

AEBR (2012) Association of European border region's website. http://www.coe.int/T/E/Legal_Affairs/Local_and_regional_Democracy/Transfrontier_co-operation/Euroregions/2Definition.asp (date accessed 18 May 2009)

Bohner, U. (2011) The European dimension of cross-border cooperation: Opening speech. In: Wassenberg, B. and Beck, J. (eds.) Living and researching cross-border cooperation, Vol. 3: The European dimension. Stuttgart: Franz Steiner Verlag, 51–58

Congress of Local and Regional Authorities (2012) The Congress of Local and Regional Authorities' website. http://www.coe.int/t/congress/default_en.asp (date accessed 15 May 2012)

Consolidated Version of the Treaty on European Union (2010) Official Journal of the European Union, C83 Volume 53, 30.3.2010. http://eur-lex.europa.eu/JOHtml.do?uri=OJ:C:2010:083:SOM:EN:HTML (date accessed 15 May 2012)

Durà-Guimerà, A. and Oliveras González, X. (2010) Recent dynamics in European cross-border cooperation: towards a new period? Paper presented at the Regional Studies Association Annual International Conference 2010, 24–26 May, Pécs, Hungary

Explanatory Report (2009) Explanatory Report to Protocol No. 3 to the European Outline Convention on Transfrontier Co-operation between Territorial Communities or Authorities concerning Euroregional Co-operation Groupings (ECGs). Utrecht. http://conventions.coe.int/Treaty/EN/Reports/Html/206.htm (date accessed 15 May 2012)

European Charter of Local Self Government (1985) http://conventions.coe.int/Treaty/EN/Treaties/Html/122.htm (date accessed 15 May 2012)

European Outline Convention on Transfrontier Co-operation between Territorial Communities or Authorities (1980) http://conventions.coe.int/treaty/en/Treaties/Html/106.htm (date accessed 15 May 2012)

Guerra, V. (2011) Le Conseil de l'Europe, premier acteur européen de la coopération transfrontalière (1957–1980)? In: Wassenberg, B. and Beck, J. (eds.) Living and researching cross-border cooperation, Vol. 3: The European dimension. Stuttgart: Franz Steiner Verlag, 155–172

Guillermo Ramirez, M. (2011) Cross-border lobbying: The Association of European Border regions (AEBR) activities within the European Union. In: Wassenberg, B. and Beck, J. (eds.) Living and researching cross-border cooperation, Vol. 3: The European dimension. Stuttgart: Franz Steiner Verlag, 283–296

Kiefer, A. (2011) The European Grouping of Territorial Cooperation (EGTC) and Euroregional Cooperation Grouping (ECG): Two legal instruments for cross-border cooperation. In: Wassenberg, B. and Beck, J. (eds.) Living and researching cross-border cooperation, Vol. 3: The European dimension. Stuttgart: Franz Steiner Verlag, 105–128

Odendahl, K. (2011) Legal instruments of transborder cooperation in Europe. In: Wassenberg, B. and Beck, J. (eds.) Living and researching cross-border cooperation, Vol. 3: The European dimension. Stuttgart: Franz Steiner Verlag, 89–104

Perkmann, M. (2003) Cross border regions in Europe: Significance and drivers of regional cross border cooperation. *European Urban and Regional Planning Studies* 10(2): 153–171

Regulation (EC) No. 1082/2006 of the European Parliament and of the Council of 5 July 2006 on a European grouping of territorial Cooperation (EGTC), Official Journal of the European Union. http://eur-lex.europa.eu/LexUriServ/LexUriServ.do?uri=OJ:L:2006:210:0019:0024:EN:PDF (date accessed 15 May 2012)

Sadowski, R. (2005) Similarities and differences of instruments and policies of the Council of Europe and the European Union in the field of transfrontier co-operation. Strasbourg: Council of Europe

Vienna Declaration (1993) Council of Europe Summit, Vienna. https://wcd.coe.int/ViewDoc.jsp?id=621771 (date accessed 15 May 2012)

Wassenberg, B. (2011) Le voisinage de proximité. Les eurorégions entre l'Ouest et l'Est. In: Wassenberg, B. and Beck, J. (eds.) Living and researching cross-border cooperation, Vol. 3: The European dimension. Stuttgart: Franz Steiner Verlag, 67–88

8 The European regional dimension

Having introduced both the history and development of European cross-border cooperation and the typical institutions responsible for promoting it, we will now focus on its regional dimension. Developments related to European regionalism have given the regions a strengthened economic development role. This is very important for entrepreneurship development, as it is the regional and local levels through which entrepreneurs come into contact with the state. The increase in global competitive pressures since the 1970s has somewhat eroded the powers of the centralised welfare state, as the decentralisation of political power became perceived as a tool for responding to the challenges of globalisation. The regional level is now widely considered the appropriate one to create the conditions by which companies can become more competitive. New relationships among levels of governments have emerged, as have relationships with non-governmental actors. Increasing global competition, the perception of the regional level as instrumental in setting the appropriate competitive conditions, and the EU's new multi-level governance ideas have also shaped the regions' developmental path. Regions increasingly compete for resources and are now considered a useful basis for policy development. The EU has played an important role in the development of governance structures at the national, regional, and local levels in its reduction of administrative barriers and institutional capacity building. This has contributed to increased regional and local power, improved relations between the public and private sectors, and the generation of new networks and partnerships.

8.1 European Union Regional Policy

The EU Regional Policy is considered to have originated in the Treaty of Rome, which called for member states to reduce regional disparities by promoting "a harmonious development of economic activities, a continuous and balanced expansion" (Treaty of Rome 1957). However, there was no specific provision for either a regional policy or regional fund. The EU's regional development policy, as outlined in the previous chapter, has existed since 1975. It was introduced to reduce existing regional economic disparities and provide both guiding principles and funding to implement Community initiatives in economically under-developed peripheral territories. It witnessed the establishment of the European Regional Development Fund (ERDF), which was seen to promote economic and territorial cohesion (as the European Social Fund was set up to address the social aspect). Allen (2005) points to the logical assumption that economic convergence among countries and regions would deliver cohesion, which would in turn deliver growth, competition, employment, and sustainable development. However, the ERDF was originally considered too small to have a major impact on reducing regional disparities. Nonetheless, the Fund provided for the creation of a Regional Policy Committee, which would act as a starting point for subsequent reforms (Allen 2005).

The Cohesion Policy for the 2007–2013 programming period was reformed to focus on the three new priority objectives – convergence, regional competition, and employment – and European territorial cooperation (Council Regulation (EC) No 1083/2006 and European Union Regional Policy 2007). The convergence objective aims to accelerate economic development and encompasses NUTS II regions whose per capita GDP is below 75% of the EU average (ibid.). The regional competition and employment objective includes all EU regions except those covered by convergence (European Union Regional Policy 2007). The European territorial objective is funded from the ERDF and aims to promote cooperation among European regions and the development of common solutions to issues such as economic development, urban, rural and coastal development, and environmental management (ibid.). The fact that cross-border cooperation has become an objective in its own right proves that it provides added value in the reduction of regional disparities across the EU. Following the 2004 enlargement and the reform of the Structural Funds (mentioned above), the need to reassess European regional policies was recognised. This need was partially met by the introduction of the European Grouping of Territorial Cooperation (EGTC) in community legislation, as discussed in the previous chapter.

The European regional level gained status over the years and is now a matter of core interest, in some ways competing with other administrative and political levels. While the context of regional politics used to be the nation state, the regional level has been given a stronger voice. New forms of regional cooperation have emerged, and the autonomy of administrative regions has increased (see Terlouw 2011). Terlouw (2011) associates regions' growing importance with the increased "importance attached to regional identity in both the external competition for resources with other regions and the internal mobilisation of regional stakeholders" (p. 1). Perkmann (2007) points to the fact that new regional policy models reflect the political support mobilised to create and maintain cross-border governance structures for cross-border space, thus allowing local actors to play a stronger role in political design and implementation. Keating et al. (2003) also suggest that "regions have emerged as a level of government in many parts of Europe [...] [but] their powers depend to a larger extent on steering and concentration of other actors" (p. 38); Heichlinger and Määttä (2006) point to the fact that "economic growth is tangible for and fostered by regional and local actors" (p. 4). They suggest that this is illustrated by "the emergence of new regional foci and local development clusters, and in the creation of new urban and local economic networks and links across national borders" (ibid., p. 4).

The level of local or regional autonomy is a crucial factor influencing the scope of local or regional authorities' involvement in regional development and design policies promoting cross-border activity. Although it is not the only factor influencing the propensity of local or regional structures to pursue cross-border cooperation, such autonomy is nonetheless regarded as key (Smallbone et al. 2007). Lack of responsibility for economic development clearly translates into a lack of capacity and scope to influence it, regardless of the degree of willingness or motivation to pursue cross-border cooperation objectives. For local and regional authorities at a practical level, this can simply mean a lack of financial and human resources or even a lack of appropriate competences. On the other hand, a high or higher level of local and regional autonomy does not guarantee that cross-border cooperation will be better developed.

8.2 European border regions

Defining a "region" from an EU perspective is difficult. As with many concepts that have become buzzwords in Europe, a specific definition is often evaded in favour of a widely assumed common understanding. This is perhaps best highlighted in the concept of a "Europe of the Regions" and is most strongly evident in the emergence of numerous regional organisations and projects and indeed the increasing importance attached to regional actors. While a multiplicity of perspectives on the concept of "region" is possible, the fact that a region is a complex structure incorporating not only political, economic, and geographical attributes but also social, cultural, and linguistic elements is widely accepted. The same is true for border regions. When speaking of cross-border regions, Perkmann (2003) defines this construct as a "bounded territorial unit comprising the territories of authorities participating in cross-border cooperation" (p. 157). In this sense, a cross-border region is not simply a functional space but is actually a socio-territorial unit with some form of strategic capacity underlined by some kind of organisational structure. The Council of Europe (1995) refers to the definition of "cross-border region" put forward by Denis de Rougemont in 1978 – a "potential region, inherent in geography, history, ecology, ethnic groups, and economic possibilities and so on, but disrupted by the sovereignty of the governments ruling on each side of the frontier" (p. 9).

It has been observed that "there are 14 200 km of internal borders inside the EU. Even if we define border regions as the area covering just 25 km of the actual border, this would still represent over 710 000 square kilometres – twice the size of Germany" (European Commission 2008, p. 40). Joachim Beck (2011) illustrates this in other terms, pointing out that approximately 40% of the territorial area of the enlarged EU comprises border regions and is home to 32% of the population of Europe. From an EU perspective, borders tend to be represented as "obstacles" to economic development. The Communication (2000/1101) from the Commission to the Member States argues that the "overall aim of the Interreg initiatives has been, and remains, that national borders should not be a barrier to the balanced development and integration of the European territory" (I.3). The same document states "the presence of borders cuts off border communities from each other economically, socially and culturally and hinders the coherent management of eco-systems" (I.3). A European Commission (2002) publication describes the aims of the Interreg Community initiative as "to lessen the 'border effect', to encourage an integrated development of cross-border areas and to promote more harmonious European regional planning" (pp. 7–8). The Community strategic guidelines on cohesion for the 2007–2013 programming period (Council Decision 2006/702/EC) reflect on the fact that "[n]ational borders are often an obstacle to the development of European territory as a whole, and can restrict its potential for full competitiveness" (p. 31). These guidelines also state that "the ultimate objective of cross-border cooperation in Europe is to integrate areas divided by national borders that face common problems requiring common solutions. Such challenges are faced by all border regions in the Union as a result of the fragmentation of markets for labour and capital, infrastructure networks, fiscal capacity, and institutions" (p. 31). The EU's policy documents tend to directly associate the phenomenon of cross-border cooperation with the economic development of border regions in order to make cross-border cooperation an object of regional policy. Documents for the 2007–2013 programming period recognise that "closer cooperation across EU regions should help speed up economic development and the achievement of higher growth" (EC 2006/702, p. 31). Attention is paid specifically to external frontiers, where cooperation with non-member countries is linked to the EU's economic development.

In fact, borders can be seen either as a kind of barrier (see above) or a point of contact (Krätke 1999) offering opportunities. In considering national borders and their possible influence on the cooperation behaviour of enterprises in border regions, two opposite effects can be identified (Leick 2010). The first relates to the concept of borders as economically disadvantaged areas, often far from the core EU markets (see Dimitrov et al. (2003) on border regions in Albania, Bulgaria, Greece, and the Former Yugoslavian Republic of Macedonia and Krätke (1999) on the German-Polish border area). The second perspective allows borders to be seen as a site of opportunity and is linked to the removal or reduction of impediments and administrative barriers. From this perspective, firms in the border area may benefit from their proximity to neighbouring foreign markets, profiting from lower transportation, trading, and entry costs. This last perspective considers spatial proximity a key motivational factor in cross-border internationalisation.

Regional economics uses spatial proximity to explain industrial districts or clusters, often based on localised links between firms or industries in smaller spatial contexts (Leick 2010). Furthermore, proximity is considered to support knowledge spillovers between firms and other regional actors and the communication of tacit knowledge between individuals (ibid.). A European Commission (2010) report based on a 2009 survey on the internationalisation of SMEs shows that the association between distance to (land) borders and involvement in international trade, while modest, is statistically significant. Investigations into how closely import to and export from cross-border regions is related to the distance between the SME engaged in international trade and a national land border show that this relationship is quite strong, particularly for export. The study shows that the closer the exporters are to the border, the higher is the percentage of exporting SMEs serving the cross-border region: "if closer than 50 km from the border the percentage is nearly twice as high as with exporters that are located more than 150 km away from the border" (European Commission 2010, p. 43). Similar results were found for importers. However, the stepping-stone theory was not supported by the study: while proximity to borders was found to be important for activities in cross-border regions, no sizeable effect on internationalisation was found.

Many scholars have discussed the importance of geographical distance in the internationalisation of firms, with the majority observing that firms are most likely to internationalise within their own region. Smallbone et al. (2007) suggest that SMEs are more likely to look to neighbouring borders than are larger firms. Others question the correlation between spatial proximity and cross-border business collaboration, usually by arguing that globalisation has increased the accessibility of more geographically distant markets. Cooperation among enterprises in neighbouring regions may be less economically important than that of enterprises connected in regions located at a distance. The 2003 Observatory of European SMEs publication on *SMEs and Cooperation* indicates that SMEs facing long distances to large markets are more likely to cooperate than SMEs in countries with short distances to large markets. However, this offers no insight into the propensity of SMEs to cooperate across borders.

While borders and cross-border regions are significant for questions of entrepreneurship and cross-border cooperation, as border conditions determine how easily people, goods, and services can flow, the potential for SME cooperation is affected by a number of determinants. Although EU integration has certainly helped lower transport and transaction costs, firm- and industry-specific factors cannot be factored out. Geographic proximity can be helpful in establishing a partnership or connection, but it is not necessary for a mutually beneficial relationship. The collaborative potential of firms in border regions is likely to be positively affected by proximity and the greater market potential, but the possible differences in regional prices and the structural deficiencies of the border region, socio-cultural factors, and firm and industrial structures may adversely impact enterprises' collaborative potential. The geographical dimension is obviously not the most relevant factor for an SME considering internationalisation. However, it can be argued that the more permeable a border is, the more likely it is that cooperation will be facilitated and encouraged: "Increased permeability of national borders paves the way for increased cooperation between firms through the creation and increased use of cross-border networks" (Smallbone et al. 2007, p. 25).

Border regions are unique and complex, each with its own set of characteristics, which then impacts the development of entrepreneurship in that region. The extent to which jurisdictions create opportunities to promote entrepreneurship will likely affect SMEs' willingness to expand across borders and set up new alliances and partnerships. In the same manner, neighbouring jurisdictions or regions can create chances for or present obstacles to the development of cooperation among SMEs. This environment is affected not only by business and legal factors but also by the wider social and cultural contexts. Thus, regional economic development policy, extending across national borders, can play a significant role in promoting business activity within certain regions.

8.3 Types of border regions

The characteristics of border regions undoubtedly impact the entrepreneurial environment and thus the potential for cross-border cooperation, both generally and entrepreneurially. It would be helpful to identify a possible typology of the regions SMEs may find themselves located in or wishing to enter when pursuing or considering cross-border cooperation.

Jessop (2002) provides a typology of cross-border regions on the basis of the region's evolution. It places particular emphasis on both the importance of past events and contextual elements. Historical relationships between companies can motivate cooperation near borders. According to Smallbone et al. (2007), other motivations may include "surplus generated from price differentials and the development of 'natural' economic spaces" (p. 25). The enlargement of the EU, particularly its eastern enlargement, has led to an EU regional typology on the basis of the NUTS III level, including regions bordering EU members, those bordering EU accession candidates, and other internal regions.

Different factors impact the different types of border regions (see Resmini 2002 and Krätke 2002). The openness of a border clearly influences activity in the cross-border region. External EU borders with a system of controls regulating activity across the border and internal EU borders with no restrictions on cross-border activities provide very different conditions for entrepreneurship and cross-border cooperation (for example, there may be barriers to material goods through tariffs or standards). Whether a region is an administrative region and thus officially designated as a region or whether it operates at a functional level will provide a very specific set of characteristics for an SME wishing to cooperate. The difference between these two types of region may be seen, for example, in the prevalent cross-border policies or the presence and development of cross-border clusters. The concepts of "administrative" and "functional" regions are quite similar to Smouts' (1998) "officially designated" and "spontaneous" regions (Smallbone et al. 2007). An officially designated region embodies the key role played by central authorities in shaping this form of regional policy, dating back to the Cold War and involving a specific strategy decided upon by states (ibid.). A spontaneous region emerged through the daily interactions of local actors, business owners, and consumers, whereas the previous interaction among the region's sectors (such as the economic, cultural, and social sectors) was considered crucially important (Smallbone et al. 2007). In this type of region, functional business clusters are considered imperative to the development of the region; in later stages of development, this type of region is seen as being more independent of the nation state with its own local administrative institutions (ibid.).

Krätke uses the concept of "new regionalism" – according to which a region is perceived as part of an international system, decoupled from the nation state – to categorise regions in the enlarged EU into "(1) structurally strong industrial centres of old European industrial states, (2) structurally weak regions of new member states and (3) relatively strong industrial locations in new member states" (Smallbone et al. 2007, p. 23). Krätke (2002) highlights the need for the regional impact of eastern EU enlargement to be "differentiated with regard to different types of regions" (p. 651), believing that advantages would accrue to the structurally strong EU regions and accession countries, while the structurally weak regions along the EU's eastern boundary would gain advantages only after overcoming domestic barriers to cross-border economic cooperation and developing a positive attitude to European integration. Smallbone et al. (2007) refer to another means of identifying regions on the basis of innovation capacity, developed by Muller and Nauwelaers (2005). The five dimensions of innovation capacity identified within this framework are knowledge creation, absorptive capacity, diffusion capacity, demand, and governance capacity (Muller et al. 2006; Smallbone et al. 2007). The regions' typology based on regional innovation systems capacity includes capital regions, regions with tertiary growth potential, skilled manufacturing platforms regions, industrially challenged regions, and lagging-behind agricultural regions (ibid.). Muller et al. (2006) emphasise the need to examine subnational regions when considering innovation capacity, as this is seen to impact the socio-economic development of a territory, either national or subnational. This is important when considering new EU member states and candidate countries with substantial regional diversity. It should perhaps also be pointed out that Smallbone et al. (2007) identify two further elements that are seen to characterise the regions of new EU member states – FDI and joint ventures in the region. Regions identified through these dimensions take into consideration the crucial aspect of involvement of businesses in a region's international business environment.

The different ways in which regions are categorised become important when considering the types of policies designed for or by these regions and in deciding whether European, national, or regional policies are best able to meet the specific needs of the region and promote its competitiveness.

8.4 Euroregions

Euroregions are considered to have emerged when the European Community was established; however, after the 1990s, a significant number of macro-regions began appearing across the European landscape. The "Euroregion" can be considered as the collective term used to describe various forms of cooperation between territorial authorities. Initiatives are occasionally referred to as "EUregions", "Euregios", "Working Communities", or "European Economic Interest Groupings". Such macro-regions typically represent either loose or more integrated cross-border structures involving both state and non-state actors and representing both public and private interests. While sharing a number of common traits, they differ significantly in scope and function. A typical key aim is attracting EU financial support or at least lobbying for some form of interregional strategy for the territory concerned. For Perkmann (2003), Euroregions' importance has three dimensions: (1) the geographical scope – small cross-border cooperation initiatives versus large-scale working communities; (2) intensity of cooperation – strategic capacity and an autonomous cross-border region versus a dependent and non-autonomous loose cooperation, and; (3) the type of actors involved – local authority versus regional authority.

Euroregions are considered by some as one of the most important forms of cross-border cooperation, constituting a "platform for the coordination of actions undertaken by different actors" (Sadowski 2005, p. 35). They represent a form of institutionalisation that benefits from both the instruments of the Council of Europe and the EU. For example, in Europe's former communist countries, Euroregions became recognised as an indispensable means of opening up communication with neighbouring countries. Operational public administration structures were considered essential, and Euroregions were perceived to contribute to the overall standard of living through enhanced economic growth.

A Euroregion is generally identifiable by the fact that some form of formal collaboration exists between territorial authorities in a defined territorial space. This usually encompasses a council, president, secretariat, and working groups with a specific focus. The Association of European Border Regions (AEBR) attributes the following characteristics to potential Euroregions:

- "an association of local and regional authorities on either side of the national border, sometimes with a parliamentary assembly;
- a transfrontier association with a permanent secretariat and a technical and administrative team with resources of their own;

- of private law nature, based on non-profit-making associations or foundations on either side of the border in accordance with the respective national law in force;
- of public law nature, based on inter-state agreements, dealing among other things, with the participation of territorial authorities" (Committee of Experts on Transfrontier Cooperation 2002, p. 16)

The impact of Euroregions on cross-border entrepreneurial activity is significant within the context of this book. It was an area of analysis during the Sixth Framework Programme project on the *Challenges and Prospects of Cross Border Cooperation in the Context of EU Enlargement* (Smallbone and Xheneti 2008). The case study regions included Bulgaria, Estonia, Finland, Germany, Greece, and Poland. The study found that a number of issues impact cross-border entrepreneurial activity (Smallbone and Xheneti 2008):

- While Euroregions are created to attract EU funding and solve the common problems faced by both sides of the border, fulfilling these objectives depends on the networking capacities in the creation of policy alliances around specific objectives and can be hampered if the competencies and resources available to the local actors are inadequate.
- A border's status and perceptions influence both the level of institutionalisation and the forms of cooperation that develop around it. This can result from differences in administrative structures and responsibilities or simply from lack of trust.
- Euroregions can fail to establish strong horizontal and vertical coordination networks. Differing traditions with regard to self-governing organisations and partnerships between the state and the private sector can prove problematic, as seen, for example, in the different policy agendas of central states and the Euroregions.
- A lack of effort to establish horizontal links with business associations and support organizations, a crucial part of gaining direct access to enterprises, is evident.
- Euroregions are not perceived by entrepreneurs as playing a role in providing contacts or information to promote cross-border cooperation.

While well-functioning cross-border cooperation structures can undoubtedly create important synergies, provide key networking opportunities, and offer impulses for regional development, there is little or no evidence to suggest that Euroregions are the most effective means of tackling the problems of a cross-border region or of promoting cross-border entrepreneurial activity.

Summary of the European Regional Dimension

1. Regional developments in Europe have placed increasing emphasis on a strengthened role for regions in economic development. The regional level is now widely considered the appropriate level on which to create the conditions for increased competitiveness.
2. Enterprises located in border regions are believed to be able to benefit from their proximity to neighbouring foreign markets. Spatial proximity can be considered a key motivational factor in cross-border internationalisation.
3. Border regions are unique and complex, each with its own specific set of characteristics impacting the development of entrepreneurship in that region. The extent to which a jurisdiction creates opportunities for the promotion of entrepreneurism is likely to affect the willingness of SMEs to expand across borders and establish new alliances and partnerships.
4. The manner in which regions are categorised is an important factor in the types of policies designed for or by these regions. This includes the question of which governance level is best for policy design in meeting the region's needs and promoting its competitiveness.
5. Well-functioning cross-border cooperation structures such as Euroregions can create important synergies, provide key networking opportunities, and offer impulses for regional development. However, there is little or no evidence to suggest that Euroregions are the most effective means of tackling the problems of a cross-border region or of promoting cross-border entrepreneurial activity.

References

Allen, D. (2005) Cohesion and the structural funds. In: Wallace, H., Wallace, W., and Pollack, M. A. (eds.) Policy-making in the European Union, 5th edn. New York: Oxford University Press, 213–242

Beck, J. (2011) Patterns of cross-border cooperation in Europe. Presentation held at the European Cross-Border Symposium, 2 March 2011, Villach, Austria

Cassin, M. and Zolin, M. B. (2008) Territorial cooperation and regional economic development: A case study. *Department of Economics Working Paper Series* No. 09-08, University of Venice

Council of Europe (1995) Handbook on transfrontier co-operation for local and regional authorities. Strasbourg: Council of Europe. https://wcd.coe.int/com.instra

net.InstraServlet?command=com.instranet.CmdBlobGet&InstranetImage=1160404&SecMode=1&DocId=1343066&Usage=2 (date accessed 16 May 2012)

Committee of Experts on Transfrontier Cooperation (2002) Report on the Current State of the Administrative and Legal Framework of Transfrontier Cooperation in Europe. Strasbourg: Council of Europe. https://wcd.coe.int/ViewDoc.jsp?id=1382343&Site=DG1-CDLR&BackColorInternet=B9BDEE&BackColorIntranet=FFCD4F&BackColorLogged=FFC679 (date accessed 6 July 2012)

Communication from the Commission to the Member States, C(2000) 1101 of 28.4.00. http://www.northernperiphery.net/managers/Library%5CRegulations%5CInterreg%20Guidelines.pdf (date accessed 16 May 2012)

Council Regulation (EC) No 1083/2006 of 11 July 2006, laying down general provisions on the European Regional Development Fund, the European Social Fund and the Cohesion Fund and repealing Regulation (EC) No 1260/1999. http://eur-lex.europa.eu/LexUriServ/LexUriServ.do?uri=OJ:L:2006:210:0025:0025:EN:PDF (date accessed 16 May 2012)

Council Decision 2006/702/EC of 6 October 2006 on Community strategic guidelines on cohesion. http://eur-lex.europa.eu/LexUriServ/LexUriServ.do?uri=OJ:L:2006:291:0011:0032:EN:PDF (date accessed 16 May 2012)

Dimitrov, M., Petrakos, G., Totev, S., and Tsiapa, M. (2003) Cross-border cooperation in South-Eastern Europe. The enterprises' point of view. *Eastern European Economics* 41(6), 5–25

European Commission (2008) Supporting the internationalisation of SMEs: Good practice selection. Luxembourg. http://ec.europa.eu/enterprise/newsroom/cf/_getdocument.cfm?doc_id=3454 (date accessed 16 May 2012)

European Commission (2010) Internationalisation of European SMEs: Final report. Brussels: Entrepreneurship Unit

European Commission (2003) SMEs and cooperation. Observatory of European SMEs 2003, no. 5. Brussels: European Commission Enterprise Publications

European Commission (2002) Structural policies and European territory cooperation without frontiers. Luxembourg. http://ec.europa.eu/regional_policy/archive/interreg3/documents/cooperation_en.pdf (date accessed 16 May 2012)

European Parliament (2005) Report on the Proposal for a Regulation of the European Parliament and of the Council on Establishing a European Grouping of Cross-border Cooperation (EGCC) (COM(2004)0496 – C6-0091/2004 – 2004/0168(COD)) Committee on Regional Development (Rapporteur: Jan Olbrycht)

European Union Regional Policy (2007) Cohesion policy 2007–13: Commentaries and official texts, Guide, January 2007. Luxembourg: Office for Official Publications of the European Communities

Heichlinger, A. and Määttä S. (2006) Background paper on good governance in delivering sustainable growth: Regions and municipalities as promoters of the Lisbon Strategy. High Level Group and Meeting on Governance and the EU, Turku, 2–3 October 2006

Jessop, B. (2002) The political economy of scale. In Perkmann, M. and Sum, N.-L. (eds.) Globalisation, regionalisation and cross-border regions. Houndmills and New York: Palgrave Macmillan, 25–49

Keating, M., Loughlin, J., and Deschouwer, K. (2003) The new regionalism in Europe: A comparative study of eight regions. Cheltenham: Edward Elgar

Krätke, S. (1999) Regional integration or fragmentation? The German-Polish border region in a new Europe. *Regional Studies* 33(7), 631–641

Krätke, S. (2002) The regional impact of EU Eastern enlargement – A view from Germany. *European Planning Studies* 10(5), 651–664

Leick, B. (2010) What determines the co-operative potential for firms in Western European and CEE border regions? A comparative micro-level analysis. *Economic and Business Review* 12(2), 109–128

Muller, E., Jappe, A., Heraud, J-A., and Zenker, A. (2006) A regional typology of innovation capacities in new member states and candidate countries. Working Papers Firms and Region, No. R1, 2006. Karlsruhe: Fraunhofer ISI Karlsruhe

Muller, E. and Nauwelaers, C. (2005) Enlarging the ERA: Identifying priorities for regional policy focusing on research and technological development in the new member states and candidate countries. Collective Report Fraunhofer ISI/MERIT prepared for the European Commission, DG Research. Karlsruhe

Perkmann, M. (2003) Cross-border Regions in Europe: Significance and Drivers of Regional Cross-border Co-operation. *European Urban and Regional Studies* 10(2), 153–171

Perkmann, M. (2007) Construction of new territorial scales: A framework and case study of the EUREGIO cross-border region. *Regional Studies* 41(2), 253–266

Resmini, L. (2002) Specialization and Growth Patters in Border Regions of Accession Countries, ZEI Working Paper B17. http://www.uni-mannheim.de/edz/pdf/zei/b02–17.pdf (date accessed 16 May 2012)

Sadowski, R. (2005) Similarities and differences of instruments and policies of the Council of Europe and the European Union in the field of transfrontier co-operation. Strasbourg: Council of Europe

Smallbone, D., Labrianidis, L., Venesaar, U., Welter, F., and Zashev, P. (2007) Challenges and prospects of cross border cooperation in the context of EU enlargement. Deliverable 7: State of the art literature review. http://www.crossbordercoop.net/Publications/Integrated_lit_review.pdf (date accessed 16 May 2012)

Smallbone, D. and Xheneti, M. (2008) Challenges and prospects of cross border cooperation in the context of EU enlargement. Deliverable 16: Policy issues related to entrepreneurship development and cross border cooperation in case study regions. http://www.crossbordercoop.net/Publications/D16_policies_governance.pdf (date accessed 26 May 2012)

Smouts, M. C. (1998) The region as a new imagined community? In: le Gales, P. and Lequesne, C. (eds.) Regions in Europe. London and New York: Routledge, 30–38

Terlouw, K. (2011) From thick to thin regional identities? *Geojournal.* DOI 10.1007/s10708-011-9422-x

Treaty of Rome (1957) http://ec.europa.eu/economy_finance/emu_history/documents/treaties/rometreaty2.pdf (date accessed 16 May 2012)

9 SME policy of the EU

Although the establishment, operation, and success of SME cross-border cooperation depends on a complex (and interrelated) set of internal and external success factors (see Chapter 4), the conditions that enable and/or constrain SME cooperation are also affected by the wider European framework conditions, including the policies and legal instruments put in place by the EU to improve and regulate the business environment. European SMEs depend heavily on their domestic markets despite the opportunities presented by the EU's enlarged single market and an increasingly globalised world. SMEs are aware of the need to both confront increasing competition from emerging and developing economies and seize newly available market opportunities. This book focuses on cross-border cooperation as one means of seizing this opportunity. Firms can improve performance by undertaking international activities to reinforce growth, enhance competitiveness, and fortify their sustainability. There is also widespread recognition of the fact that SMEs face tough times. The global economic downturn, burdensome bureaucratic procedures, and cash flow difficulties (including access to financing) are just some of the challenges facing European SMEs.

If cross-border cooperation is to be considered by SMEs as a means of overcoming current challenges, they need to be fully aware of the framework conditions underpinning possible cooperation activities. In cross-border activities taking place within Europe, the policy measures adopted by the EU and the Council of Europe to create a business friendly environment are particularly relevant, some of which were briefly alluded to in Chapter 4 and will be discussed in more detail here.

9.1 Policy background

We have already described the role of cooperation among institutions in a regional setting as a potential driver of sustainable long-term cooperation between border regions. This institutionalisation of cooperation can, but will not necessarily, provide the appropriate framework conditions by which businesses may find contacts, identify potential partners, or access information on how to obtain the resources necessary for developing potential collaborations (Smallbone et al. 2007). Smallbone and his colleagues point out that the EU established the concept of the Euroregion to provide the legal framework conditions necessary for promoting cross-border cooperation. While the powers of Euroregions may be more limited than those of local or regional authorities, they can still play an important role in providing interventions that promote the formation of cross-border partnerships. Euroregions are just one form of integrated regional development fostering economic and regional development. Policies specifically aimed at encouraging cross-border cooperation among enterprises at local, regional, and national levels are likely to be affected by a wider range of policies at the supranational level. Thus, a good coordination of supranational EU policies and domestic policies is crucial. This need for coordination has resulted in new policy development and delivery models, both horizontally, among the various policy fields, and vertically, among the various levels of governance. In this chapter, the EU's role in coordinating and regulating SME-related policies to promote an SME-friendly business environment that encourages cooperation will be further discussed.

Many refer to SMEs as the backbone of Europe's economy (Lopriore 2009, COM[2007] 592 final); thus, their growth is considered crucial for the wellbeing of the economy. The 2008 Commission Communication *Think Small First – A Small Business Act for Europe* describes SMEs as having become "even more important as providers of employment opportunities and key players for the wellbeing of local and regional communities" (COM[2008] 394 final, p. 2). A more recent study (EIM 2011) on whether SMEs create more and better jobs (also supported by the European Commission) echoes this view, indicating that, between 2002 and 2010, 85% of net new jobs were created by small and medium-sized enterprises. The study further highlights that new firms, those younger than five years, provide an overwhelming majority of these jobs. With this in mind, policy-making for European SMEs can make an important contribution to the overall economic development of the EU. SMEs' role in economic growth and job creation is constantly acknowledged at the highest political levels; the Commission sees support for SMEs as one of its economic growth, job creation, and economic and social cohesion priorities. The Lisbon Growth and Jobs Strategy gave SMEs center stage by placing their needs high on its agenda. The 2007–2013 programming period, outlined in the previous chapter, also saw an increased focus on SMEs in various support programmes (COM[2008] 394 final): "The European Cohesion Policy supports actions to promote the adaptability of workers, entrepreneurs and enterprises with some € 13.5 billion over the period 2007–2013. A significant part of this amount is directly targeted at SMEs. In addition, it is estimated that support for self-employment and business start-ups will total € 2.8 billion" (COM[2008] 394 final, p. 15). The Single Market Review (COM[2007] 724 final) re-emphasises the need to deliver more results and provide more tangible benefits for SMEs. It calls attention to the fact that, unlike for large enterprises, SMEs' participation in the Single Market is impeded by a number of factors, including differing approaches to taxation, language, and cultural and consumer barriers. On the back of this review, the Commission decided to examine a range of initiatives that are necessary to better unleash the untapped potential of SMEs: the result was the Small Business Act.

The Commission's adoption of a definition for SMEs was considered an important milestone in EU SME Policy (European Commission Recommendation No. 361/2003). The existence of a common definition for SMEs is regarded as a major step towards an improved SME business environment, better facilitating the implementation of SME policies. The unified SME definition came into force in 2005 and is considered important in its implications for policies applied through the exclusive competencies of the EU. As presented in Chapter 1, enterprises qualify as micro-, small-, or medium-sized enterprises on the basis of headcount, turnover, and balance sheet ceilings. The implementation of the definition has since been reviewed twice, in 2006 and 2009, and adapting the definition has not been deemed necessary (C[2006] 7074) and SEC[2009] 1350 final).

In its efforts to create an SME-friendlier environment, the EU has prioritised a number of key policy areas, such as reducing red tape for SMEs, increasing the SME focus of the support programmes provided by the EU, improving regulation, and making it easier and quicker to establish businesses across the EU, all of which also impact SME cross-border cooperation activities. Efforts to reduce the administrative burden on SMEs, for example, can be seen in the 2007 Action Programme endorsed by the European Council and designed to reduce administrative burdens resulting from EU legislation by 25 % by 2012 (COM[2009] 544 final).

The "triple helix" model of innovation (Leydesdorff and Etzkowitz 1996), which points to the importance of the microeconomic business environment and the value of interlinking business, universities and research institutes, and public actors in innovation, is evident in the European Commission's policy for the business sector. Recently, the EU's SME policy has begun to focus very much on regional innovation systems and clusters that boost competitiveness (Lopriore 2009). Lopriore (2009) suggests that "[t]his new emphasis in EU policy can be seen in the work done by the European Commission in favouring innovation and clustering among companies, as well as inter-cluster cooperation, including cross-border cooperation" (p. 32). One means of helping SMEs develop their innovation capacity and contribute to Europe's competitiveness was the Small Business Act.

9.2 The Small Business Act

Introduced in 2008, the Small Business Act for Europe (SBA) is a multifaceted initiative aiming to (among other things) help small businesses access research funds, protect their intellectual property, and collaborate in areas of common interest. The SBA was adopted in order to ensure a more business-friendly environment and strengthen SMEs' competitiveness, eliminating potential or existing obstacles to growth and job creation (COM[2008] 394 final). This framework policy promotes entrepreneurship, aiming to entrench the "Think Small First" principle in both law and policy making throughout the EU and its member states. The "Think Small First" concept requires that SMEs are taken into account before introducing new laws, analysing the effect legislation will have on small businesses, and generally providing support for SMEs. While not legally binding, the SBA is considered to coordinate the actions of member states, identify good practices, guarantee that EU policies are SME-friendly and monitor the performance of individual member states. The SBA replaces and builds on the European Charter for Small Enterprises. The Charter was adopted by the Feira European Council in June 2000, outlining the need for a small-business-friendly environment across the EU. Concrete fields of action were identified (including evaluating existing measures), and emphasis was placed on ensuring that the needs of small businesses were taken into consideration by EU policy makers. Given the scope and focus of this book, a detailed analysis of the SBA would be neither useful nor possible; however, certain of its basic aspects relevant to SME collaboration across borders will be briefly outlined.

The SBA is essentially designed around the following 10 principles and comprises specific policy and legislative initiatives to be taken at the EU and member-state levels in order to guarantee their implementation:

> *"I Create an environment in which entrepreneurs and family businesses can thrive and entrepreneurship is rewarded*
> *II Ensure that honest entrepreneurs who have faced bankruptcy quickly get a second chance*
> *III Design rules according to the "Think Small First" principle.*
> *IV Make public administrations responsive to SMEs' needs*
> *V Adapt public policy tools to SME needs: facilitate SMEs' participation in public procurement and better use State Aid possibilities for SMEs*
> *VI Facilitate SMEs' access to finance and develop a legal and business environment that is supportive of timely payments in commercial transactions*

VII Help SMEs to benefit more from the opportunities offered by the Single Market
VIII Promote the upgrading of skills in SMEs and all forms of innovation
IX Enable SMEs to turn environmental challenges into opportunities
X Encourage and support SMEs to benefit from the growth of markets" (COM[2008] 394 final, p. 4).

The SBA should guarantee that EU policies are SME-friendly while improving the regulation of SMEs and providing better coordinated and more effective support for SMEs. A 2011 review of the SBA reports the progress made to date in implementing the act and outlines the actions necessary to respond to the challenges of the economic crisis. The review points to the fact that more must be done for SMEs and places a particular emphasis on three areas requiring more attention, all of which are relevant to SMEs involved in or planning to begin cross-border cooperation (COM[2011] 78 final):

- *Think small first*, relating to all initiatives aiming at creating an SME-friendly environment, including both legislative and administrative dimensions.
- *Access to finance*, strengthening measures directed at improving SMEs' financial situation.
- *Access to markets*, incorporating measures designed to facilitate SME access to EU-internal markets and fast-growing markets outside the EU.

The European Commission plays a decisive role in steering and monitoring implementation of the SBA throughout all EU member states. The SBA country factsheets for each state (and ten additional countries, including from the Western Balkans), produced annually by the Directorate General Enterprise and Industry, present in-depth information on SBA implementation in each country in order to improve understanding of the recent trends and national policies affecting SMEs. These prove a crucial source of statistics and SME policy information for each of the member states and facilitate a more stringent monitoring of the SBA across the EU (see DG Enterprise and Industry 2012). Statistical SME monitoring and research is an important part of SME policy and should not be overlooked. The SBA factsheets can be a useful source of information for businesses wishing to undertake cooperation activities in the countries they cover.

Following the review of the Small Business Act for Europe (COM[2011] 78 final) mentioned above, the Commission established a network of SME envoys comprising a high-ranking official from each of the member states' national administrations in order to drive and monitor SBA implementation at the member-state level. The Directorate General for Enterprise and Industry also has its own SME envoy in order to ensure that the EU's administrative and legislative conditions are more SME-friendly. To date, only one of the SBA's legislative initiatives has not been adopted; however, it is currently under review by the Council. It is an initiative considered particularly important for cross-border business within the EU – a regulation providing for a Statute for a European Private Company (SPE): "The SPE has been designed to address the current onerous obligations on SMEs operating across borders, who need to set up subsidiaries in different company forms in every Member State in which they want to do business. In practical terms, the SPE would mean that SMEs can set up their company in the same form, no matter if they do business in their own Member State or in another. Opting for the SPE will save entrepreneurs time and money on legal advice, management and administration" (European Commission 2012). The Commission's review of the SBA urges member states to adopt the statute promptly, thereby emphasising its value in reducing administrative burdens for SMEs in terms of cross-border business (COM[2011] 78 final). However, the Council did adopt a number of other initiatives that have helped improve the general SME business environment and are particularly beneficial to those SMEs that engage in cross-border cooperation, such as a 2010 Directive on e-invoicing that places e-invoices on an equal footing with paper invoices and an optional cash accounting scheme that makes it possible for enterprises (with a turnover under € 2 million) to delay VAT accounting until payment has been received from their customers (COM[2010] 695 final; COM[2011] 78 final).

9.3 SME policy needs

While the SBA clearly helps alleviate the problems faced by SMEs in their daily operations, both domestically and across borders, European SMEs are still seen to face a number of challenges that could be addressed at the European policy level. A number of key policy areas of interest to SMEs engaged in or wishing to engage in cross-border activities require further action, as will be discussed briefly below.

The EU's current patent system, as outlined in Chapter 5, is not considered favourable to promoting competitiveness or innovation. SMEs find the patent system both costly and burdensome (Wegefelt and Schramm Rasmussen 2011). The system is seen as decentralized and fragmented, and the language requirements are believed to incur extremely high costs. The European business community's demands for a reformed system focus on the need to guarantee high quality and legal certainty at a reasonable cost. In cases of patent infringement, businesses must take parallel legal action in each European country, which is both expensive and complex. These demands appear to have been heard, as a unified patent system and a European patent court have been agreed upon. It now remains to be seen how effectively this system will be implemented. Wegefelt and Schramm Rasmussen (2011) describe this development as one of the crucial final steps towards a single market for knowledge and innovation.

There is currently no common EU corporate tax base, implying that the EU, with its 27 different tax systems, is clearly at a disadvantage. It is costly and complex for European businesses to operate in more than one member state, directly contradicting the underlying principles of a single market (ibid.). In order to remedy this situation, the European Commission has proposed a Common Consolidated Corporate Tax Base (CCCTB) with a set of common rules for calculating taxable profits as an option that would not replace national systems. It is considered important that this CCCTB remain voluntary; otherwise, SMEs operating in only one member state might face unnecessary added burdens. The CCCTB would essentially allow companies to benefit from a one-stop-shop system for filing their tax returns, allowing them to consolidate the profits and losses incurred across the EU (COM [2011] 121/4). Member states would still be responsible for setting their own corporate tax rate. While this solution would go some way in reducing the current tax obstacles facing companies, it would not resolve the fundamental problem – the existence of 27 different tax systems.

A further challenge facing EU businesses is the Value Added Tax (VAT) system. The current VAT rules are complex and contribute to administrative burdens for businesses, thereby making it difficult to fully profit from the development of both European and global trade. One recent improvement to the system, the optional cash accounting scheme, has been outlined above. Otherwise, reporting obligations for businesses have increased due to the shift in risk from the member states to businesses. Meanwhile, national exemptions have increased the compliance burdens for businesses. Occasionally, it is suggested that the burdens are so extensive that it is often easier to trade with non-EU countries than with EU states (Wegefelt and Schramm Rasmussen 2011), while businesses claim that the complexity of the VAT rules is making the EU a less attractive place to invest (European Commission 2012b). The shift in services taxation to the country of consumption has led to calls for a closer harmonisation of VAT systems and easier access to the required information (Wegefelt and Schramm Rasmussen 2011). A study conducted by the Confederation of Danish Industry indicates that 90% of export-oriented SMEs have little to no knowledge of the VAT rules of other EU member states (ibid.).

It is often argued that Europe needs to more extensively adopt common international standards for accounting and auditing to address their lack of transparency and their high costs for business. Currently, the voluntary use of the International Financial and Reporting Standards (IFRS), an accounting standard geared for SMEs, is not permitted. The recent revision of the 8th Accounting Directive did envision the use of International Standards on Auditing (ISAs) in the EU; however, this has not yet been implemented (Wegefelt and Schramm Rasmussen 2011). As part of the Commission's aim to simplify the transparency and reporting requirements for smaller listed companies, a directive has been proposed that simplifies the EU accounting framework "by revising the basic requirements for annual and consolidate accounts (4th and 7th Directive) of limited liability companies" (COM[2011] 78 final, p. 8). However, this is not believed to go far enough. Full adoption of global standards would certainly facilitate cross-border services in auditing: "A flexible and internationally oriented accounting system would cater for the needs of European businesses operating in different parts of the world" (Wegefelt and Schramm Rasmussen 2011, p. 61).

A number of other obstacles continue to influence SMEs' decision to engage in cross-border activities. Enterprises still lack the instruments to resolve conflicts with customers in other nation states and make payment across borders, which is perceived as costly and burdensome (COM[2011] 78 final). The Commission plans to introduce measures to facilitate cross-border debt recovery. Some 60% of cross-border debt remains unrecovered (COM[2011] 78 final). The general conditions for SMEs wishing to engage in cross-border trade are not yet optimal. A number of proposals to redress the current shortcomings are under review by the Commission, such as a legislative proposal on Alternative Dispute Resolution schemes as an alternative to costly and lengthy court proceedings, including an online dispute resolution system for e-commerce transactions. Differences among company and contract laws are also believed to discourage businesses from expanding to other member states. The prevailing legal conditions for SMEs merit their own discussion and will be briefly dealt with in the following section.

9.4 Legal environment of European SMEs

Globalisation, e-commerce developments, and the general growth of cross-border trade present a new set of challenges to the existing legal framework for European company law. While the landscape changes, the regulatory framework must also change. There are several problems with the current legal framework for business operations; in particular, the legal treatment of companies involved in cross-border business transactions remains problematic. The key challenge continues to lie in finding the appropriate balance between (1) providing the right set of instruments to business in order to guarantee freedom of establishment and cross-border mobility, and (2) not hampering competitiveness through excessive and complicated legislation.

Among the first areas of legislation to be harmonised at the European level were those necessary to achieve a single market, including company law and accounting, both essential for cross-border business. Clearly, SMEs benefited from these policies in many ways, ranging from new possibilities and opportunities related to access to new markets to the development of trade and partnerships across borders. A unified single market brought about a new mobility for firms, improved and more equitable competition conditions among states, improved relations among states (particularly in their commercial relations), and, crucially, a fresh impetus for cross-border cooperation activities, ranging from establishing agencies, branches or subsidiaries, to investment and mergers and acquisitions.

The EU's company law provides the fundamental legal framework necessary for European companies to operate within and across the Single Market, thereby ensuring the freedom of establishment, free movement of capital, and the elimination of barriers to cross-border business. Traditionally, EU company law relied on a distinction between public and private limited companies as the basis of the choice of company form. However, a more contemporary component of company law instead relies on a distinction between companies whose shares are listed and those whose shares are not (Reflection Group 2011). The objectives outlined by the European Commission for company law include "providing equivalent protection for shareholders and other parties concerned with companies; ensuring freedom of establishment for companies throughout the EU; fostering efficiency and competitiveness of business; promoting cross-border cooperation between companies in different member states; and stimulating discussions between member states on the modernisation of company law" (European Commission 2012a). The harmonisation of company law has proven essential in eliminating the obstacles posed by the differing legal systems in different member states that had hampered companies wishing to operate across borders and develop on a European scale (Moussis 2012). Harmonisation, while respecting member states' different legal conditions, enables companies to offer their services and products across the entire EU.

Freedom of establishment was one of the key measures introduced in respect to company law (see TREU 2010). Article 49 of the Consolidated Version of the Treaty on the Functioning of the European Union (ex article 43 Treaty Establishing the European Community) outlines the framework conditions for the right of establishment, under which any restrictions on the freedom of establishment of nationals from one member state in another member state are prohibited. It states that "[f]reedom of establishment shall include the right to take up and pursue activities as self-employed persons and to set up and manage undertakings, in particular companies or firms within the meaning of the second paragraph of Article 54, under the conditions laid down for its own nationals by the law of the country where such establishment is effected, subject to the provisions of the Chapter relating to capital" (TREU 2010, p. 69). While this guarantees that activities taking place in accordance with the law of one member state will not meet any administrative problems while establishing in other member states, the actual situation is more complex. The real economic and legal problems accompanying establishment and the likelihood of conflict among various national measures continue to be problematic (Moussis 2012). Nevertheless, this article does harmonise a number of important aspects of company law in the Member States through European Council directives.

It is useful here to draw attention to the fact that a number of different legal instruments are employed in order to ensure harmonisation of company law. These include a directly binding regulation, directives requiring national implementation, and simple recommendations. Efforts to achieve a single Community framework for enterprises took three decades. In 2001, the Council adopted two legislative instruments that led to the creation of the European company: the regulation on the statute for a European Company (Council Regulation [EC] No 2157/2001) and a supplementary directive on the involvement of employees (Council directive 2001/86). New rules were agreed upon for associations and cooperative and mutual societies, and a European Economic Interest Grouping was created (see European Parliament 2012 for further detail or Reflection Group 2011 on the future of EU Company Law).

Regulation (EC) No 2157/2001 on company statutes mandated that a company could be established in the form of a public limited liability company, known under the Latin name *Societas Europaea* (SE). These different forms for cooperation were outlined in Chapter 5 and will not be discussed again here. The directive on the involvement of employees (Council Directive 2001/86) aims to guarantee that the employee involvement practices existing within the companies are protected in companies involved in establishing an SE. This is important given the very different operating practices throughout the member states regarding how employee representatives are involved in company decision-making.

A series of recommendations on cross-border mobility made by the Reflection Group on the Future of EU Company Law (2011) offer some insight into the most relevant issues concerning the legal environment of SMEs. It is considered important that the EU harmonisation process make it possible for national companies to transfer their registered office from one Member State to another, thus changing the applicable company law regime. The right to transfer the registered offices of national companies is, however, not thought to require a major harmonisation of national law as regards international private law and conflict-of-laws provisions. It is believed that the Directive on cross-border mergers should be applicable *mutatis mutandis*, including the system established to protect stakeholders, particularly shareholders, employees, and creditors. The Council recommends that national companies should have the right to engage in cross-border divisions and that a legal regime for cross-border conversions and divisions be introduced. The Reflection Group considers that the Directive's provisions on cross-border mergers require a review. It also believes that the EU company forms created to supplement Member States' national law forms should be carefully based on practical needs-based evidence, be as flexible as those of national companies, and not impinge upon national arrangements.

The reality is that while freedom of establishment is now possible within the EU, it is still not possible for a company to move out of the member state in which it was established and into another member state, while preserving its legal capacity (Reflection Group 2011). Nor is corporate mobility yet considered a reality. It is widely accepted that more needs to be done in order to ensure the principle of free corporate mobility, by introducing further cross-border measures. While corporate mobility is possible through cross-border mergers, it is a very costly and complicated process, and is thus much less feasible for SMEs. Company law and corporate governance are two inextricably linked policy fields; some corporate governance rules are also inherent in company law.

Legislators would do well to reassess some of the challenges still facing cross-border business. The diversity of national corporate firms needs to be taken into consideration in any new policy or legislative proposals. It should be noted again that, while the policies may theoretically be in place, their practical impact largely depends on the delivery methods used to put them in place. It is widely believed that policies introduced at the European level aimed at promoting cross-border cooperation among SMEs must remain flexible enough to facilitate the needs of participating firms in their very diverse regional settings (Moussis 2012). Some argue the case for non-legislative options for company regulation – the introduction of so-called "soft laws" and contractual freedom – in keeping with the "one-size-does-not-fit-all" concept (Reflection Group 2011; Wegefelt and Schramm Rasmussen 2011). Nonetheless, companies need a set of efficient and practical cross-border instruments. Wegefelt and Schramm Rasmussen (2011) emphasise the need for a company's right to cross-border conversion and national companies' right to engage in cross-border divisions while also ensuring the protection of stakeholders. The report of the Reflection Group on the future of EU company law makes the following recommendation in this regard: "A legal regime for cross-border conversions and cross-border divisions should be introduced, either via separate directives or by amending the Directive on cross-border mergers into a joint Directive on cross-border mobility. The regime should apply to limited liability companies and later be expanded to other company forms" (Reflection Group 2011, p. 22). Wegefelt and Schramm Rasmussen (2011) also reiterate the need for a European Private Company to be introduced in order to meet the particular needs of SMEs.

There is a clear need to revisit some of the challenges still facing cross-border business throughout the European Union. While some revision or expansion of policies promoting SME cross-border cooperation is necessary, these must remain flexible enough to incorporate the needs of firms operating in Europe's very diverse regional settings.

Summary of the SME policy of the EU

1. The European Commission's Small Business Act for Europe is a key framework policy promoting entrepreneurship in Europe and aiming to entrench the "Think Small First" principle in law and policy making across the EU.
2. A Common Consolidated Corporate Tax Base for the EU has been proposed by the European Commission. If adopted, it would reduce the com-

plexity and costs for SMEs operating in more than one member state. Current VAT rules across the Union are considered complex and burdensome and make it difficult for SMEs to fully benefit from both European and global trade. An optional cash accounting scheme makes it possible for businesses with a turnover of less than € 2 million to delay accounting until payment has been received.

3. It is argued that the EU needs to adopt common international accounting and auditing standards to improve the business environment for SMEs.
4. The key challenge in the SMEs' legal environment is providing the right set of instruments that will guarantee businesses freedom of establishment and cross-border mobility without hampering competitiveness through excessive and complicated legislation.
5. It is generally accepted that a legal regime for cross-border conversions and divisions must be introduced in the EU. Such a regime should first apply to limited liability companies and subsequently be expanded to other company forms.

References

Council Directive 2001/86/EC of 8 October 2001 supplementing the Statute for a European company with regard to the involvement of employees. *Official Journal of the European Communities.* http://eurlex.europa.eu/LexUriServ/LexUriServ.do?uri=OJ:L:2001:294:0022:0032:EN:PDF (date accessed 22 May 2012)

Council Regulation (EC) No 2157/2001 of October 2001 on the Statute for a European company (SE). *Official Journal of the European Communities*

DG Enterprise and Industry (2012) SME policy review webpage. http://ec.europa.eu/enterprise/policies/sme/facts-figures-analysis/performance-review/#h2-3 (date accessed 22 May 2012)

EIM (2011) Do SMEs create more and better jobs? http://ec.europa.eu/enterprise/policies/sme/facts-figures-analysis/performance-review/pdf/do-smes-create-more-and-better-jobs_en.pdf (date accessed 22 May 2012)

European Commission (2012) European private company webpage. http://ec.europa.eu/internal_market/company/epc/index_en.htm (date accessed 22 May 2012)

European Commission (2012a) European Commission company law webpage. http://ec.europa.eu/internal_market/company/index_en.htm (date accessed 22 May 2012)

European Commission (2012b) Green paper on the future of VAT: Towards a simpler, more robust and efficient VAT system, COM (2010) 695 final. http://eur-lex.

europa.eu/LexUriServ/LexUriServ.do?uri=COM:2010:0695:FIN:EN:PDF (date accessed 22 May 2012)

European Commission Recommendation 361/2003/EC concerning the definition of micro, small and medium-sized enterprises, *Official Journal of the European Union* (20.5.2003). http://eur-lex.europa.eu/LexUriServ/LexUriServ.do?uri=OJ:L:2003:124:0036:0041:en:PDF (date accessed 22 May 2012)

European Commission Report (2006) 7074 on the implementation of the Commission recommendation (2003/361/EC) of 6 May concerning the definition of micro, small and medium-sized enterprises. http://ec.europa.eu/enterprise/policies/sme/files/sme_definition/sme_report_en.pdf (date accessed 22 May 2012)

European Commission COM (2007) 592 final, Communication from the Commission to the Council, the European Parliament, the European Economic and Social Committee and the Committee of the Regions: Small and medium-sized enterprises – Key for delivering more growth and jobs. A mid-term review of modern SME policy. Brussels, 4.17.2007. http://eur-lex.europa.eu/LexUriServ/LexUriServ.do?uri=COM:2007:0592:FIN:en:PDF (date accessed 22 May 2012)

European Commission Communication COM (2007) 724 final from the Commission to the Council, the European Parliament, the European Economic and Social Committee and the Committee of the Regions. A single market for 21st century Europe. http://eur-lex.europa.eu/LexUriServ/site/en/com/2007/com2007_0724en01.pdf (date accessed 22 May 2012)

European Commission Communication COM (2008) 394 final from the Commission to the Council, the European Parliament, the European Economic and Social Committee and the Committee of the Regions, "Think Small First" – A "Small Business Act" for Europe. http://eur-lex.europa.eu/LexUriServ/LexUriServ.do?uri=COM:2008:0394:FIN:EN:PDF (date accessed 22 May 2012)

European Commission Communication COM (2009) 544 final from the Commission to the Council and the European Parliament, Action programme for reducing administrative burdens in the EU sectoral reduction plans and 2009 actions. http://eur-lex.europa.eu/LexUriServ/LexUriServ.do?uri=COM:2009:0544:FIN:EN:PDF (date accessed 22 May 2012)

European Commission Staff Working Document SEC (2009) 1350 final on the implementation of the Commission recommendation (2003/361/EC) of 6 May concerning the definition of micro, small and medium-sized enterprises. Retrieved from http://ec.europa.eu/enterprise/policies/sme/files/sme_definition/sme_report_2009_en.pdf (date accessed 22 May 2012)

European Commission Communication COM (2011) 78 final from the Commission to the Council and the European Parliament, Review of the "Small Business Act" for Europe. http://ec.europa.eu/enterprise/policies/sme/small-business-act/files/sba_review_en.pdf (date accessed 22 May 2012)

European Commission Proposal for a Council Directive on a Common Consolidated Corporate Tax Base (CCCTB) COM (2011) 121/4. http://ec.europa.eu/taxation_

customs/resources/documents/taxation/company_tax/common_tax_base/com_2011_121_en.pdf (date accessed 22 May 2012)

European Parliament (2012) Company law, authored by Panizza, R. (2008) http://circa.europa.eu/irc/opoce/fact_sheets/info/data/market/legislation/article_7200_en.htm (date accessed 22 May 2012)

Leydesdorff, L. and Etzkowitz, H. (1996) Emergence of a triple helix of university-industry-government relations. *Science and Public Policy* 23(5), 279–286

Lopriore, M. (2009) Small and medium-sized enterprises – Key for delivering more growth and jobs: A mid-term review of modern SME policy in Europe. *EIPASCOPE* 2009/2, 31–36

Moussis, N. (2012) Webpage based on the book by Moussis, N. (2011) Access to European Union law, economics, policies. http://europedia.moussis.eu/books/Book_2/ (date accessed 22 May 2012)

Reflection Group (2011) European Commission Report of the Reflection Group on the Future of European Company Law, 5 April 2011, Brussels. http://ec.europa.eu/internal_market/company/docs/modern/reflectiongroup_report_en.pdf (date accessed 22 May 2012)

Smallbone, D., Labrianidis, L., Venesaar, U., Welter, F., and Zashev, P. (2007) Challenges and prospects of cross border cooperation in the context of EU enlargement. Deliverable 7: State of the art literature review. http://www.crossbordercoop.net/Publications/Integrated_lit_review.pdf (date accessed 22 May 2012)

TREU (2010) Consolidated Version of the Treaty on the Functioning of the European Union, 30.03.2010. *Official Journal of the European Union*. http://eurlex.europa.eu/LexUriServ/LexUriServ.do?uri=OJ:C:2010:083:0047:0200:EN:PDF (date accessed 22 May 2012)

Wegefelt, P. and Schramm Rasmussen, H. (eds.) (2011) Europe fast forward: Business priorities for growth. Copenhagen: Confederation of Danish Industries

10 EU initiatives supporting cross-border cooperation among SMEs

One of the main challenges for the EU and its member states concerning initiatives to support cross-border cooperation among SMEs is to create the appropriate conditions in which entrepreneurs are encouraged to follow through on cooperation activities and where the cooperation's potential gains clearly outweigh its costs and risks.

As seen in the previous chapters, an extensive range of EU-, national-, and regional-level policies impact SME development. Some are designed specifically for SMEs, while others affect SMEs inadvertently. The same is true of the EU policies and initiatives impacting SMEs' cross-border cooperation activities. At the national and local levels, chambers of commerce, business associations, SME agencies, commercial consultants, and trade promotion organisations all deal with activities that may assist cross-border cooperation among SMEs, such as matchmaking, trade fairs, business missions, and market studies: "A recent survey of EU SMEs with international experience found that over half (63 %) of such companies recorded an improvement in performance following participation in an international support programme" (European Commission 2011, p. 6). Support programmes can be understood as a set of tangible SME support activities. With regard to support programmes, it is imperative that local situations be borne in mind in order to provide the most efficient and effective support services and gain the most synergies. A "bottom-up approach" for SMEs wishing to enter cooperation with enterprises in another nation state is crucial. This approach is clearly endorsed by the European Commission in its efforts to involve SMEs across the EU in its consultations, policy-making, and provision of localised support networks like the Enterprise Europe Network. Only through this type of approach can gaps in services be recognised and decisions made regarding where EU-level action (in conjunction with national, local, and regional action) can provide the most value. As cooperation activities are fluid and changeable, so too must be the support measures for SMEs involved in or entering cooperation. "The visibility of the services already in place is not always sufficient and SMEs still face considerable distances when it comes to [...] entering into business cooperation with international partners" (COM[2011] 702 final, p. 8). This is particularly important given that a Commission study found that 47 % of EU SMEs reported a lack of adequate public services and 44 % a lack of adequate information as barriers to the business environment of EU-EEA markets (European Commission 2010).

Access to information is often considered a key factor in enterprises' ability to develop cross-border cooperation: "General information on the potential benefits and risks of internationalisation and/or business partnerships is necessary to raise awareness of the operations presented by different forms of CBC and to facilitate the informed decisions of enterprises" (Smallbone and Xheneti 2008, p. 10). Programmes designed to improve this access to information have become an important part of EU initiatives aimed at supporting enterprises. However, studies show that entrepreneurs are often either unaware of the benefits of participating in cross-border cooperation or doubtful that there will be any advantages or benefits for their businesses (Smallbone et al. 2007). Entrepreneurs and small businesses often feel decoupled from the policy-making process, despite efforts to include them. Local authorities and organisations looking for funding support are most likely to be involved in cross-border cooperation activities. As has been previously outlined, this can also be seen to have merit, as it helps lay the foundation for longer-term and possibly institutionalised forms of cooperation at the regional level (ibid.); this can also benefit SMEs interested in cross-border cooperation by providing stability and useful contact points on either side of the border.

Traditionally, programmes to support SME internationalisation have focused on promoting exports. The first European Internationalisation Agency (otherwise known as Trade Promotion Agencies or Export Promotion Agencies) was founded as early as 1999 in Finland (see European Commission 2007). While most policy makers are become increasingly aware of the need to provide support measures for internationalisation that do not focus on export alone, a recent analysis of European policy measures shows that more than 70 % of the world's internationalisation programmes (both national and regional) still focus on export (European Commission 2008). A European Commission report based on a 2009 survey on the internationalisation of SMEs points to two interesting policy conclusions drawn from the results on SMEs' awareness and use of public programmes that might assist their access to foreign markets: (i) larger enterprises are more aware of the available support measures and use them more often, and (ii) the vast majority of internationally active enterprises state that they do not use public support measures (European Commission 2010). However, the 2011 report *Opportunities for the Internationalisation of European SMEs* shows that those enterprises that do take advantage of support programmes are positive about their effects (European Commission 2011). This study lists some 300 support measures undertaken by member states and the EU to assist European SMEs in gaining access to seven key target markets – Brazil, China, India, Japan, Russia, South Korea, and the Ukraine. Most of them, because of their general nature, are applicable beyond the seven markets identified. While the study focuses on the opportunities for EU SMEs in markets outside the EU and the role of business support for companies attempting to access these markets, it also offers interesting insights into support provision for SMEs' international activity in general. It is worth noting again that this study also confirmed that some three quarters of all internationally active SMEs are not aware of the available support measures. At the same time, "from among the 27 % that are aware, only about 26 % – which is 7 % of all internationalised SMEs – report using such support" (ibid., p. 7).

The European Commission offers numerous programmes and measures, both financial and non-financial, focused on providing support to SMEs. The Small Business Act discussed in the previous chapter provides ample evidence of the European Commission's recognition of the essential role SMEs play in the European economy. As is clearly evidenced above, the European SME is often not aware of the programmes and instruments available at the EU level. The following section outlines some of the main non-financial programmes and measures provided by the EU to SMEs, which should provide them with an overview of the support currently available to them as well as measures that may be of interest in the future. However, it must be noted that this list is selective and thus by no means exhaustive and that programmes and priorities change on a multi-annual basis. Nevertheless, the list should prove a useful introduction to EU initiatives supporting SMEs both generally and specifically concerning cross-border activities.

10.1 Non-financial EU initiatives supporting SME cross-border activities

Among the support needs of businesses involved in or wishing to become involved in cross-border activities, finance is likely to be the need most commonly expressed by businesses, along with labour and legal advice and help finding partners (cf. Smallbone and Xheneti 2008). With regard to access to finance, the application procedures for the financial support provided by EU and other national programmes are very often considered too complex, time-consuming, and bureaucratic, thus unattractive to SMEs with limited resources.

The principles of EU-level SME support are outlined below:

- "Providing support to SMEs only if the private sector is not offering support at reasonable conditions (i.e., there is a market failure);

- Beginning with the needs of SMEs, rather than concentrating on what agencies can currently provide;
- Avoiding stand-alone initiatives;
- Aiming to build the general management capacity of enterprises, as well as addressing the immediate problem" (European Commission 2011, p. 9)

The Europe 2020 strategy calls for raising the profile of internationalisation support. It should perhaps be noted again that the characteristics favouring entry into and success in a cooperation closely mirror those of internationalisation. The European Commission conducted public stakeholder consultations in 2009 and 2011 that revealed a general concern regarding an uncoordinated increase in support schemes relating to SMEs and internationalisation and the unsatisfactory use of fiscal resources (cf. COM[2011] 702 final). A better coordination of activities at the European, national, and regional or local levels would certainly prove beneficial and has been recognised by the Commission as deserving more attention.

A crucial support network, and certainly one of the most relevant European networks for cross-border cooperation, is the European Commission's Enterprise Europe Network (EEN). This, along with the SBA, represents one of the EU's major SME-supporting initiatives. It combines the former Euro Info Centre and the Innovation Relay Centre networks and aims to contribute to both the innovative capacity of SMEs and Europe's overall competitiveness (Enterprise Europe Network 2012). The EEN plays an important role in bringing businesses together, "in particular in the area of long term SME cooperation" (European Commission 2008, p. 25). The Enterprise Europe Network is a key element in the SME-support infrastructure, providing information and advice, organising partnership-building activities, and offering innovation and technology-transfer services. Informing enterprises regarding EU legislation, programmes, and funding opportunities are among the Network's main activities. One of the benefits of the Network is that it has direct access to the European Commission. The EEN helps SMEs benefit from the EU's internal market and supports internationalisation beyond the EU. Generally, EEN partners are hosted in member states by business support organisations at national and local levels. There are approximately 600 local partners worldwide spread across EU member states, candidate countries, members of the European Economic Area, and major economic areas such as China, Russia, South-Korea, Mexico, and the US (Enterprise Europe Network 2012; COM[2011] 702 final).

The Commission's renewed Market Access Strategy (COM[2007] 183) is also seen as a key contribution to European SMEs wishing to internationalise.

First, the partnership approach, linking the European Commission, member states, and the EU business community, provides an important benefit to SMEs both within and outside the EU: Market Access Teams are located in key export markets, and a Market Access Database provides information on tariffs and other non-tariff barriers in third countries (see Market Access Database 2012). The European Customs Information Portal (ECIP) is a website that provides practical information on EU legislation, news, links to databases, documents, e-learning tools, and procedures used by national customs administrations (European Customs Information Portal 2012). The European Union has a number of external business centres that are also relevant to the EU's market access support for SMEs. The EU's external business centres can be found in both China and India (see European Business and Technology Centre 2012). For example, there is currently a European Business and Technology Centre in New Delhi and further antennae are planned for Mumbai, Kolkata, and Bangalore (European Commission 2012). The centre in New Delhi, opened in 2009, is led by Eurochambres in partnership with 16 business and research organisations from four different sectors (biotech, energy, environment, and transport) and is co-financed by the European Commission (European Commission 2012). The centre aims to become the point of contact for European companies and research bodies wishing to enter the Indian market. A European Support Centre for SMEs focussing on the Chinese market is also funded by the European Commission and provides "free, hands-on business support to SMEs from the European Union, facilitating their access to the Chinese market" (EU SME Centre 2012).

As part of its Competitiveness and Innovation Programme, the Commission is planning to launch an in-depth "mapping" and analysis of the support services currently available in EU and non-EU countries in order to identify their gaps and overlaps (COM[2011] 702 final). This should substantially respond to the stakeholder criticisms regarding the proliferation of uncoordinated support schemes for SMEs wishing to internationalise. While initially implemented only for priority markets, this work will be followed by an awareness-raising campaign that should be of interest to all SMEs interested in cross-border cooperation. Additionally, Market Access Teams in EU Delegations involved in this exercise will "bring together and coordinate local organisations, for example chambers of commerce, European Business Organisations and Enterprise Europe Network partners, in order to identify synergies and gaps in existing local SME support activities" (COM[2011] 702 final, p. 8). COM[2011] 702 final encourages member states to voluntarily open up their services in non-member countries to all EU SMEs and recommends that "where necessary, top-up schemes of financing at EU level should be considered, subject to the future multiannual financial framework, as a means of facilitating cross-border cooperation and access to complementary expertise among service providers, thereby optimising the use of scarce public funds" (p. 12).

The European Commission recognises the importance of SME growth and innovation and is aware that SMEs often need to find the right partners to do this, entering into strategic business cooperation and networks with international partners. Clusters and business networks are seen as allowing SMEs to benefit from business connections and formal and informal knowledge transfers, which can in turn make the development of partnerships abroad easier: "SMEs have easier access to global value chains, develop strategic alliances with research organisations in counterpart clusters or networks, expand their commercial activities abroad, including public procurement, and obtain appropriate skills and tailored professional advice" (COM[2011] 702 final, p. 13; see also Meier zu Köcker et al. 2011). As facilitators of SME internationalisation, it is suggested that cluster and network organisations should also be integrated into SME internationalisation support schemes. With this in mind, a call for proposals under the EU's Competitiveness and Innovation Programme was launched in March 2011 to stimulate international cooperation through regional and national cluster programmes. It is believed that a European Cluster Cooperation Platform, set up under the European Cluster Excellence Initiative, will contribute greatly to the promotion of international cluster cooperation for the benefit of SMEs. Clusters are important for SMEs interested in cooperation, as they provide a suitable business environment for collaboration. Those SMEs that are involved in clusters are likely to cooperate with research institutions, suppliers, customers, and other competitors located in the same geographic space.

Another initiative worth mentioning is related to public procurement. The SMEs' access to public procurement is still considered suboptimal. For example, the SBA Review notes that it is necessary "to further facilitate SMEs' access to public procurement which represents 17% of the EU GDP, notably through further simplification" (COM[2011] 78 final, p. 11). As part of a new procurement initiative launched in March 2012, the Commission aims to ensure that all companies are on an equal footing in competing in the public procurement market and aims to enhance the incentives encouraging the EU's trading partners to open up their public procurement markets to interested EU parties, including SMEs (European Commission 2012a).

With regard to the EU's current and future efforts to mainstream SME internationalisation into other EU policies and improve the environment for SMEs' international activities, the Commission plans to undertake a range of further measures, some of which are summarised below:

- Support the establishment of a business-friendly environment in enlargement, neighbouring, and developing countries, in particular for SMEs;
- increase efforts to eliminate remaining tariff and non-tariff barriers in non-EU countries;
- set up contact points for SMEs in the trade and economic sections of all relevant EU Delegations (foreseen as part of the work of Market Access Teams);
- draw attention to the aim of making markets more open and friendly to small businesses in regulatory talks held with partner governments;
- make SMEs more aware of the economic benefits of trading internationally through improved communication and of the possible autonomous tariff suspensions and quotas; assessing the autonomous tariff suspensions and quotas on SMEs will be the focus of a future consultation. (COM [2011] 702 final)

Given the extensive range of EU measures available to aid SMEs in their internationalisation and cross-border cooperation activities and the measures in place at the national, local, and regional levels, it seems obvious that emphasis should be placed on coordinating the numerous current activities. The Communication *Small Business, Big World* also highlights this need for "a more coherent and integrated approach to SME support" (COM[2011] 702 final, p. 7).

10.2 Financial initiatives supporting European SMEs

The question of access to finance plagued SMEs even before the onset of the recent financial crisis. With banks often less inclined now than they were before the crisis to lend to businesses, this can make the extra costs incurred in cross-border cooperation even more difficult to finance. In addition to the tools and measures used by the Commission to analyse and monitor European financial markets and make them more responsive to SME needs, an SME Finance Forum was established in 2010 in order to bring together financial institutions and organisations representing SMEs and address issues relating to SMEs' access to financing. The EU supports financial intermediaries (such as banks, guarantee funds, and leasing companies) providing financing to SMEs through loan guarantees. Currently, this guarantee facility is funded under the Competitiveness and Innovation Framework Programme (CIP). The Commission Communication *A Budget for Europe 2020* (COM[2011] 500 final Part I) proposes increasing the amounts allocated to three particular policy areas: research and innovation, education, and SME development. *A Budget for Europe 2020* (COM[2011] 500 final Part II) suggests that "[p]articular effort is needed to promote the development of SMEs" (p. 17) and sees this effort as needed in the key market failures that limit SME growth, such as access to financing. The budget should provide crucial equity and debt financing through innovative financial instruments, while also supporting activities promoting SME development at the European level. The overall financial framework aims to increase the participation of small businesses in funding programmes, addressing the funding aspects considered problematic by SMEs: "simplifying rules, reducing the costs of participation, accelerating award procedures and providing a 'one-stop shop' to make life easier for the beneficiaries of EU funding" (p. 17). The Commission plans to establish a *Competitiveness and SME Programme* to replace the non-innovation part of CIP, while the innovation part of CIP will be included in the *Common Strategic Framework for Research and Innovation* along with all its research and innovation support for SMEs (COM[2011] 500 final Part II).

The *Competitiveness and SMEs Programme* is particularly interesting in the context of SMEs and cross-border cooperation, as it will focus on measures promoting "more dynamic and internationally-competitive SMEs" (COM [2011] 500 final Part II, p. 18). One of its key measures relates to access to financing through innovative financial instruments, particularly for venture capital (VC) for start-up and growth investments:

> "*(1) An* ***equity facility*** *for growth-phase investment, which will provide commercially-oriented reimbursable equity financing primarily in the form of VC through financial intermediaries to SMEs. The following two measures are envisaged in this regard:*
>
> – *Investments in VC funds that operate across borders within the EU and are focused on investing in growth-oriented enterprises, thereby supporting the development of an EU-wide VC market.*
> – *A 'fund-of-funds' (or 'European fund') investing across borders in VC funds that subsequently invest in enterprises, particularly in their international expansion phase.*

*(2) A **loan facility**, providing direct or other risk sharing arrangements with financial intermediaries to cover loans for SMEs. The facility would generate a high leverage effect and would provide cross-border or multi-country lending that could not easily be achieved through facilities at the national level" (COM[2011] 500 final Part II, p. 18).*

Beginning in 2008, the European Investment Bank also reinforced its commitment to SMEs. Both the Commission and member states are working together to improve the market's equity investment efficiency and are striving to create a more open venture capital market: "The Commission aims to encourage Member States to learn from good practices by supporting business angel investments, in particular across borders, and through cooperation with venture capital funds" (European Commission 2011a). The Commission is also increasing efforts to improve SME cash flow, as was briefly outlined in the previous chapter. This is evident in its revision of the Late Payment Directive, aimed at better protecting creditors (European Commission 2011a). State aid rules for SME support have been simplified to facilitate member states' SME support. A handbook on Community state aid rules was made available in 2009 to provide concise and simplified information on state aid legislation (European Commission 2009).

Better and easier access to EU SME funding is a key challenge for the EU. This is reiterated in the recommendations made by Wegefelt and Schramm Rasmusse (2011) in *Europe Fast Forward: Business Priorities for Growth*: "A reinvigoration of SME investments is essential and should be promoted through the various relevant EU policies. This implies further development of well- designed financing instruments and greater simplification efforts to allow SME participation in EU funded programs" (p. 16).

Table 10.1 outlines some of the financial schemes currently available to SMEs. The financial schemes presented in this table do not provide funding directly to SMEs but are provided via intermediary financial institutions, such as banks. The aim of these financial instruments is to increase the amount of credit available to SMEs, while also encouraging an increased SME lending capacity among financial intermediaries (European Commission 2012).

Table 10.1 Financial instruments

Name	Website	Additional information
Competitive-ness and Inno-vation Frame-work Pro-gramme (CIP)	http://ec.europa.eu/cip/index_en.htm http://ec.europa.eu/enterprise/policies/finance/cip-financial-instruments/index_en.htm http://eif.europa.eu/	The European Investment Fund (EIF) manages the following three schemes: 1. The High Growth and Innovative SME Facility (GIF) aims to increase available equity for innovative SMEs both in their early stages (GIF1) and in the expansion phase (GIF2). 2. The SME Guarantee Facility provides additional guarantees to guarantee schemes, concentrating on addressing market failures in four areas: (i) access to loans of SMEs with growth potential; (ii) provision of microcredit; (iii) access to equity or quasi-equity; (iv) securitisation. 3. A Capacity Building Scheme supporting financial intermediaries in some Member States.
Joint European Resources for Micro and Medium Enterprises (JEREMIE)	http://eif.europa.eu/jeremie/ http://ec.europa.eu/regional_policy/funds/2007/jjj/jeremie_en.htm	This is a joint initiative of the European Commission and the European Investment Fund with the European Investment Bank, aiming to improve access to financing for micro- to medium-sized enterprises. It focuses on the supply of micro-credit, venture capital financing and guarantees, and other forms of innovative financing.
Joint Action to Support Micro-finance Institu-tions in Europe (JASMINE)	http://ec.europa.eu/regional_policy/funds/2007/jjj/micsro_en.htm http://www.eif.org/what_we_do/microfinance/JASMINE/index.htm	JASMINE is a joint initiative of the European Commission, the European Investment Fund, and the European Investment Bank and complements JEREMIE. This scheme aims to develop the supply of micro-credit in Europe by providing technical assistance to micro-finance institutions and financing the activities of non-bank financial institutions.

Name	Website	Additional information
European Investment Funds (EIF)	http://eif.europa.eu/ http://eif.org/EIF_for/sme_finance/index.htm	The EIF's own investment focuses on the following aspects: – VC funds and business incubators that support SMEs, particularly new and technology-oriented ones – Guarantee instruments providing guarantees to financial institutions encompassing credits to SMEs
European Investment Bank (EIB) loans	http://eib.europa.eu http://eib.europa.eu/projects/topics/sme/index.htm http://eib.europa.eu/projects/topics/sme/intermediaries/index.htm	These loans are awarded via intermediaries for tangible or intangible SME investments and to provide SMEs with a stable working capital base. Loans are available for between 2 and 12 years, for a maximum of € 12.5 million per loan.
European Progress Microfinance Facility (EPMF) for Employment and Social Inclusion	http://ec.europa.eu/social/main.jsp?langId=en&catId=836 http://www.eif.org/what_we_do/microfinance/progress/index.htm http://ec.europa.eu/social/main.jsp?catId=983&langId=en.	This is a new facility providing microcredit to small businesses and people who have lost their jobs and want to start their own small businesses. It aims to complement other existing instruments, such as the ESF

Source: Adapted from European Commission (2012)

The European Commission's (2012) document *European Union Support Programmes for SMEs: An Overview of the Main Funding Opportunities Available to European SMEs* includes a section on financial initiatives relating specifically to the internationalisation of SMEs (see Table 10.2). This is of particular interest for SMEs wishing to enter some form of cross-border cooperation outside the EU as part of an internationalisation process. Again, these schemes do not generally provide funding directly to SMEs but indirectly via intermediaries and/or public authorities. The following table outlines the sources of funding relating to EU candidate and neighbourhood countries.

Table 10.2 Internationalisation of SMEs

Name	Website	Additional information
Instrument of Pre-Accession Assistance (IPA)	http://ec.europa.eu/regional_policy/funds/ipa/index_en.htm	The IPA has been running since January 2007, replacing other Commission instruments for candidate countries. It focuses on assistance for transition and institution building, cross-border cooperation, regional development, human resources, and rural development.
European Neighbourhood Policy	http://ec.europa.eu/world/enp/index_en.htm	Launched in 2004, this aims to establish collaboration with EU neighbours through political relationship building and economic integration. Currently, 16 neighbour countries are incorporated into this policy, and actions are financed through the European Neighbourhood Policy Instrument (ENPI).
Neighbourhood Investment Facility (NIF)	http://ec.europa.eu/world/enp/index_en.htm http://ec.europa.eu/europeaid/where/neighbourhood/regional-cooperation/irc/investment_en.htm	Financed through ENPI.
East-investment programme	http://ec.europa.eu/europeaid/work/ap/aap/2010_en.htm http://www.enpi-info.eu/ http://www.enpi-info.eu/maineast.php?id=315&id_type=10	This programme supports the improvement of the business environments in Armenia, Azerbaijan, Belarus, Georgia, Moldova, and the Ukraine. SMEs are supported in their internationalisation processes, improving networking and encouraging trade development.
European Bank for Reconstruction and Development programmes (EBRD)	http://www.ebrd.com/pages/sector/financial/sme/shtml http://www.ebrd.com/pages/about/policies/msme.shtml http://www.ebrd.com/pages/workingwithus/tambas.shtml http://www.ebrd.com/	The EU/EBRD SME Finance facility provides financing to SMEs in 11 Central European countries, including EU accession states and new member states. Financing is provided through local banks, leasing companies, and equity funds. Non-financial support is provided through the TAM (Turn Around Management) and BAS (Business Advisory Services) programmes,

Name	Website	Additional information
	pages/workingwithus/tambas/guide.pdf	designed to help private enterprises adapt to a market economy.
EIB loans for SMEs in Eastern Neighbourhood countries	http://www.eib.europe.eu/projects/regions/eastern-neighbours/index.htm?lang=en	Towards the end of 2009, the European Investment Bank launched SME loans in Eastern Neighbourhood countries.
EIB loans for SMEs in Mediterranean partner countries (FEMIP)	http://eib.org/projects/regions/med/	The FEMIP grants loans to small businesses in the Mediterranean region, particularly for projects aiming to boost the economic infrastructure of the area.
AL-Invest IV	http://ec.europa.eu/europeaid/where/latin_america/regional-cooperation/al-invest/index_en.htm	Programme supporting the internationalisation of SMEs in Latin America through a network of operators from Europe and Latin America.
EU Gateway Programme	http://www.eu-gateway.eu	The EU Gateway Programme (2008–2015) is designed to complement export promotion activities already in place in certain high-growth potential sectors (such as healthcare and medical technology) in Japan and South Korea.
EU-Japan Industrial Cooperation Programmes	http://www.eu-japan.eu/gloabal/business-training.html	This incorporates a set of annual programmes also open to SMEs. Enterprises are offered indirect support via training programmes.
Understanding China	http://understanding-china.eu	This is a programme run by Eurochambres and other stakeholders aimed at helping European companies better understand the Chinese economy and improve their competitiveness in the Chinese market.
EU-China Managers Exchange and Training Programme (METP)	http://www.metp.net.cn/metp3/english/index_asp_ColumnId=271	This programme provides language and business culture training for Chinese and European managers.

Source: Adapted from European Commission (2012)

Before concluding this chapter on EU initiatives supporting SME cross-border cooperation, two further sections included in the Commission's document on funding opportunities for SMEs should be mentioned (European Commission 2012). The first relates to EU Structural Funds. As has been mentioned in previous chapters, EU Structural Funds are special funds designed to promote economic and social cohesion within the EU. These are of particular relevance to cross-border activities, as they aim to reduce regional disparities across Europe. However, within the framework of these funds, direct aid to SMEs to co-finance their investments is possible only in regions identified as "convergence" (i.e. less economically developed) regions; SMEs in other regions can be indirectly funded through actions considered high priority due to their perceived high leverage effect, such as entrepreneurship training, support services, business incubators, technology transfer mechanisms, and networking (ibid.). Programmes running as part of the Structural Funds are managed at the national and regional levels and are co-financed by the European Commission. Table 10.3 includes basic information on the funding sources incorporated into the EU Structural Funds.

Table 10.3 Structural funds

Name	Website	Additional information
European Regional Development Fund	http://ec.europa.eu/regional_policy/funds/feder/index_en.htm	Largest SME-supporting fund. Aims to strengthen and improve the competitiveness of SMEs, improve regional and local business environment for SMEs, promote the interregional and cross-border cooperation of SMEs, and invest in human resources.
European Social Development Fund	http://ec.europa.eu/employment_social/esf	Supports SMEs' economic and social changes.
European Agricultural Fund for Rural Development (EAFRD)	http://europa.eu/legislation_summaries/agriculture/general_framework/l60032_en.htm	Designed to support the development of rural areas and the competitiveness of agriculture and forestry

Source: Adapted from European Commission (2012)

The second section on SME funding opportunities included in the document outlined above but not yet discussed in this chapter refers to funding for specific thematic areas. Thematic funding is generally designed by European Commission departments to focus on a specific set of objectives relating to thematic areas. This type of funding can be applied for directly by SMEs and other bodies. The general prerequisites required of projects seeking funding from any of these programmes are that the projects be sustainable, value-added, and transnational (European Commission 2012). The transnational element encourages cooperation among partners in different territories, making them particularly interesting for SMEs interested in engaging in cooperative alliances. As a rule, co-funding is necessary, with the EU covering only part of the costs (cf. European Commission 2012). Tables 10.4–10.7 have been adapted from the Commission's document on SME funding opportunities.

Table 10.4 Thematic area: environment, energy, and transport

Name	Website	Additional information
LIFE +	http://ec.europa.eu/environment/life/funding/lifeplus.htm	Three strands: Nature and Biodiversity, Environment Policy and Governance, and Information and Communication.
Competitiveness and Innovation Framework Programme (CIP)	http://ec.europa.eu/cip/index_en.htm	CIP areas of interest: a) Entrepreneurship and Innovation Programme (EIP) b) Intelligent Energy Europe Programme (IEE) c) Information and Communication Technologies Policy Support Programme (ICT-PSP).
Marco Polo II	http://ec.europa.eu/transport/marcopolo/index_en.htm	Programme to reduce road congestion, improve the environmental performance of the freight transport system, and contribute to an efficient and sustainable transport system.

Source: Adapted from European Commission (2012)

Table 10.5 Thematic area: innovation and research

Name	Website	Additional information
Seventh Framework Programme for Research and Technological Development (2007–2013), FP7	http://cordis.europa.eu/fp7/home_en.html	Cooperation programme Ideas programme People programme Capacities programme
Competitiveness and Innovation Framework Programme (CIP)	http://ec.europa.eu/cip/index_en.htm	Two strands: a) Entrepreneurship and Innovation Programme (EIP) b) ICT Policy Support Programme
EUREKA	http://www.eurekanetwork.org	Eureka is a network of market-oriented, industrial R&D organisations. Eurostars Joint Programme finances small businesses participating in international projects in innovation and research.

Source: Adapted from European Commission (2012)

Table 10.6 Thematic area: education and training

Name	Website	Additional information
Integrated Action Programme in Lifelong Learning, 2007–2013	http://ec.europa.eu/education/lifelong-learning-programme/doc78_en.htm	Four programmes under the Integrated Action Programme in Lifelong Learning: COMENIUS, ERASMUS, GRUNDTVIG, and LEONARDO DA VINCI (most relevant to enterprises).
Erasmus for young entrepreneurs (initiated in 2009)	http://ec.europa.eu/enterprise/entrepreneurship/support_measures/erasmus/index.htm http://www.erasmus-entrepreneurs.eu	Programme provides practical and financial assistance for new entrepreneurs wishing to spend time in an enterprise in another EU country.

Source: Adapted from European Commission (2012)

Table 10.7 Thematic area: culture and media

Name	Website
CULTURE 2007–2013	http://ec.europa.eu/culture/our-programmes-and- actions/doc411_en.htm
MEDIA 2007–2013	http://ec.europa.eu/information_society/media/index_en.htm

Source: Adapted from European Commission (2012)

While not all of the funding initiatives listed in this chapter relate specifically to cross-border cooperation, to maintain as comprehensive a list of support initiatives for European SMEs as possible, the most important support schemes have been mentioned. The key challenges in the EU's support for SMEs undertaking cross-border cooperation is coordinating activities with those of the member states and designing activities that create conditions at the local and regional levels that encourage SMEs to become involved in cooperation activities.

Summary of the EU initiatives supporting SME cross-border cooperation

1. It is considered crucial that a "bottom-up approach" be taken in the support of SMEs wishing to enter some form of cross-border cooperation. Therefore, it is imperative that EU initiatives in support of SME cross-border cooperation bear in mind the local situations in order to provide the most efficient and effective support services and gain the most synergies.
2. The visibility of the available support services for SME cross-border cooperation is considered insufficient. Access to information is a key factor influencing the decision to develop cross-border cooperation. Access to information regarding the benefits and risks of business partnerships is necessary to raise awareness of the potential of cross-border cooperation.
3. A crucial SME support network, and one of the most relevant in Europe for cross-border cooperation, is the European Commission's Enterprise Europe Network (EEN).
4. Financing is one of the needs most commonly expressed by businesses involved in or wishing to get involved in cross-border activities, as are support for labour, legal advice, and help finding partners.

5. Cooperation activities are fluid and changeable; so too must be the support measures for SMEs involved in or entering cooperation. The EU programmes and priorities supporting SMEs change on a multi-annual basis.

References

European Business and Technology Centre (2012) European Business and Technology Centre website. http://www.ebtc.eu// (date accessed 2 June 2012)

European Commission (2007) Final report of the expert group on supporting the internationalisation of SMEs. http://ec.europa.eu/enterprise/policies/sme/files/support_measures/internationalisation/report_internat_en.pdf (date accessed 2 June 2012)

European Commission (2008) Supporting the internationalisation of SMEs – Good practice selection. http://ec.europa.eu/enterprise/policies/sme/files/support_measures/internationalisation/internat_best_en.pdf (date accessed 2 June 2012)

European Commission (2009) Handbook on community state aid rules for SMEs – Including temporary state aid measures to support access to finance in the current financial and economic crisis (29.02.2009). http://ec.europa.eu/competition/state_aid/studies_reports/sme_handbook.pdf (date accessed 2 June 2012)

European Commission (2010) Internationalisation of European SMEs – Final report. http://ec.europa.eu/enterprise/policies/sme/market-access/files/internationalisation_of_european_smes_final_en.pdf (date accessed 2 June 2012)

European Commission (2011) Opportunities for the internationalisation of European SMEs – Final report. http://ec.europa.eu/enterprise/policies/sme/market-access/files/web_internationalisation_opportunities_for_smes_final_report_aug_2011_en.pdf (date accessed 2 June 2012)

European Commission (2011a). Thinking big for small businesses – What the EU does for SMEs. http://ec.europa.eu/enterprise/policies/sme/files/thinking_big_en.pdf (date accessed 2 June 2012)

European Commission (2012) European Union support programmes for SMEs: An overview of the main funding opportunities available to European SMEs. http://ec.europa.eu/enterprise/newsroom/cf/_getdocument.cfm?doc_id=7264 (date accessed 2 June 2012)

European Commission (2012a) European Commission levels the playing field for European business in international procurement markets. European Commission Press Release, 21 March 2012. http://europa.eu/rapid/pressReleasesAction.do?reference=IP/12/268&format=HTML&aged=0&language=EN&guiLanguage=en (date accessed 2 June 2012)

European Commission Communication COM(2007) 183 final from the Commission to the European Parliament, the Council, the European Economic and Social

Committee and the Committee of the Regions. Global Europe: A stronger partnership to deliver market access for European exporters. http://trade.ec.europa.eu/doclib/docs/2007/april/tradoc_134507.pdf (date accessed 2 June 2012)

European Commission Communication COM(2011) 78 final from the Commission to the Council, the European Parliament. *Review of the "Small Business Act" for Europe.* http://ec.europa.eu/enterprise/policies/sme/small-business-act/files/sba_review_en.pdf (date accessed 2 June 2012)

European Commission Communication COM(2011) 500 final Part I from the Commission to the European Parliament, the Council, the European Economic and Social Committee and the Committee of Regions. A budget for Europe 2020, 29 June 2011. http://ec.europa.eu/budget/library/biblio/documents/fin_fwk1420/MFF_COM-2011–500_Part_I_en.pdf (date accessed 2 June 2012)

European Commission Communication COM(2011) 500 final Part II from the Commission to the European Parliament, the Council, the European Economic and Social Committee and the Committee of Regions. A budget for Europe 2020 – Part II Policy fiches, 29 June 2011. http://ec.europa.eu/budget/library/biblio/documents/fin_fwk1420/MFF_COM-2011-500_Part_II_en.pdf (date accessed 2 June 2012)

European Commission Communication COM(2011) 702 final from the Commission to the European Parliament, the Council, the European Economic and Social Committee and the Committee of the Regions. Small business, big world – A new partnership to help SMEs seize global opportunities. Brussels, 9.11.2011. http://ec.europa.eu/enterprise/policies/sme/market-access/files/com_2011_0702_f_en.pdf (date accessed 2 June 2012)

European Customs Information Portal (2012) European Customs Information Portal website. http://ec.europa.eu/ecip/index_en.htm (date accessed 2 June 2012)

Enterprise Europe Network (2012) Enterprise Europe Network website. http://portal.enterprise-europe-network.ec.europa.eu/about/about (date accessed 2 June 2012)

European Union SME Centre (2012) European Union SME Centre website. http://www.eusmecentre.org.cn/ (date accessed 2 June 2012)

Market Access Database (2012) Market Access Database website. http://madb.europa.eu/mkaccdb2/indexPubli.htm (date accessed 2 June 2012)

Meier zu Köcker, G., Müller, L., and Zombori, Z. (2011) European clusters go international: Networks and clusters as instruments for the initiation of international business cooperation. Berlin: Institute for Innovation and Technology

Smallbone, D. and Xheneti, M. (2008) Challenges and prospects of cross border cooperation in the context of EU enlargement. Deliverable 16: Policy issues related to entrepreneurship development and cross border cooperation in case study regions. http://www.crossbordercoop.net/Publications/D16_policies_governance.pdf (date accessed 26 May 2012)

Wegefelt, P. and Schramm Rasmussen, H. (eds.) (2011) Europe fast forward: Business priorities for growth. Copenhagen: Confederation of Danish Industries

Part III:
A managerial perspective on cross-border cooperation

Dietmar Sternad

11 Selecting the right cooperation partner

The success of any cooperation is strongly contingent on finding the right partners. It is thus remarkable that many SMEs do not pay adequate attention to partner selection. In a study of 46 Dutch companies, Nijssen et al. (1999) found that few used formal procedures to find international partners. Most managers relied on informal personal contacts instead. However, Nijssen et al.'s research shows that using a formalised search process and thoroughly evaluating potential partners contributed to a higher satisfaction with the selected partner and thus with cooperation. For Elmuti and Kathawala (2001), partner selection "is the most intensive process in the formation of an alliance. Yet done correctly, [it helps to] ensure a higher quality, longer lasting relationship" (p. 214). Figure 11.1 below provides an overview of a framework for a rational partner selection process.

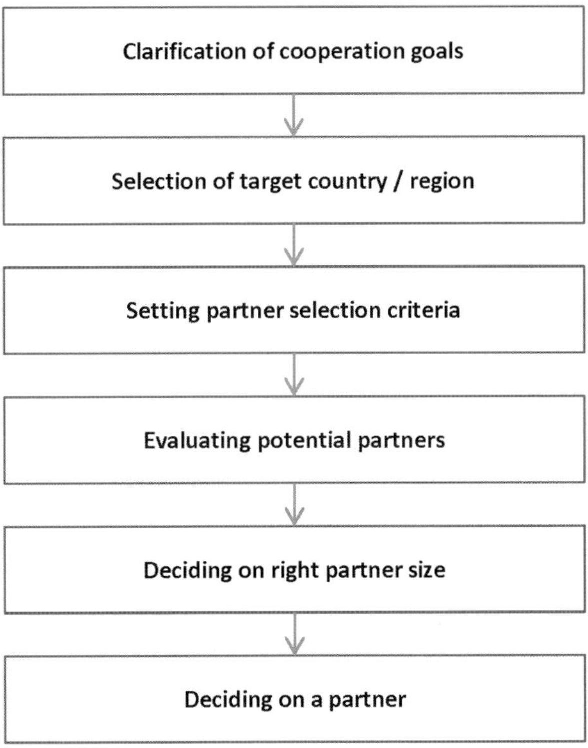

Fig. 11.1 The partner selection process

Source: Author

Partner selection takes place within three categories of firms: friends, acquaintances, and strangers (Li et al. 2008). In Li et al.'s terms, "friends" are potential partners who are already well known from previous interactions and with whom a considerable amount of mutual trust has already been built; "acquaintances" are also known to a company but only through a limited number of interactions and with whom there is a lower level of trust; "strangers" are completely unknown to each other. Previous positive experience with partners was found to be connected to a higher willingness to execute larger contracts with them (Hitt et al. 2004). Higher trust can therefore increase one's commitment to a partnership. However, the more partners know of each other, the higher the possibility for knowledge transfer, leading to an increased risk of opportunistic behaviour and an "increase[d] risk of exposing a firm's core competence" (Li et al. 2008, p. 328). Engaging strangers with whom one has no prior cooperation history as partners also has its advantages. Strangers can bring new ideas, information, and know-how to a partnership (Beckman et al. 2004). These views all emphasise the importance of not only looking for resource compatibility when searching for a potential partner but also assessing how to protect the firm's resources within a tight partnership.

11.1 Criteria for the selection of a country or region

Before selecting a partner – whether a friend, acquaintance, or stranger – companies need to decide on a country or region for cross-border cooperation. Wood et al. (2009, p. 240) present six criteria or *strategic considerations* that SMEs can use to analyse potential target regions:

1. Demand or sourcing facilities for an SME's products or services (including factors such as the level of market development, sourcing quality, and competition levels);
2. Openness to an SME's business (e.g., transfer barriers such as tariffs or quotas and legal restrictions on foreign businesses);
3. Continued openness to business (political stability and risk assessment);
4. Infrastructure and technology availability (including manufacturing, communication, and distribution infrastructure and technology);
5. Economic potential (degree of economic development and the stability of or projected increase in consumption levels);
6. Internal coherence (cultural issues such as the level of cultural unity).

As with selecting partners, selecting a target country or region is not always a formalised rational process. It is often based not on a logical sequence of decisions but on existing relationships or opportunism (Andersen and Buvik 2002). The theory known as the "Uppsala model" proposes that SMEs usually follow an establishment chain in which they prefer to first enter countries at a close psychic distance from their home countries (Johanson and Vahlne 1977). A more rational approach to selecting target markets would first establish criteria for a potential market, such as those described above, followed by in-depth research into the market conditions in the particular industry.

11.2 Partner selection criteria

After a firm has decided upon a target country or region, it needs to find an appropriate cooperation partner. Before deciding on a partner, a firm evaluates the *attractiveness* of potential partners, defined as "the degree to which an initiating firm in a particular alliance project sees a partner as desirable, favorable, appealing, and valuable" (Shah and Swaminathan 2008). Wood et al. (2009) emphasise the need to have both a "strategic congruence" and a "tactical congruence" between cooperation partners. They see strategic congruence as a fit between both business opportunities and cultural factors, such as values or organisational culture. Tactical congruence refers to the capacity to organise the day-to-day coordinative aspects of potential partnerships.

Finding the right partner requires thinking about the criteria that a partner must meet. Geringer (1991) distinguishes between task-related selection criteria, associated with the resources and capabilities necessary to achieve a firm's strategic goals, and partner-related selection criteria, which relate to the ability of a potential partner to engage in efficient and effective cooperation. Partner-related criteria include a potential partner's national or organisational culture, prior experience with the partner, trust between the management teams, and firm size and structure. Examples of task-related criteria are experienced, technically skilled people, access to distribution systems, contacts with the government, and patents, licenses, and trademarks (ibid.). Combining resources and capabilities allows firms to create competitive advantage. According to Child et al. (2005), "[i]f competitive advantage from the joint value chain seems unlikely, then the success of an alliance would be doubtful regardless of its nature and form" (p. 102).

The quite comprehensive list of selection criteria for international alliances proposed by Dacin et al. (1997) is presented in Table 11.1. In their study of international managers, they found that the prioritisation of partner selection criteria differed across countries: while Korean executives focused on technical capabilities and industry attractiveness, their American counterparts emphasised financial assets and managerial capabilities.

Table 11.1 Partner selection criteria in international alliances

Partner selection criteria	Definition	Examples
Financial assets	Resources that reflect liquidity/financial health	Lines of credit; costs of capital; debt-equity positions
Complementarity of capabilities	The degree to which a partner's resources can be used in conjunction with those of your firm	Complementary distribution channels that can be used to market your firm's products
Unique competencies	Abilities or skills possessed by a partner but not by other firms	A partner that can produce a product that cannot be imitated by other firms
Industry attractiveness	The degree to which an industry presents a favourable environment in which to achieve a firm's goals	An industry composed of a small number of competitors and/or a potentially large number of buyers
Cost of alternatives	The cost to your firm of alternatives to the alliance	For example, the cost to set up your own subsidiary in the target market
Market knowledge/access	The expertise or ability of a partner to effectively operate in a market or industry	Understanding competitors and customers; experience with government regulations; knowledge of culture
Intangible assets	Assets not reflected in the financial statements	Firm reputation; brand name; human resources
Managerial capabilities	The ability of managers to guide their firm efficiently and effectively	For example, the ability to build consensus among groups; the ability to recognise demographic changes in customers

Partner selection criteria	Definition	Examples
Capabilities to provide quality product/service	The ability of a partner to provide buyers with the quality of products they desire	Low defect rates; strong manufacturing facilities
Willingness to share expertise	The degree to which a partner is willing to allow your firm to acquire capabilities	Sharing technological knowledge; sharing marketing know-how
Partner's ability to acquire your firm's special skills	The ability of a partner to learn/acquire the skills your firm possesses	Experience in acquiring skills from alliances
Previous alliance experience	The number of alliances in which a partner is engaged	Prior participation in formal alliances
Special skills that you can learn from your partner	The ability of your firm to learn/acquire the skills the partner possesses	Partner has technology or marketing know-how that your firm does not possess but wishes to learn
Technical capabilities	The ability of a partner to develop new process or product technologies	Significant R&D operations; develops and commercialises new products

Source: Slightly adapted from Dacin et al. (1997), p. 10

In Glaister and Buckley's empirical research (1996), criteria related to the possibility of entering new international markets were dominant. They included, for example, providing the opportunity to gain a presence in new markets, offering faster market entry, or facilitating international expansion. In Glaister's (1996) study of alliances between U.K. and other Western European firms, local cultural knowledge and relationships with major buyers were the most important partner selection criteria. These findings are supported by Moan et al. (2010), who also found in case studies of Norwegian firms that access to major buyers, networks, and distribution channels in the target market and access to local market knowledge were among the most important partner selection criteria for cross-border cooperation. In addition, trust and personal chemistry between the management teams, resource complementarity, firm reputation, financial status, and financial risk-sharing also ranked high on the list of selection criteria.

Another framework, combining the proposals of Kale and Singh (2009) and Shah and Swaminathan (2008), suggests that potential partners should be evaluated using a four-tier criteria system:

(a) *Partner complementarity*: Do the partners bring distinct resources to the partnership that the other partners need but lack? Are they offering capabilities or other qualities in which their counterpart is deficient?
(b) *Partner commitment*: Are the partners willing to contribute resources to the cooperation, even when they need to make short-term sacrifices in pursuit of longer-term common benefits?
(c) *Partner compatibility*: Do the partners have matching cultures and work styles?
(d) *Potential financial payoff*: What opportunities for market access and cost reduction does a partner offer?

The relative importance of these factors can vary according to the situation and the requirements of the potential partners. In a study of alliances in the biotechnology industry, Rothaermel and Boecker (2008) observe that cooperation based on complementarity between old and new technology companies was more likely when the new technology firm was younger (e.g., an entrepreneurial start-up), while cooperation involving "older" new technology firms was more often based on similarities. Kale and Singh (2009) argue, on the other hand, that partner commitment is crucial when the overall cooperative goal is known, though the way to achieve it may be unclear.

Using a similar approach, Brouthers et al.'s (1995) "4C" scheme also implies the importance of complementary skills and compatible goals, while adding cooperative cultures and commensurable risk. A cooperative culture, they argue, can be difficult to maintain in cross-border cooperation, as national cultures differ in their learning propensity, which can lead to asymmetry between the partners. As an example, Brouthers et al. (1995) mention that "US companies are generally not good at learning from their alliance partners, whereas the Japanese want to learn *everything*. Many foreign firms want to use American firms to their maximum benefit" (p. 20). Commensurable risk refers to the stakes for the partners involved in a cooperation – an equivalent risk level (e.g., the risk of losing proprietary competencies or the financial risk involved in the partnership) and mutual dependence. As Brouthers et al. (1995) state, "[i]f nothing is at risk there is less of an incentive to stay together" (p. 22).

In a European context, Franco (2010) studies 114 partnerships by Portuguese companies and identifies the following as the main factors in partner choices: reputation, resource contribution, complementarity, organisational culture, and local/regional identity. The most interesting contribution of this study is, however, its emphasis on the personality of the entrepreneur, which also plays a key role in SMEs' partner selection.

11.3 The decision among potential partners

Clearly, many frameworks for cross-border cooperation partner selection criteria have been proposed. As the "perfect" partner who fulfils all the necessary criteria hardly exists, management must first define its cooperation goals and then specify the criteria that a potential partner must fulfil to enable the company to achieve these goals.

Geringer (1991) argues that managers evaluate the current and potential competitive position and then decide upon the most salient partner selection criteria in order to fill the capability gaps in an effort to achieve the intended future strategic position. These arguments are supported by an empirical study of Danish firms engaged in partnerships. Their partner selection criteria were based mainly on the firm's strategic motivation (Nielsen 2003). Chen et al. (2008) suggest that the weighting of partner selection criteria should depend on the primary cooperation motives. If the main goal of cooperating is gaining competitive advantage in a foreign market, the criteria will emphasise complementarity of resources and capabilities. If, on the other hand, a company has all the relevant technology and product-based advantages and is entering into cooperation primarily to gain access to a specific market or target group, criteria such as reputation, market knowledge, access to appropriate distribution channels, market position, and relationships with key players in the market will be weighted more heavily than other criteria.

Decision makers should therefore be clear about the general cooperation objectives before thinking about the relevant criteria they will use to evaluate whether the potential partners would be conducive to reaching the objectives.

Shah and Swaminathan (2008) argue that the type of project and the complexity of the processes involved in the cooperation influence partner selection. Specifically, they found that a partner choice should be contingent on two factors: first, process manageability – the amount of interaction and communication needed to fulfil the cooperative task, including the management time, communication, personnel, energy, and stress involved; second, outcome interpretability – the degree to which the outcome of a common project is easy to define and understand. When both process manageability and outcome interpretability are high, potential financial payoff is the most salient criteria. When process manageability and outcome interpretability are low, trust becomes more important.

Following an example from Hollensen (2007), companies can use a framework to evaluate potential cooperation partners. First, they would set the criteria they see as the most important determinants for successful cooperation. For example, a subset comprising the criteria from Table 11.1 relevant to the partnership at hand could be applied. Second, these criteria would be weighted according to their relative importance. Finally, in a scoring model, the potential cooperation partners would be ranked, with the total scores indicating their relative suitability as a partner. An example of the evaluation framework is presented in Table 11.2 below:

Table 11.2 A framework for cooperation partner evaluation

		Potential partner A		Potential partner B		Potential partner C	
Criteria	**Weight**	**Rating**	**Score**	**Rating**	**Score**	**Rating**	**Score**
Financial strength	*5*	5	25	8	40	2	10
Complementarity of capabilities	*4*	7	28	2	8	8	32
Unique competencies	*5*	3	15	2	10	6	30
Market knowledge/access	*5*	9	45	4	20	6	30
Managerial capabilities	*4*	6	24	8	32	5	20
Willingness to share expertise	*4*	10	40	2	8	3	12
Partner's ability to acquire your firm's special skills	*2*	7	14	7	14	5	10
Previous alliance experience	*2*	2	4	7	14	5	10
Special skills that you can learn from your partner	*3*	5	15	5	15	7	21
Technical capabilities	*2*	4	8	8	16	4	8
Overall score			218		177		173

Scales: weights – 1 (standard), 2 (of some importance), 3 (success factor), 4 (prerequisite), 5 (critical success factor); scores: from 0 (not important) to 10 (very important)

(Source: Author, using criteria based on Dacin et al. 1997)

An extended model could divide the criteria further into "must-have" and "nice-to-have" criteria, with criteria in the first category essential to the decision about whether to even consider entering into cooperation with a potential partner.

After the selection criteria are applied to the potential partners, they should also be closely evaluated as to the likelihood of the partnership succeeding. Dyer et al. (2001) propose that two factors should be considered here: (a) the partner's resources and capabilities; and (b) the cultural fit of the partner. As an example of a cultural fit analysis, Dyer et al. (2001) have reported on a firm's examination of the "potential partner's corporate values and expectations, organizational structure, reward systems and incentives, leadership styles, decision-making processes, patterns of human interaction, work practices, history of partnerships, and human resources practices" (p. 39). Sarkar et al. (2001) believe that inter-firm cooperation is more likely to succeed when the partners are "different, yet similar" (p. 369), complementing each other by combining their different resources and capabilities while sharing values and being culturally compatible. Strategic and cultural fit are also seen as two necessary partner qualities by Child et al. (2005).

It makes sense to invest time and effort into finding and selecting the right partners for cross-border cooperation. A thorough selection process can help to avoid misunderstandings, conflicts, disappointments, and failures.

11.4 The size of partner firms

One issue of particular relevance for SMEs selecting a potential cooperation partner is the size of the partner firm. Large partner firms, according to Lu and Beamish (2006), offer two important assets: resources and reputation. They propose that access to financial resources enables cooperative ventures involving large companies to establish themselves in a market quickly and to strengthen their ability to survive in difficult times. Large companies also often control distribution, marketing, or manufacturing resources that SMEs can use to leverage their unique technologies or competencies (Alvarez and Barney 2001). When companies present large, well-known firms as partners, this can positively affect their credibility and social legitimacy (Barringer and Harrison 2000). This legitimacy can, in turn, through inter-organisational endorsement, enhance the capacity of a firm to acquire financial and human resources and set up a local network (Stuart et al. 1999).

Despite the advantages of having a large-scale partner, important drawbacks also exist. Of significant concern is the superior negotiating strength of larger companies, which makes it possible for them to overrule smaller cooperation partners in conflict events, as Alvarez and Barney (2001) report when an SME manager describes his company's large firm partner by saying, "They are just bullies" (p. 140). Large firms are often initially very interested in the specific technology or know-how that SMEs have to offer. Once they have absorbed the relevant knowledge, however, they sometimes start to (a) underinvest in the cooperative venture or (b) raise unreasonable demands that the SME is unable to meet, thereby exploiting the partnership for their own gain (Alvarez and Barney 2001). Because of the power imbalance, large firms are more inclined to act negatively if their stake in a cooperative venture is relatively small. Lu and Beamish (2006) found that larger companies were less likely to exploit joint ventures with SMEs selfishly when they owned a larger part of the shares.

It is therefore necessary to assess not only the potential benefits of a specific partnership but also the risks. Bronder and Pritzl (1992) suggest that the following questions should be asked during a partner selection process:

> *"What are the risks associated with realizing these potentials within a reasonable timeframe? What are the sources of these risks? Is our partner really interested in the alliance or is he planning a hidden takeover? How stable is the business environment and the industry? What is the influence of the parent company?" (p. 417)*

Finally, when selecting a partner, it is crucial to evaluate whether you share long-term goal-congruency or, at least, non-conflicting goals (Child et al. 2005). One partner's aim to attain the leading position in the target market at the expense of the other in the long term might not constitute a solid basis for successful cooperation.

A summary of how to find the right cooperation partners

Finding the right partners is crucial to the success of any cooperative endeavour. In this chapter, we have explored some of the key points that need to be considered during the partner selection process:

1. Although uncommon for SMEs, formalised partner search and evaluation processes add to the quality of the selection and therefore to the chance of starting successful cooperation.
2. Before selecting a partner, a company should be clear about which country and which region or sub-region to target.

3. To evaluate the attractiveness of potential partners, it is necessary to establish partner selection criteria. These can be task-related or partner-related and are designed to evaluate whether a potential cooperation partner is committed, compatible, complementary in resources and capabilities, and able to provide opportunities for market access or cost reduction and thus for financial payoff.
4. The relative weights of the selection criteria depend on the goals and strategic aims that a company wants to achieve in a cooperative venture. In addition to assessing the objective criteria, it also makes sense to assess the cultural fit and goal congruency between partners.
5. For SMEs, it is crucial to consider the size of a partner firm, as larger companies can offer access to valuable resources and reputation but are also more prone to exploit the partnership due to their stronger negotiating power.

References

Alvarez, S. A. and Barney, J. B. (2001) How entrepreneurial firms can benefit from alliances with large partners. *Academy of Management Executive* 15(1), 139–148

Andersen, O. and Buvik, A. (2002) Firms' internationalization and alternative approaches to the international customer/market selection. *International Business Review* 11(3), 347–363

Barringer, B. R. and Harrison, J. S. (2000) Walking a tightrope: Creating value through interorganizational relationships. *Journal of Management* 26(3), 367–403

Beckman, C., Haunschild, P., and Phillips, D. (2004) Friends or strangers? Firm-specific uncertainty, market uncertainty, and network partner selection. *Organization Science* 15, 259–275

Bronder, C. and Pritzl, R. (1992) Developing strategic alliances: A conceptual framework for successful co-operation. *European Management Journal* 10(4), 412–420

Brouthers, K. D., Brouthers, L. E., and Wilkinson, T. J. (1995) Strategic alliances: Choose your partners. *Long Range Planning* 28(3), 18–25

Chen, S.-H., Lee, H.-T., and Wu, Y.-F. (2008) Applying an approach to partner selection for strategic alliance. *Management Decision* 46(3), 449–465

Child, J., Faulkner, D., and Tallman, S. (2005) Cooperative strategy, 2nd edn. Oxford: Oxford University Press

Dacin, M. T., Hitt, M. A., and Levitas, E. (1997) Selecting partners for successful international alliances: Examination of U.S. and Korean firms. (cover story). *Journal of World Business* 32(1), 3–16

Dyer, J. H., Kale, P., and Singh, H. (2001) How to make strategic alliances work. *MIT Sloan Management Review* 42(4), 37–43

Elmuti, D. and Kathawala, Y. (2001) An overview of strategic alliances. *Management Decision* 39(3), 205–217

Franco, M. (2010) Partner selection criteria in cooperative agreements: Influence from contextual factors. *International Journal of Business Environment* 3(3), 267–291

Geringer, J. M. (1991) Strategic determinants of partner selection criteria in international joint ventures. *Journal of International Business Studies* 22(1), 41–62

Glaister, K. W. (1996) UK-Western European strategic alliances – motives and selection criteria. *Journal of Euromarketing* 5(4), 5–35

Glaister, K. W. and Buckley, P. J. (1996) Strategic motives for international alliance formation. *Journal of Management Studies* 33(3), 301–332

Hitt, M. A., Ahlstrom, D., Dacin, M. T., Levitas, E., and Svobodina, L. (2004) The institutional effects on strategic alliance partner selection in transition economies: China vs. Russia. *Organization Science* 15(2), 173–185

Hollensen, S. (2007) Global marketing, 4th edn. Harlow et al.: Financial Times Prentice Hall

Johanson, J. and Vahlne, J. E. (1977) The internationalization process of the firm: A model of knowledge development and increasing foreign market commitment. *Journal of International Business Studies* 8(1), 23–32

Kale, P. and Singh, H. (2009) Managing strategic alliances: What do we know now, and where do we go from here? *Academy of Management Perspectives* 23(3), 45–62

Li, D., Eden, L., Hitt, M. A., and Ireland, R. D. (2008) Friends, acquaintances, or strangers? Partner selection in R&D alliances. *Academy of Management Journal* 51(2), 315–334

Lu, J. W. and Beamish, P. W. (2006) Partnering strategies and performance of SMEs' international joint ventures. *Journal of Business Venturing* 21(4), 461–486

Moen, Ø., Båkas, O., Bolstad, A., and Pedersen, V. (2010) International market expansion strategies for high-tech firms: Partnership selection criteria for forming alliances. *International Journal of Business and Management* 5(1), 20–30

Nielsen, B. B. (2003) An empirical investigation of the drivers of international strategic alliance formation. *European Management Journal* 21(3), 301

Nijssen, E. J., Douglas, S. P., and Calis, G. (1999) Gathering and using information for the selection of trading partners. *European Journal of Marketing* 33(1/2), 143–162

Rothaermel, F. and Boeker, W. (2008) Old technology meets new technology: Complementarities, similarities, and alliance formation. *Strategic Management Journal* 29(1), 47–77

Sarkar, M. B., Echambadi, R., Cavusgil, S. T., and Aulakh, P. S. (2001) The influence of complementarity, compatibility, and relationship capital on alliance performance. *Journal of the Academy of Marketing Science* 29(4), 358–373

Shah, R. H. and Swaminathan, V. (2008) Factors influencing partner selection in strategic alliances: The moderating role of alliance context. *Strategic Management Journal* 29(5), 471–494

Stuart, T. E., Hoang, H., and Hybels, R. C. (1999) Interorganizational endorsements and the performance of entrepreneurial ventures. *Administrative Science Quarterly* 44(2), 315–349

Wood, V. R., Pitta, D. A., and Franzak, F. J. (2009) Successful strategic alliances with international partners: Key issues for small- to medium-sized enterprises. *Journal of Business Innovation and Research* 3(3), 232–251

12 Cooperative negotiations in an intercultural context

When two or more parties decide to cooperate, they do so because, on one hand, they have a common interest, and on the other, they are pursuing their own independent interests, which they seek to protect in the partnership. Reconciling independent interests with the common interest is the domain of cooperative negotiations. Effective negotiation is a necessary precondition for reaching an agreement on how to work together, which resources to share and divide in which proportion, and how to deal with potential difficulties. However, negotiations do not end when the agreement is signed. Contracts cannot provide for all eventualities. Partner interests evolve and change over time. Thus, in a complex and dynamic business environment, cooperative relationships are characterised by the constant flow of negotiation and re-negotiation.

Negotiations, by nature, include cooperative and conflicting elements. Negotiators want to achieve something together – that is why they negotiate in the first place – but they typically also strive to maximize their individual outcomes. However, in long-term relationships, such as strategic cross-border partnerships, it is important to keep the interests in balance and to enable all parties to benefit continually from the joint effort.

In cross-border partnerships, the different cultures and institutional systems of the participants adds to the complexity of the negotiations, which are, in any case, already complex endeavours. In cross-cultural negotiations, it is important to consider that "[w]hen two people communicate, they rarely talk about precisely the same subject, for effective meaning is flavoured by each person's own cognitive world and cultural conditioning" (Herbig and Gulbro 1997, p. 158). There is always a possibility of misunderstanding if the statements and behaviours of one partner are evaluated in the cultural frame of another. For example, while those socialized in a particular culture may be task-oriented or focus mainly on the legal and financial aspects of an agreement, those accustomed to different cultural norms may emphasize interpersonal factors (Gulbro and Herbig 1995). As Mintu-Wimsatt and Gassenheimer (1996) noted, "[i]n a negotiation context, researchers believe that cultural orientation dictates how people process and interpret information and also affects which strategies and tactics to pursue" (p. 22). Therefore, as cultural differences increase, so do the possibility of miscommunication and the amount of time and energy necessary for the interaction (Gudykunst and Kim 1992).

12.1 General approaches to negotiation

Parties may take two general routes during negotiations: the *competitive approach* and the *problem-solving approach*. While in the competitive approach, emphasis is placed on convincing the other party of one's own ideas, thereby also using influencing tactics such as bluffing or threatening, the problem-solving approach is directed towards achieving a win-win situation by understanding the needs and interests of the other party and attempting to find a mutually beneficial solution. The problem-solving approach has been found to be more conducive to creating and maintaining successful long-term business relationships (Mintu-Wimsatt and Gassenheimer 2000). A key precondition for the success of the problem-solving strategy is that both parties actively seek to elicit information about their negotiation partners' needs, interests, and preferences (Chaisrakeo and Speece 2004).

Pruitt and Rubin (1986) have proposed a dual-concern model, which includes concern for the partner's outcome as well as one's own. If negotiators value the outcomes of both parties, they apply *problem solving* (or *integration*) as the main strategy. High concern for oneself and low concern for the other leads to *contending* strategies; low emphasis on one's own and high emphasis on the other party's outcomes, to *yielding* strategies; and low concern for both, to *inactivity*. A further, "middle-of-the road" strategy is *compromise*, where the parties meet halfway, as they are not able to fulfil all their original demands (Child et al. 2005). In a cross-cultural study performed in Greece, Russia, and the UK, Fraser and Zarkada-Fraser (2002) observed a preference for the problem-solving approach in all countries. This general preference for win-win solutions was also supported by Ready and Tessema's (2009) empirical work. In Fraser and Zarkada-Fraser's study, however, British negotiators showed significantly less willingness to compromise than did their Russian and Greek counterparts. As contending and yielding strategies were less common in all countries, the authors concluded that, compared to cultural variations, personal differences or other situational variables better explain the differences in the approach to negotiations.

In addition to the general approach, negotiators can also choose to use different tactics for influencing other parties. Kipnis and Schmidt (1985) have proposed a classification of hard, soft, and rational influence tactics. Hard tactics include demanding, threatening, and generally acting in an assertive, forceful manner. Soft tactics rely more on interpersonal skills to wield influence, such as emphasizing mutual obligations and reciprocity. They also include using other people to influence the negotiating partner.

Rational influence tactics build on the power of logical arguments as well as on objective data.

When considering influencing tactics, an ethical dimension is always involved. Lewicki and Robinson (1998) propose five categories of unethical negotiation behaviour (p. 673):

1. Misrepresentation of information (either to the other party or to the media);
2. Traditional competitive bargaining tactics, such as hiding a bottom line, starting with demands that are intentionally set too high, or undermining the other party's confidence;
3. Bluffing (e.g., making false threats and false promises);
4. Manipulation of the opponent's network (e.g., trying to undermine the support of the counterpart's network);
5. Inappropriate information gathering (e.g., by paying informants or obtaining information in exchange for bribes).

In their study, Lewicki and Robinson were able to determine cross-cultural differences in the acceptance levels for various tactics. Americans, for example, showed a significantly more positive attitude towards competitive bargaining and bluffing than did negotiators from other nations. Therefore, we need to be aware that what is considered as unethical negotiation behaviour can be contingent upon cultural standards. Negotiators must be aware that tactics that are perfectly acceptable in their own countries might be considered unfair or even offensive in other cultures. As discussed in the following section, cultural differences in strategies and tactics are not the only way in which culture may intrude upon international negotiations.

12.2 Cross-cultural differences in negotiation behaviour

Many researchers have taken a closer look at how people from different cultural backgrounds differ in the way they perceive and subsequently act in negotiations. Chaisrakeo and Speece (2004), for example, show that the extent of problem-solving orientation, defined as the tendency to adopt cooperative and needs-focused behaviour in negotiations, may be influenced by cultural factors. Mintu-Wimsatt and Gassenheimer (1996) also found that the propensity to take risks or to generally act in a cooperative way can be contingent on culture and observed the extent of importance that negotiators from different cultures place on organizational versus personal interests. People from different cultures could also experience different emotions during the negotiation process. Ulijn et al. (2005) found that Chinese negotiation participants were considerably more angry at themselves, anxious, apprehensive, and uncertain than their Dutch counterparts; the authors attributed this to core cultural norms, such as maintaining close social ties and the need to avoid the risk of losing face.

Decision structures within companies may also vary according to country. Sebenius (2002) proposed that while negotiating across national borders, one should always ask the following questions about the other parties: "Who are the players? Who decides what? What are the informal influences that make or break the deal?" (p. 77). Sebenius takes Germany as an example, wherein strategic decisions – especially in medium-sized companies – usually involve not only top management but also the supervisory board, shareholders (especially in family-owned firms), and labour representatives. In Southeastern Europe, on the other hand, informal networks comprising players from different firms and institutions may also play an important role in influencing the manner in which companies formulate strategies, thus also affecting the alliances in which they are entering (Grødeland 2011). Again, in other countries, like Italy or France, seniority and rank play an important role. Understanding these power and influence relationships is essential for determining how to negotiate with whom.

Several attempts have been made to classify the different cultural influences on negotiations. Fraser and Zarkada-Fraser (2002) suggested four main aspects of culture that have particular relevance for cross-cultural negotiations: (1) cultural norms regarding how to behave and how to express one's feelings; (2) cultural norms regarding relationship-building; (3) the importance of group relationships and how people within a culture relate inside and outside of groups, and (4) the attitude that people have toward time, especially the degree of future-orientation.

Schuster and Copeland (1996) suggest that the amount of time people spend on tasks in negotiations compared to the amount of time spent on relationships varies across different cultures. People in Northwestern European countries have proven to be more task-oriented, and those in Mediterranean Europe, more relationship-oriented. Typical Southern Italians, according to this general model, are usually expected to spend more time in getting to know their counterparts personally than are negotiators from Northern Germany.

A more comprehensive framework that attempts to integrate prior research has been proposed by Fells (2009) and classifies possible cultural differences in negotiation perceptions and behaviour into three basic categories: (1) general orientation and objectives, (2) approach to the negotiation task, and (3) negotiators (Fig. 12.1).

1. General orientation and objectives

Contract	⟷	Relationship
Ongoing	⟷	Sporadic contact/implementation
High time sensitivity	⟷	Low time sensitivity
High risk taking	⟷	Low risk taking
External basis for trust	⟷	Internal basis for trust
Specific agreement	⟷	General agreement

2. Approach to the negotiation task

Bottom-up approach	⟷	Top-down approach
Direct communication	⟷	Indirect communication
High emotionalism	⟷	Low risk emotionalism
Form of reasoning and persuasion		

3. Negotiators

Skill-based selection	⟷	Status-based selection
Group-oriented org.	⟷	Leader-oriented organization
Formal style	⟷	Informal style
Business commitment	⟷	Individual commitment
Personal disclosure	⟷	Social topics

Fig. 12.1. Possible cultural differences in negotiations

Source: Adapted from Fells (2009, p. 158) who summarized the works of Salacuse (2004), Schuster and Copeland (1996), Weiss (1994), Gesteland (2005), and Sebenius (2002)

The original appeared as a table in Fells, R. (2009) Effective Negotiation: From Research to Results, published by Cambridge University Press. Reprinted with kind permission of the publishing house

Sebenius (2002) also warns us not to neglect the differences in "softer" cultural factors, such as greeting norms, degrees of formality in dressing and behaviour, offering gifts, acceptance of body contact and eye contact, food and dining, body language, and punctuality. The use of tools might also be judged differently in different cultural contexts. As Fells (2009) remarks, while some cultures emphasize the dimension of relationship in the exchange of information, others will use PowerPoint.

Each of these categorizations of the cultural influences on negotiations elucidates that these issues are by no means trivial, but are in fact complex and multidimensional. They become even more so when we consider additional social aspects. Not everyone from the same nation behaves alike as per the cultural norm: consider Queen Elizabeth II, David Beckham, Professor Stephen Hawking, and Mick Jagger. Although all of them are British, we can nevertheless assume that they do not behave according to the same social norms. People are influenced not only by their national culture but also by the groups in which they were socialized. They are affected by hierarchical culture (e.g., managers versus blue-collar-workers), professional culture (e.g., accountants versus marketing people), the cultures of the organizations they are working for and the sectors or industries in which these organizations are based, and the culture of their particular generation. Therefore, negotiators need to recognize and understand cultural differences while avoiding falling into the trap of cultural stereotyping.

Nevertheless, negotiators of cross-border cooperation need to be aware of the cultural differences between nations and regions. To foster intercultural understanding, it is possible to seek outside help. Herbig and Gulbro (1997) determined a positive correlation between the use of external agents, such as translators or bicultural brokers, and successful cross-cultural negotiations. The use of national and cultural experts was found to be more effective than the use of technical experts.

Outside help, however, is no substitute for acquiring an understanding of intercultural communication skills. *Cultural awareness* (being able to predict the effect of one's own behaviour on others), *cultural sensitivity* (understanding and sensitivity to verbal and non-verbal cues), and *cultural adroitness* (effective communication with people from other cultures) were found to be generally conducive to successful cross-cultural negotiation (Chaisrakeo and Speece 2004). As Gulbro and Herbig (1995) note, "[s]uccess at this cross-cultural negotiation table means being able to see through the eyes of the people across the table, and understanding their cultural values and assumptions" (p. 19).

An important caveat should be raised at this point. When entering in negotiations with potential partners that cross cultural borders, the entire context of the country needs to be considered. As Fells (2009) pointed out, "[n]o amount of cross-cultural sensitivity training is going to compensate for agreeing to a supply contract without knowing how the local financial system operates [...] It will not compensate for being unaware that your agreement with a local manufacturer to produce your product under licence also requires approval from the local government authority [...] In short, any proposal requires an understanding of the local business system" (p. 161).

12.3 Bargaining power

In cross-border negotiations, as in all other types of negotiations, in addition to understanding cultural and other country-specific influences, it is also necessary to be aware of the relative power distribution in the exchange relationship. To assess these power structures, it is crucial to understand the partners' perceived dependence on one another. The party with a higher dependence on the other is usually the less powerful one in the negotiation (Emerson 1962). This also means that SMEs can function as the more powerful party in a negotiation with a big multinational conglomerate, if the large cooperation depends more on what the SME has to offer. The higher a party values the outcome that it can get from cooperating, the higher the dependence and the lower the chance of obtaining these highly needed outcomes through other channels. The potential to achieve the outcomes elsewhere has been operationalized as "BATNA", an acronym for "best alternative to the negotiated agreement" (Pinkley et al. 1994). A negotiator's BATNA is neither static nor unchangeable. It may be influenced – at least in theory – in four different ways (Kim and Fragale 2005):

a) Negotiators can attempt to increase their BATNA (e.g., through actively searching for new alternatives to cooperating);
b) Negotiators can try to decrease their counterpart's BATNA (e.g., through offering very specific competence for an alliance that cannot be acquired elsewhere);
c) Negotiators can try to decrease their perceived value of the counterpart's contribution (e.g., seeing the specific cooperation as less strategically important for one's own business); or
d) Negotiators can attempt to increase the counterpart's perceived value of one's own contribution (e.g., through improving one's competence).

The short-term capacity to alter a power relationship in general and that of BATNAs in particular is often very limited. If the relative BATNA could be changed, the parties would in any case try to change it, in which case, they would arrive at different BATNAs than those they would bring to the negotiation table. In their study, Kim and Fragale have shown that having a better BATNA is an advantage only if a small bargaining zone exists. In the case of a large bargaining zone, which in itself offers more room to manoeuvre, superior contributions can yield a stronger effect on negotiation performance than BATNAs.

In experimental settings, it was found that negotiators who saw themselves in a more powerful position compared to their counterparts displayed a tendency to use hard influence tactics (Bacharach and Lawler 1981), whereas those who perceived themselves as the weaker party often resorted to soft tactics (Rubin and Zartman 1995). In Rao and Schmidt's (1998) study, negotiators who had the feeling that their counterparts had alternatives often resorted to softer tactics. In the same study, it was revealed those who believed that their firms would enter in future cooperation with the other party showed a higher propensity to employ rational tactics characterised by a large exchange of information. Moreover, according to Rao and Schmidt, in this specific case, negotiators from the US tended to use soft tactics when dealing with firms from countries like Eastern Europe and Asia that were culturally very different from the US. A possible reason is that the negotiators were trying to adapt to the cultural style of their partners, as eastern cultures are usually defined as being high context cultures, wherein nonverbal and indirect communication – and therefore indirect influencing styles – are more common than in typical Western low context cultures, wherein people state more directly what they want or expect (Hall 1976). A summary of the characteristics of high context and low context communication is presented in Fig. 12.2.

Low context communication		High context communication
Meaning conveyed primarily through explicit statements	↔	Content is also conveyed through facial expressions, gestures, environment, and status of the negotiators
Precise, relevant, clear statements	↔	Broad-ranging, indirect statements
Open expression of feelings and opinions	↔	More reserved, trying to maintain harmony within their group
Information-seeking through questioning	↔	Information sought through inference and indirect means
Silence tends to be filled with words	↔	Silence conveys meaning

Low context countries (examples)	High context countries (examples)
Germany	France
UK	Spain
Scandinavia	Russia

Fig. 12.2 Characteristics of high context and low context communication

Source: Based on Copeland and Griggs (1986), Fells (2009), and Hall (1976)

12.4 The negotiation process

Differences between low context (e.g., in Anglo-Saxon nations) and high context cultures (e.g., in Southern European nations) can also affect the behaviour of negotiators at different stages of the negotiation process. Negotiations, as previously mentioned, have both a cooperative and a competitive side. Olekalns et al. (1996) suggest that negotiators repeatedly move between cooperative and competitive modes during the process of negotiation. Adair and Brett (2005) propose a four-stage model, wherein they conceptualize the negotiation process as a "dance" with the actors moving forward and backwards in cooperation and competition. Adair and Brett describe the main characteristics of the four stages as follows:

Negotiation stage 1: Relational positioning

When negotiations begin, the parties usually exhibit two types of behaviour: first, they try to build a relationship with the other side, and then, they try to position themselves strategically. A relationship needs to be built on mutual trust. People will usually attempt to find out how much they can trust their counterparts and assess whether the counterpart is working in a cooperative or competitive mode. Trust can be built through open, friendly communication and also by revealing pieces of sensitive information, as sharing information is a sign of a willingness to cooperate. On the other hand, the parties also need to define their positions in the negotiation, which will usually involve a more competitive stance. Initial offers often become cognitive anchors for subsequent negotiations. Therefore, they need to be carefully selected.

Negotiation stage 2: Identifying the problem

When negotiators discover that a mere exchange of position does not bring them closer to a mutually acceptable solution, they usually direct their discussion toward concrete issues in a more cooperative mode. An important characteristic of this stage is the intense exchange of information about the issue as well as the underlying interests of the parties. Exchange of information, specifically regarding interests, was found to be conducive at the early stages of negotiations for subsequent successful outcomes (Lytle et al. 1999). In the words of Adair and Brett (2005), "[w]hat negotiators do in the first half of the negotiation has a significant impact on their ability to generate integrative solutions with joint high gains" (p. 47).

Negotiation stage 3: Generating solutions

If the issue is well defined and the underlying interests of all sides are understood, it makes sense to proceed to the next stage of the negotiation process, wherein the negotiating parties try to combine their individual priorities with their understanding of their counterpart's needs in order to suggest alternative solutions in the form of "offers". These offers are compared to one's limits and alternatives and are either (a) accepted, (b) rejected, or (c) integrated and developed further. The parties very often rely on the power of argument and persuasion during this stage.

Negotiation stage 4: Reaching an agreement

After opening up the space for different alternatives in stage 3, the parties need to move toward a commonly acceptable solution. In this final stage, if both sides wish to reach an agreement, they use reciprocal counter-offers and concessions in addition to persuasive methods. The frequency of offers is generally much higher than in the previous stage. Ideally, this leads to the proposal of one offer in which all sides can meet within their limits (or, in the case of a compromise, slightly outside of the limits of all parties) and with an outcome that is more attractive for all sides than the BATNAs of the partners.

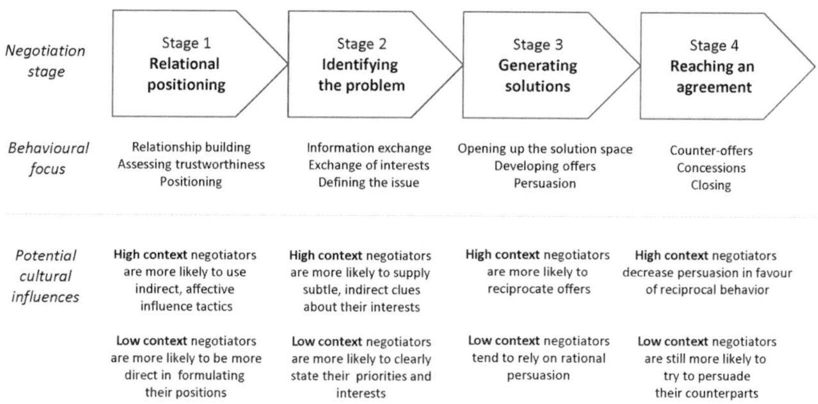

Fig. 12.3. The negotiation process and potential cultural influences

Source: Graphic presentation by the author based on contents from Adair and Brett (2005)

Adair and Brett (2005) suggest that culture, specifically differences between high context cultures and low context cultures, can influence all four stages of the negotiation process (see Fig. 12.3). They also found one common denominator between both high context and low context cultures: clearly stating interests and priorities, rather than only indirectly sharing important information that is embedded within the offers, leads to higher joint gains.

12.5 The role of the quality of communication experience

Understanding the partner's cultural predispositions, needs, and interests is a major precondition for the problem-solving approach to negotiation, which is also termed an "integrative" approach, as it attempts to integrate the expectations of all parties.

The key to successful integrative negotiations is the open exchange of information. Liu et al. (2010) suggest that the *quality of communication experience*, which they define as the clarity, responsiveness, and comfort that people perceive in negotiations, can lead to both higher joint gains and higher satisfaction levels for the partners. Clarity is thereby seen as the extent to which negotiators are able to comprehend the message and meaning of what is being communicated by their counterparts. Responsiveness refers to the degree to which partners signal their understanding of the others' statements and emotions and show an adequate response to them. Comfort was defined by Liu et al. as "a condition of positive affect of ease and pleasantness when interacting with each other" (p. 6). This cross-cultural study also revealed that the perceived quality of the communication experience was significantly lower in intercultural negotiations than in within-culture negotiations. Further, it is also possible that one party experiences more clarity, responsiveness, and comfort in a certain negotiation situation than the other does. The authors found that it is often easier for high context negotiators to understand low context negotiators, who are more direct in their proposals and in voicing their interest, than for low context negotiators to understand high context negotiators, who have a more indirect and ambiguous communication style. On the other hand, low context negotiators – although more easily understood – could also be seen as discomforting or offensive by their high context counterparts who are not used to such direct communication. Since the quality of communication experience was found to be conducive to good negotiation results for both sides, it was proposed that intercultural negotiators should pay close attention to (a) maintaining clarity in communication (e.g., re-checking whether they correctly understood a term or a statement), (b) showing responsiveness to the words and emotions of their counterparts (by adapting to their behavioural norms and styles), and (c) ensuring that the negotiations are taking place in a setting that is perceived as comfortable by all parties.

A summary of the preconditions for successful cross-border cooperation negotiations

From this chapter's discussion, we can summarize some of the main ideas regarding how to conduct cross-cultural cooperation negotiations successfully as follows:

1. Actors in cross-border negotiations are influenced by the cultures in which they have been socialized. An awareness of the cultural influences on negotiators' perceptions and behaviours is therefore essential.
2. Across cultures, people usually prefer a problem-solving (or integrative) approach to negotiation. In long-term partnerships, there is no alternative to integrating the interests of all parties for achieving joint gains.
3. Negotiation is a two-sided process. It is therefore necessary to understand the interests, relative power positions (BATNAs), and cultural influences of all parties involved in the negotiation.
4. Cultivating high quality communication – maintaining clarity, showing responsiveness, and providing a comfortable environment for all negotiation partners – has a positive influence on the negotiation process.
5. It always makes sense to follow the "golden rule" of respecting your cooperation partners: Treat others as you would like them to treat you.

References

Adair, W. L. and Brett, J. M. (2005) The negotiation dance: Time, culture, and behavioural sequences in negotation. *Organization Science* 16(1), 33–51

Bacharach, S. B. and Lawler, E. J. (1981) Bargaining: Power, tactics and outcomes. San Francisco: Jossey Bass

Chaisrakeo, S. and Speece, M. (2004) Culture, intercultural communication competence, and sales negotiation: A qualitative research approach. *Journal of Business and Industrial Marketing* 19(4), 267–282

Child, J., Faulkner, D., and Tallman, S. (2005) Cooperative strategy, 2nd edn. Oxford: Oxford University Press

Copeland, L. and Griggs, L. (1986) Going international: How to make friends and deal effectively in the global marketplace. New York: Plume

Emerson, R. M. (1962) Power-dependence relations. *American Sociological Review* 27(1), 31–40

Fells, R. (2009) Effective negotiation: From research to results. Cambridge: Cambridge University Press

Fraser, C. and Zarkada-Fraser, A. (2002) An exploratory investigation into cultural awareness and approach to negotiation of Greek, Russian and British managers. *European Business Review* 14(2), 111–127

Gesteland, R. R. (2005) Cross cultural business behavior. Copenhagen: Copenhagen Business School Press

Grødeland, Å. B. (2011) Networks and informal power structures in South East Europe. In: Sternad, D. and Döring, T. (eds.) Handbook of doing business in South East Europe. Houndsmills: Palgrave Macmillan, 109–149

Gudykunst, W. B. and Kim, Y. Y. (1992) Communicating with strangers: An approach to intercultural communication. New York: McGraw-Hill

Gulbro, R. and Herbig, P. (1995) Differences in cross-cultural negotiation behavior between industrial products and consumer products firms. *Journal of Business and Industrial Marketing* 10(3), 18–28

Hall, E. T. (1976) Beyond culture. New York: Doubleday

Herbig, P. and Gulbro, R. (1997) External influences in the cross-cultural negotiation process. *Industrial Management and Data Systems* 97(4), 158–168

Kim, P. H. and Fragale, A. R. (2005) Choosing the path to bargaining power: An empirical comparison of BATNAs and contributions in negotiation. *Journal of Applied Psychology* 90(2), 373–381

Kipnis, D. and Schmidt, S. M. (1985) The language of persuasion. *Psychology Today* 4, 40–46

Lewicki, R. J. and Robinson, R. J. (1998) Ethical and unethical bargaining tactics: An empirical study. *Journal of Business Ethics* 17(6), 665–682

Liu, L. A., Stahl, G. K., and Chei, H. C. (2010) Quality of communication experience: Definition, measurement, and implications for intercultural negotiations. *Journal of Applied Psychology* 95(3), 469–487

Lytle, A. L., Brett, J. M., and Shapiro, D. L. (1999) The strategic use of intersts, rights, and power to resolve disputes. *Negotiation Journal* 15(1), 31–49

Mintu-Wimsatt, A. and Gassenheimer, J. B. (1996) Negotiation differences between two diverse cultures: An industrial seller's perspective. *European Journal of Marketing* 30(4), 20–39

Mintu-Wimsatt, A. and Gassenheimer, J. B. (2000) The moderating effects of cultural context in buyer-seller negotiation. *The Journal of Personal Selling and Sales Management* 20(1), 1–9

Olekalns, M., Smith, P. I., and Walsh, T. (1996) The process of negotiating: Strategy and timing as predictor of outcomes. *Organizational Behavior and Group Decision Processes* 68(1), 68–77

Pinkley, R. L., Neale, M. A., and Bennett, R. J. (1994) The impact of alternatives to settlement in dyadic negotiation. *Organizational Behavior and Human Decision Processes* 57(1), 97–116

Pruitt, D. G. and Rubin, J. Z. (1986) Social conflict: Escalation, stalemate, and settlement. New York: Random House

Rao, A. and Schmidt, S. M. (1998) A behavioral perspective on negotiating international alliances. *Journal of International Business Studies* 29(4), 665–693

Ready, K. J. and Tessema, M. T. (2009) Perceptions and strategies in the negotiation process: A cross cultural examination of U.S. and Malaysia. *International Negotiation* 14(3), 493–517

Rubin, J. Z. and Zartman, I. W. (1995) Assymetrical negotiations: Some survey results that may surprise. *Negotiation Journal* 11(4), 349–364

Salacuse, J. W. (2004) Negotiating: The top ten ways that culture can effect your negotiation. *Ivey Business Journal* 69(1), 1–6

Schuster, C. and Copeland, M. (1996) Cross-cultural communication: Issues and implications. In: Ghauri, P. and Usunier, J. (eds.) International business negotiations. Oxford: Pergamon, 131–152

Sebenius, J. K. (2002) The hidden challenges of cross-border negotiations. *Harvard Business Review* 80(3), 76–85

Ulijn, J., Rutkowski, A.-F., Kumar, R., and Zhu, Y. (2005) Patterns of feelings in face-to-face negotiation: A Sino-Dutch pilot study. *Cross Cultural Management* 12(3), 103–118

Weiss, S. E. (1994) Negotiation with "Romans". *Sloan Management Review* 35(2/3), (2): 51–61; (3): 85–99

13 Choosing a governance structure

When an alliance is formed, the partners need to decide on its governance structure – the general arrangements of their work together – including "all combinations of legal and social control mechanisms which coordinate and safeguard the alliance partners' resource contributions, and define their administrative responsibilities and the division of rewards from their joint activities" (de Man and Roijakkers 2009). A governance system generally includes three types of mechanisms: coordination mechanisms, control or monitoring mechanisms, and incentive (motivation) mechanisms (Albers 2010; Jensen 1983). Coordination is necessary in a partnership, as the partner firms perform different tasks and activities in order to achieve joint goals. Monitoring is important to keep opportunistic behaviour under control. Finally, an incentive structure is needed to induce the partners to act in a way beneficial to the partnership rather than just to their own goals. Coordination mechanisms include direct supervision, mutual adjustment, and standardisation; monitoring can be organised formally (e.g., by setting key performance indicators or a reporting system) or informally; incentives include rules about "sharing the pie" – distributing the positive outcomes of cooperation between the partners (Albers 2010).

There are three basic forms of governance in cross-border cooperation (Kale and Singh 2009):

(1) equity-based governance;
(2) contract-based governance; and
(3) relationship-based governance.

In equity-based cooperation such as in international joint ventures, all the partners hold shares in a common firm. Kale and Singh (2009) recommend using equity-based forms of cooperation when opportunistic behaviour is expected. If the partners have a stake in a common company, they share both profits and losses. Thus, equity-based forms of cooperation closely tie the fate of the partners together, as all involved parties participate either positively or negatively in the joint company's results. A joint business, however, also needs a basic resource endowment, which can sometimes form a hurdle for SMEs. When partnering with large-scale corporations, smaller firms should be aware that under changing conditions, for example when additional contributions or increases in share capital are needed or demanded, they run the risk of not being able to go along with the stronger partners given their financial constraints, thus diluting their position in the joint firm or, in extreme cases, being thrown out altogether. Moreover, some cooperation types, for example a joint R&D project with a limited timeframe, are not suitable for an equity joint venture approach.

The second form of governance, contract-based cooperation, generally preserves the independence of the firms involved in the partnership yet still formalising the terms of the interaction, the contributions of the parties, and the procedures required for terminating cooperation. Contracts are effective in clearly determining the expectations partners hold of each other. They can also help them avoid conflicts in rather stable environments, in which it is easy to predict contingencies (Lumineau and Malhotra 2011). When the environment is dynamic and characterised by a high level of uncertainty, however, it is hard to formulate effective provisions for all possible circumstances on paper. Under these conditions, therefore, contractual agreements are less effective, and non-contractual governance structures are preferable; likewise when partners' expectations are only vaguely defined up-front (ibid.). If potential partners do not know exactly what to expect from cooperation, it is clearly difficult to put these poorly defined expectations into contract form.

The third form of governance mechanism is sole reliance on trust, without any formal equity exchange or contractual arrangement. Such relationship-based cooperation is less protected by the law but does have advantages, especially for SMEs, which in more formal arrangements must bear transaction costs such as those for notaries to set up contracts and for lawyers when trying to enforce them. Resorting to relationship-based cooperation can therefore help to avoid contracting costs and monitoring costs, as no third party is required as an arbitrator when partners trust each other (Kale and Singh 2009). In addition, there are fewer adaptation costs, as these kinds of arrangements are more flexible in adapting to environmental developments (ibid.). There are considerations beyond the cost-driven ones when deciding between governance modes, however. The quality of the existing relationships can be important here. Gulati and Nickerson (2008) observe, for example, that higher levels of existing trust increased the tendency to choose less-costly non-formal forms of alliance governance over contract-based and equity-based forms.

Table 13.1 summarises the three main forms of governance and their main advantages and disadvantages for SMEs planning to enter cross-border cooperation. The choice of governance mode can also be contingent on the *main risk* perceived by the partners. De Man and Roijakkers (2009) propose that formal control mechanisms should be preferred in situations where there is a high relationship risk and a low performance risk. In this case, the formal arrangements can act as a safeguard against opportunistic behaviour. If performance risk is perceived as high and relationship risk as low, though, a trust- or relationship-based cooperation may be the better choice, as partners who trust each other can focus fully on the task rather than expending their energy monitoring the behaviour of their counterparts.

Table 13.1 Advantages and disadvantages of cooperation governance modes

Governance structure	Advantages for SMEs	Disadvantages for SMEs
Equity-based cooperation	less incentive for opportunistic behaviour; clearly determined share in partner contributions and profits; clear centralised control mechanism	basic resource endowment needed; costs of starting/acquiring a company; not suitable for short-term cooperation; large partners have more potential to dilute SMEs' share
Contract-based cooperation	preserves the firm's independence; clearly defines partners' expectations; can avoid conflicts in stable environments	contracting costs; monitoring and enforcing costs; less suitable for dynamic environments large companies usually have more resources for legal disputes in the case of conflict
Relationship-based cooperation	low set-up costs; more flexible and adaptable; usable also when partners' expectations are still vaguely defined	less legal protection in the case of deceitful or opportunistic behaviour–not enforceable; high level of trust needed as a precondition

Source: Author

Several internal and external factors need to be taken into account when choosing the most suitable governance form for a cross-border alliance. Hoetker and Mellewigt (2009) found evidence that the *type of main assets* that are contributed to a partnership can influence the choice of governance structure: while property-based assets can be more easily controlled by formal means, relational governance methods are more suitable for cooperation that is mainly based on knowledge-related assets, which are more difficult to control owing to their embeddedness in a firm's specific routines and culture.

Moreover, national cultural differences can influence the choice of governance mode. Tallmann and Shenkar (1994) suggest that equity modes of governance will be preferred to contractual modes if the parent companies come from individualistic national cultures. The choice of governance structure affects not only the legal and financial situation, power distribution, and management structures of an alliance, but also its tax structure. As they differ from country to country, these effects are not discussed here, but managers should be aware of them.

Teng and Das (2008) argue that two further contingency factors are particularly important for the choice of governance form of cooperation. The first factor is *alliance management experience*, with more experienced firms having less need to rely on equity-based governance structures deemed necessary when there is not enough trust between the partners. The second factor is especially relevant for cross-border cooperation – the *internationality of the partners*. The authors refer to Brouthers (1995) here, who points out that partners engaging in cross-border cooperation shoulder an additional category of risk he terms "international risk", caused by cultural and institutional differences, and differences in technological standards and business practices. To overcome these additional obstacles, equity-based forms of cooperation are more suitable, as the joint legal unit is usually based in one country and institutional environment and, through its structural integration, can also foster cultural integration (Teng and Das 2008). In their empirical study, Teng and Das found clear support for their hypotheses that (a) alliance experience is positively linked with choosing a contract-based governance structure and that (b) cross-border cooperation generally shows a tendency towards equity-based mechanisms.

In the following sections, we will explore some of the specifics of each of the three (equity-, contract-, and relationship-based) governance modes.

13.1 Specifics of equity-based joint ventures

When SMEs try to internationalise, they need three key resources: knowledge about the local market environment, reputation, and financial capital (Lu and Beamish 2006). If they do not have control over all of these necessary resources, SMEs can form joint ventures to obtain them in collaboration with partners. Joint ventures are created when firms join some of their resources, forming a separate company that is then jointly owned by the partners (Barringer and Harrison 2000). When firms create cross-border joint ventures, they try to use the specific knowledge of a local partner instead of taking the long way round and creating this knowledge base themselves. Local companies are more likely to be able to use an existing network of relationships, as they understand the local business culture, the local legal system, the local competitors, and the needs of the local customers (Lu and Beamish 2006).

Kent (1991, p. 388) sees five basic reasons for companies to engage in international joint venture (IJV) agreements:

(1) creating market power by jointly using resources or generating economies of scale;
(2) risk reduction through risk sharing;
(3) acquiring information;
(4) overcoming legal or cultural barriers; and
(5) turning potential competitors into partners, thus becoming able to influence the level of rivalry in the industry.

The local partner in an IJV might be interested in cooperating with an international firm to acquire specific know-how and capabilities. The ability of an IJV to perform successfully depends on the transfer of technology or skills from the foreign parent firm(s) (Lane et al. 2001). Lyles and Salk (1996) found, for example, that Hungarian IJVs that effectively transferred knowledge from their foreign parents achieved superior financial performance. It is not always in the interest of the technology owner, though, for its partners to acquire full know-how, thus allowing them to offer certain products or services independently and develop into competitors. In an IJV, the risks and rewards of the common endeavour are shared. In the case of equity sharing, "partner firms realize that their interests are intertwined and hence opportunistic behavior tends to be discouraged" (Teng and Das 2008, p. 727).

There are three ways for companies to enter into joint ventures abroad (Li et al. 2009): control, in which the foreign firm holds a higher share of the ownership than the local partner, a minority share, or collaboration through a 50/50 agreement. Holding a majority ownership in the IJV, according to Li and his colleagues, provides the partner the advantage of being more in control of knowledge transfer, thus reducing the risk of the misuse of know-how. The advantages of a collaborative and more balanced ownership structure, meanwhile, lie in the "shared fate of the partners [...]" and the "balanced authority [that] increases both partners' perceived safety in making contributions and minimizes their fear of exploitation" (ibid., p. 869). Therefore, it has been argued that both forms of governance promote performance – the control mode by enabling the acquisition of more advanced technology, the collaborative mode by creating a positive and trustful atmosphere between the partners. Taking these considerations into account, Li et al. propose an inverse U-shaped type of relationship, in which an optimal level of foreign IJV ownership exists and in which the benefits from control and collaboration are balanced. In other words, an optimal ownership solution needs to take into account that the foreign partners want control over their knowledge as well as a sufficient share in the profits of the business and that the local partner needs to feel committed as they have the possibility of acquiring know-how and getting their fair share of the business: 50/50 is thereby not always the right solution. As Li et al. (2009) note, "the balancing of control and cooperation requires similar (and not necessarily identical) levels of partner ownership stakes" (p. 881).

In any case, parent firms need to design a system for controlling their IJVs. Kumar and Seth (1998), drawing primarily from Killing (1983) and Schaan (1983), identify six types of control mechanisms for IJVs:

(1) integrative mechanisms (e.g., through direct managerial contact, liaison personnel, and task forces);
(2) the internal role of IJV board directors (e.g., participation of board directors in strategic planning and monitoring);
(3) cultural socialisation of IJV managers (e.g., through training, temporary inpatriation, and regular meetings);
(4) incentive plans for IJV managers (to align the interests of parents and IJV managers);
(5) IJV board structure (influencing the votes on strategic issues);
(6) IJV top management staffing (with managers trusted by the parent companies).

These control mechanisms can be used in combination. Kumar and Seth (1998) suggest that the higher the strategic interdependence of a parent company with an IJV, the tighter or more complex the control mechanisms should be. Majority equity ownership does not necessarily mean full operational control, however, as other partners' managers or employees are often needed for the effective implementation of a cooperation strategy (Child et al. 2005).

13.2 Specifics of contract-based cooperation

Contract-based cooperation usually shows a lower level of structural integration than equity-based alliances (Teng and Das 2008). Contracts are used as safeguards against opportunistic partner behaviour and as coordination mechanisms that clearly state the expectations regarding tasks and the contributions of all parties involved; they also provide procedures for decision-making and conflict resolution during cooperation (Faems et al. 2008). Cooperation is, in essence, an exchange relationship. Contracts, which provide a legally binding framework codifying each party's rights, responsibilities, and duties, determine the *structure* of cooperation, which in turn constitutes the basic condition for the *process* of the cooperative exchange (Luo 2002).

Mowery et al. (1996) distinguish between unilateral contract-based alliances and bilateral contract-based alliances. Cooperation is unilateral and contract-based if the firms conduct their alliance-related tasks on their own and just exchange property rights, such as, for example, in distribution agreements or in licensing agreements in which one company grants another the right to use a brand name or technology in return for cash payment. Under such an arrangement, both sides remain separate in their identity and ownership (Child et al. 2005). Compared to bilateral contract-based alliances, there is relatively little integration involved in this cooperation. For cooperative relationships that are tightly intertwined, with partners frequently directly working together and joining resources to create a joint outcome, Mowery et al. use the term "bilateral contract-based alliance". Examples include joint production facilities or research and development cooperation. In this case, it is less useful to formulate very specific contracts, as it is not possible to predict all the contingencies of such an evolving form of cooperation.

Contracts serve three general aims: first, they should direct the behaviour of the partners into a cooperative one that facilitates a positive exchange for the common good while preventing opportunism; second, they should be formulated in an unambiguous way, so that the partners know what to expect from each other; third, they should have limited rigidity, to allow cooperation to remain adaptable to changing circumstances (Luo 2002).

Contractual agreements represent an inherent trade-off between contract completeness and adaptability. Luo's (2002) empirical research results suggest that there is an optimal level of contract completeness, after which cooperation performance declines due to too much rigidity. As Luo remarks, "[i]n practice, overly specific terms may bring up rigidity while overly adaptive guidelines may increase enforceability costs or plant the seeds for opportunism and conflict" (p. 916). Thus, contracts for cross-border cooperation should be specific in their expectations while retaining the flexibility to allow the partnership to adapt to a changing environment.

Cooperation contracts usually include at least two types of provisions – the stronger *enforcement provisions* regulating how to deal with intellectual property and breaches of important contract clauses, and the weaker *coordination provisions* relating to information flow and the coordination mechanisms employed to manage the partnership (Reuer and Arino 2007). Of particular importance are contractual safeguards. Parkhe (1993) identifies a list of the safeguard clauses often used in cooperation agreements:

"*(1) periodic written reports of all relevant transactions;*
(2) prompt written notice of any departures from the agreement;
(3) the right to examine and audit all relevant records through a firm of CPAs[1]*;*
(4) designation of certain information as proprietary and subject to confidentiality provisions of the contract;
(5) non-use of proprietary information even after termination of agreement;
(6) termination of agreement;
(7) arbitration clauses;
(8) lawsuit provisions." (p. 829)

Child (2005) also points out the need to establish clear mechanisms for resolving disputes. According to Hagedoorn and Hesen (2007), the type of partnership also has an influence on which contract clauses are employed. They observe that, in both equity joint ventures and close non-equity partnerships, there is a prevalence of internal dispute resolution procedures, usually followed by arbitration rather than litigation. On the other hand, court procedures as conflict solving mechanisms are more common in cooperation based on licensing contracts. In any case, providing guidelines on dealing with conflicts and contingencies is a major task that contracts can fulfil. There are two types of provisions for dealing with such issues: first, it is possible to formulate general principles, processes, or guidelines on how to deal with conflicts and contingencies; second, specific contract clauses can be established for anticipated changes, such as changes in export regulations or customs and tariff systems (Luo 2002).

1 CPA: Certified Public Accountant

Cooperation contracts are also a means of establishing clear rules on how the partner contributions will be valued. A fair valuation of the assets partners are contributing is essential to successful cooperation. Child et al. (2005, pp. 138–140) suggest that the following factors should be taken into consideration in the valuation of partner assets used in cooperation:

- *Fixed assets*: considering the cost of the assets, their uniqueness and specificity, replacement value, and net present value of the future revenue streams that can be generated from the asset.
- *Working capital*: either at face value or discounted (e.g., for bad debts).
- *Know-how*: a partner's specific expertise being contributed to the alliance, valued, for example, according to "man hours".
- *Relationships*: contacts and networks are often of value to the alliance.
- *Brand names*: discounted cash-flow and net present value methods can be used to value intangible assets.
- *Technology*: technology transfer can be valued using, for example, time-based methods (as for other types of know-how) or a commission on future sales.

A precise definition of rights and duties was found to be a major success factor in SME cooperation (Hoffmann and Schlosser 2001). Good cooperation contracts can provide the opportunity to openly state mutual expectations in written form, so that all parties involved know their rights and duties. Lumineau and Malhotra (2011) also observe that an integrative, consensual approach to conflict resolution is more frequently used than a rights-based approach in alliances based on more detailed contracts, possibly due to a better understanding of the partners' needs and interests through a longer and more thorough contract negotiation period. It is therefore essential that potential partners make their expectations explicit in the process of forming their cooperation, in order to anticipate and avoid conflicts that may appear at later stages of the partnership (De Mattos et al. 2009). As well as they might have been negotiated, however, contracts always remain incomplete, as they can hardly make provisions for all possible future contingencies (Malhotra and Murningham 2002). They cannot totally substitute for trust and a good relationship among the partners.

13.3 Specifics of relationship-based cooperation

Relationship-based forms of cooperation governance involve processes that build trust and social identification, such as, for instance, frequent direct managerial communication and meetings, expert committees and project groups, the development of a shared vision and shared values, joint decision-making and problem-solving, and the filling of key positions with personnel who can be trusted (Hoetker and Mellewigt 2009). When partners show their commitment to the joint undertaking and to the effort to build and maintain a good partnership reciprocally, trust is built, helping to reduce the perceived risk of opportunistic behaviour (Uzzi 1997). Thus, relationship-based governance mechanisms "minimize contracting costs by allowing the parties to move forward with a less fully specified contract under the assumption that contingencies will be addressed in good faith and shirking will not occur" (Hoetker and Mellewigt 2009, p. 1030). While formal governance mechanisms can operate independently of specific individuals, relationship-based cooperation usually strongly relies on relationships among specific persons (Hoetker and Mellewigt 2009). Relationships between firms can therefore also change if key people involved in cooperation leave the partner companies.

One of the major questions in relationship-based cooperation is how to maintain control over the common endeavour. One strategy uses staffing–filling the relevant roles in the cooperative venture with trusted people. Another approach is maintaining frequent interaction with the key people managing cooperation and using project management tools. A comprehensive typology of control mechanisms that can be used between firms was composed by Bjørn (1997) and is presented in Table 13.2.

Table 13.2 An overview of control mechanisms for cooperation

Control mechanism	What the mechanism does	Examples
Input control	Facilitates action on grounds of controlled conditions	Transfer prices, distribution of resources, information management, training and personnel management
Behavioural control	Specifies the correct way to do work	Policies, plans, specification of methods, rules, direct supervision

Control mechanism	What the mechanism does	Examples
Output control	Specifies intended results, monitors and rewards their achievement	Targets, budgets, reporting of results, performance-related pay
Value socialization	Defines and creates common values	Organizational cultures expressed through belief systems, rituals, traditions
Adaptation socialization	Makes people familiar with each other's values and practices	Skills standardization, peer pressure, culture sensitivity programmes
Personal involvement	Signals what partner managers think is important	Visits and participations by managers, spoken communication
Hierarchical structure	Emphasizes and supports partner and alliance goals	Boards of directors, appointment of managers, reporting lines
Lateral structure	Influences people to interact across formal boundaries	"Gatekeepers" between partners and cross-partner teams

Source: Child et al. (2005), p. 224 based on Bjørn (1997)

From Cooperative Strategy: Managing Alliances, Networks, and Joint Ventures by John Child, David Faulkner & Stephen Tallman (2005). By permission of Oxford University Press

In their study of different joint venture control mechanisms, Choi and Beamish (2004) observed that split management control led to superior cooperation performance. In split management control, each partner maintains control of those activities connected to their firm-specific advantages. Thus, the distinct competences of the partner firms can also be fully used in cooperation. In the context of cross-border cooperation, it needs to be pointed out that culturally induced preferences for certain control mechanisms can occur. Egelhoff (1984) observes, for example, that U.S. multinational companies relied more extensively on output control, while their European counterparts tended to prefer behavioural control and putting their own staff into key positions.

Poppo and Zenger (2002) point out that firms do not have to make an exclusive decision between formally-based or relationship-based cooperation. Both forms of governance can complement and even reinforce each other. Trust between cooperation partners has the capacity to increase the performance of cooperative exchanges regardless of whether cooperation governance structure is more or less formal (Gulati and Nickerson 2008). Cooperation based on both interpersonal trust and legally binding commitments has a broader and more stable base. When standing on more pillars, the joint building is less likely to break down. Contractual and relational governance mechanisms also cross-influence each other. As Faems et al. (2008) note, "the initial contract design substantially influences relational dynamics at operational and managerial levels, which in turn determine how the contract is applied" (p. 1072). The nature of the relationship, on the other hand, can influence the way contracts are drafted and agreements made.

A summary of the choice of governance mode for cross-border cooperation

When entering into cross-border cooperation, the partners need to decide what mechanisms they will use to coordinate and monitor their common venture. Generally, the governance of cooperation can be equity-based, contract-based, or relationship-based. When choosing a governance structure, firms should take into account that:

1. Each form of governance has its advantages and disadvantages. While international joint ventures provide clear centralised control systems and a way to curb opportunistic behaviour, contractual agreements preserve the independence of firms, and relationship-based forms of cooperation are very flexible and adaptable to changing environmental circumstances in dynamic markets.
2. Equity-based international joint ventures, in which all partners hold shares in a separate, jointly owned company, provide a mechanism by which to share risks and returns, to align partner interests, and to overcome legal (trade) and cultural barriers. In order to ensure the achievement of the individual goals, however, the parent firms also need to set up functioning control mechanisms for their joint company.
3. Contract-based cooperation clearly sets out the partners' mutual expectations about their contributions, rights, and duties. A balance needs to be struck between detailed and unambiguous contract provisions on the one hand and maintaining adaptability and flexibility on the other. Major clauses in cooperation contracts include regulations on how to value the contributions of the partners, how to deal with breaches of partner obligations, how to coordinate and manage the partnership, and how to terminate cooperation.

4. Relationship-based cooperation relies mainly on trust as a mechanism for building a mutually beneficial partnership. Frequent personal interactions, positive reciprocity, and joint decision-making and problem-solving foster the development of trust. It needs to be added, however, that relationship-based cooperation needs control, for example in the form of high personal involvement, value socialisation, or cross-partner teams.
5. The choice among the governance modes is not exclusive. Joint ventures can be complemented with additional contractual cooperation provisions, and both formal structures of governance profit from good partner relations. Fundamentally, the governance system must ensure (a) that mutual expectations and roles are clearly understood by all partners, (b) that procedures and rules for managing and controlling cooperation are in place, and (c) that the partners agree on how to deal with conflicts.

References

Albers, S. (2010) Configurations of alliance governance systems. *Schmalenbach Business Review* 62(3), 204–233

Barringer, B. R. and Harrison, J. S. (2000) Walking a tightrope: Creating value through interorganizational relationships. *Journal of Management* 26(3), 367–403

Bjørn, L. B. (1997) Managing uncertainty in transnational headquarters-subsidiary interfaces: Danish companies in Japan and Germany. Unpublished Ph.D. dissertation, University of Aarhus, Denmark

Brouthers, K. D. (1995) The influence of international risk on entry mode strategy in the computer software industry. *Management International Review* 35(1), 7–28

Child, J., Faulkner, D., and Tallman, S. (2005) Cooperative strategy, 2nd edn. Oxford: Oxford University Press

Choi, C.-B. and Beamish, P. W. (2004) Split management control and international joint venture performance. *Journal of International Business Studies* 35(3), 201–215

de Man, A.-P. and Roijakkers, N. (2009) Alliance governance: Balancing control and trust in dealing with risk. *Long Range Planning* 42(1), 75–95

De Mattos, C., Salciuviene, L., Auruskeviciene, V., and Thomas, S. (2009) Investigating the importance of matching expectations of contributions to SME's international strategic alliance formation. *Economics and Management* 14, 375–380

Egelhoff, W. G. (1984) Patterns of control in U.S., U.K. and European multinational corporations. *Journal of International Business Studies* 15(2), 73–83

Faems, D., Janssens, M., Madhok, A., and Van Looy, B. (2008) Toward an integrative perspective on alliance governance: Connecting contract design, trust dynamics, and contract application. *Academy of Management Journal* 51(6), 1053–1078

Gulati, R. and Nickerson, J. A. (2008) Interorganizational trust, governance choice, and exchange performance. *Organization Science* 19(5), 688–708

Hagedoorn, J. and Hesen, G. (2007) Contract law and the governance of inter-firm technology partnerships – an analysis of different modes of partnering and their contractual implications. *Journal of Management Studies* 44(3), 342–366

Hoetker, G. and Mellewigt, T. (2009) Choice and performance of governance mechanisms: Matching alliance governance to asset type. *Strategic Management Journal* 30(10), 1025–1044

Hoffmann, W. and Schlosser, R. (2001) Success factors of strategic alliances in small and medium-sized enterprises – an empirical survey. *Long Range Planning* 34(3), 357–381

Jensen, M. C. (1983) Organization theory and methodology. *Accounting Review* 58(2), 319–339

Kale, P. and Singh, H. (2009) Managing strategic alliances: What do we know now, and where do we go from here? *Academy of Management Perspectives* 23(3), 45–62

Kent, D. H. (1991) Joint ventures vs. non-joint ventures: An empirical investigation. *Strategic Management Journal* 12(5), 387–393

Killing, J. P. (1983) Strategies for Joint Venture Success. New York: Praeger

Kumar, S. and Seth, A. (1998) The design of coordination and control mechanisms for managing joint venture-parent relationships. *Strategic Management Journal* 19(6), 579–599

Lane, P. J., Salk, J. E., and Lyles, M. A. (2001) Absorptive capacity, learning, and performance in international joint ventures. *Strategic Management Journal* 22(12), 1139–1161

Li, J., Zhou, C., and Zajac, E. J. (2009) Control, collaboration, and productivity in international joint ventures: Theory and evidence. *Strategic Management Journal* 30(8), 865–884

Lu, J. W. and Beamish, P. W. (2006) Partnering strategies and performance of SME's international joint ventures. *Journal of Business Venturing* 21(4), 461–486

Lumineau, F. and Malhotra, D. (2011) Shadow of the contract: How contract structure shapes interim dispute resolution. *Strategic Management Journal* 32(5), 532–555

Luo, Y. (2002) Contract, cooperation, and performance in international joint ventures. *Strategic Management Journal* 23(10), 903–919

Lyles, M. A. and Salk, J. E. (1996) Knowledge acquisition from foreign parents in international joint ventures: An empirical examination in the Hungarian context. *Journal of International Business Studies* 29(2), 154–174

Malhotra, D. and Murningham, J. K. (2002) The effects of contracts on interpersonal trust. *Administrative Science Quarterly* 47(3), 534–559

Mowery, D. C., Oxley, J. E., and Silverman, B. S. (1996) Strategic alliances and interfirm knowledge transfer. *Strategic Management Journal* 17 (Special Issue *Winter*), 77–91

Parkhe, A. (1993) Strategic alliance structuring: A game theoretic and transaction cost examination of interfirm cooperation. *Academy of Management Journal* 36(4), 794–829

Poppo, L. and Zenger, T. (2002) Do formal contracts and relational governance function as substitutes or complements? *Strategic Management Journal* 23(8), 707–725

Reuer, J. and Ariño, A. (2007) Strategic alliance contracts: Dimensions and determinants of contractual complexity. *Strategic Management Journal* 28(3), 313–330

Schaan, J. L. (1983) Parent control and joint venture success: The case of Mexico. Unpublished doctoral dissertation, University of Western Ontario, Canada

Tallman, S. B. and Shenkar, O. (1994) A managerial decision model of international cooperative venture formation. *Journal of International Business Studies* 25(1), 91–113

Teng, B.-S. and Das, T. K. (2008) Governance structure choice in strategic alliance. *Management Decision* 46(5), 725–742

Uzzi, B. (1997) Social structure and competition in interfirm networks: The paradox of embeddedness. *Administrative Science Quarterly* 42(1), 35–67

14 Managing the cooperative relationship

Managing cooperation is not easy, as the interests of at least two partners are always involved, which could come into conflict with each other. Dacin et al. (1997) remind us of the importance of being sensitive to the needs of one's partner: "For an alliance to be successful over time, both partners must achieve their objectives" (p. 15). In addition to the partners' expectations, different cultural and institutional contexts need to be taken into account, and, adding to the complexity, managing cooperation often requires working with people over whom one has no direct authority (Child 2005). In such an environment, building and maintaining good partner relationships becomes essential. Considering the potentially diverging partner interests, it is also important to focus on the risks involved in cooperation, especially the risk of opportunistic partner behaviour. Before we further discuss the management of relationships and risk, we will take a closer look at one of the most crucial stages in cooperation, its operational launch.

14.1 The first steps

Doz (1996) found that the small steps partners take at the beginning of a partnership can have significant consequences for the subsequent phases of cooperation. He argues that, from the beginning, all partners informally monitor and evaluate the moves of the others, "watch[ing] each other for unexplained divergence between what they see as the task requirements and the behaviour of the partners *vis-à-vis* those requirements, which might denote lack of competence, lack of flexibility, or ultimate "unspeakable" motives beyond the efficiency of the alliance. In other words, they read in the behaviour of the partner clues about the partner's competencies, capability to adjust, and trustworthiness" (p. 77). It is therefore necessary to take care of the "small things" one says and does in the first phase of cooperation, as they can have a tremendous influence on a partner's perception of one's firm and of the potential benefits and risks of the alliance. In cross-border cooperation, the early encounters carry the risk of cultural misunderstanding. On the other hand, early positive reciprocity can build trust and commitment strong enough to form the basis of a sustained positive outcome for cooperation. Paying more attention to the partner firms and their expectations in the early stages of cooperation is an investment that can pay off handsomely later. One of the special tasks at the start of cooperation is to "establish the right tone" (Yoshino and Rangan 1995, p. 123). The way partners communicate and interact with each other in the early stages of their partnership will have a considerable influence on the later development of cooperation.

After the very first steps, alliances need to evolve. Ring and Van de Ven (1994) propose a framework for the development of inter-firm cooperation, which is presented in Figure 14.1.

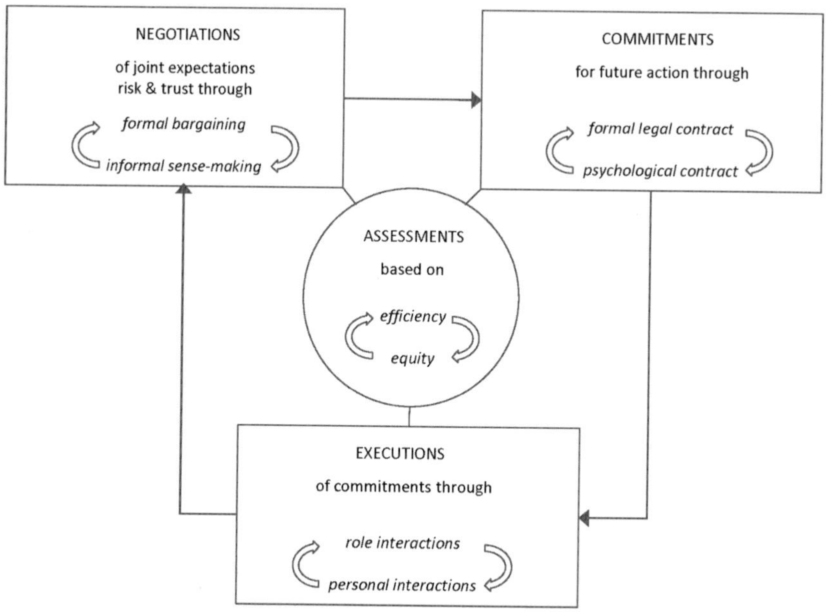

Fig. 14.1 A framework for the development of cooperation

Source: From "Developmental processes of cooperative interorganizational relationships" by P. S. Ring and A. H. Van de Ven (1994) Academy of Management Review 19(1), p. 97

Ring and Van de Ven's framework consists of the three stages through which cooperation repeatedly passes, not sequentially but cyclically. In the negotiation stage, the cooperation partners explore their options and generate joint expectations about the investments needed and the potential risks and benefits of cooperation. They also assess the uncertainties involved and whether they can trust their counterparts. The two main evaluation criteria for the possibility of exchange are *efficiency* ("Are cooperation itself and the form of cooperation the least costly way of obtaining the desired benefits?") and *equity* ("Are the input-output relations considered fair by all sides?"). If the parties are willing to cooperate, they make commitments to the others, in the form of either signed formal contracts or unwritten “psychological contracts” by which the mutual expectations and obligations are well understood although not formally coded. In the final execution stage, the cooperation partners establish actions according to their prior agreements. Then, the partners assess whether the actions are being efficiently and equitably executed. As environmental conditions change, conflicts arise, or new requirements or expectations emerge, the cooperation partners need to engage in a constant re-negotiation of their partnership, thus starting a new loop in the cycle. As Ring and Van de Ven (1994) point out, “[a]s these transactions are repeated through time, and meet basic norms of equity and efficiency, the parties may feel increasingly secure in committing more of their available resources and expectations in subsequent cycles [of cooperation]” (p. 101). Cooperation often starts out in a very small manner, with limited commitment, and becomes stronger and more comprehensive over time after taking several turns through this development cycle. Ring and Van de Ven’s model also shows that it takes time to build a relationship based on mutual understanding and trust before cooperation can operate at full potential.

As trust between firms is of crucial importance, one of the most important decisions in the starting phase of a collaboration is whom to put in charge of managing the cooperative efforts and of being the link with the partner firm. It is important that the managers in charge of cooperation have the necessary interpersonal, negotiation, and cooperation-specific skills. Cross-border cooperation managers must also have the necessary intercultural skills. It would not make sense, for example, to put a technical production manager without any marketing knowledge or international experience in charge of cross-border sales and marketing cooperation. Additionally, the persons responsible for cooperation should have adequate standing in their own firms. Dyer et al. (2001) point out that “[o]ne reason that alliances fail is the inability of one partner or another to mobilize internal resources to support the initiative” (p. 40). In other words, if nobody from one of the firms cares about the partnership, the venture will not work. Das (2005) argues that there is a risk that managers might be socialised in the partner’s culture and be eventually “enticed away” (p. 716) from their own firms. This is especially critical in the case of employees with key skills or know-how.

Who is responsible for the management of cooperation? Some authors argue that successful cooperative strategies require a dedicated ‘alliance function’ in the partner companies (Kale et al. 2002), a unit in which alliance-management know-how would be concentrated. Small and medium-sized enterprises (SMEs), however, often do not have enough resources to set up a dedicated alliance function. Thus, individuals with other functions must assume the additional responsibility of taking care of the development of cooperation. In micro enterprises, this will often be the top manager of the company.

14.2 Managing the relationship

Good personal relationships between the managers of the partner firms are an important precondition for successful cooperation. Child et al. (2005) propose that a key factor for fruitful cooperation is the positive attitude of the partners towards it, which they find is shown through strong *commitment* on the part of the top and middle management of the partner firms, through mutual *trust*, and (particularly important for cross-border cooperation), through a *sensitivity towards cultural differences* and a willingness to engage in a process of *mutual sense-making*. The first two, commitment and trust, are considered by Child et al. (2005) as key factors: "No amount of energy and clear direction will compensate for their absence. And it should be noted that commitment can exist without trust and vice versa, but both are necessary for a lasting and stable relationship" (p. 7).

Nakos and Brouthers (2008) define commitment as the "willingness of partner firms to maintain a stable relationship and the degree to which an alliance partner expects the alliance to continue into the future" (p. 125) and argue that higher levels of commitment will usually lead to an increase in cooperative behaviour and a decrease in opportunistic behaviour. Their research also shows that process control – trying to influence the behaviour of a cooperation partner – can mediate between alliance commitment and the performance of the cooperative venture.

Trust includes (a) expectations about being fairly treated without opportunistic behaviour by the partner and (b) having confidence that the partner will act with high reliability and integrity (Kale and Singh 2009). Schoorman et al. (2007) define trust as a "willingness to be vulnerable" (p. 347) – having the courage to put oneself into a vulnerable position, expecting that the partner will reciprocate. One can also develop trust by ensuring that all commitments are met and fostering interpersonal bonds between the representatives of the cooperation partners (Kale and Singh 2009; Schreiner et al. 2009). Certain routines help maintain trust between partners, specifically those that signal that the partners are committed to a continuing relationship (Dyer and

Chu 2011). One key to developing and maintaining a trustful relationship is keeping one's promises (Spence et al. 2008). The main precondition for developing a trustful relationship is mutual understanding between the cooperation partners (Child et al. 2005). Understanding the partner's values and modes of thinking and acting can enhance the effectiveness of cooperation. However, one needs to understand that "[c]ultural differences could inhibit the development of mutual understanding and trust" (ibid., p. 59). Building trust is therefore particularly challenging in cross-border cooperation, as it usually lacks the common legal-institutional and cultural systems that instil trust (ibid.). It is not only national cultural differences that are important. Trust in cooperation needs to develop on multiple levels – at the firm level, at the level of the groups interacting between the firms, and at the individual level (Currall and Inkpen 2002). As Child et al. (2005) notice, "[t]he interface between the two (and sometimes more) company cultures is the crucible of potential achievement. Sensitivity to each other's cultures is vital to effective joint operation." (p. 8)

To understand cooperative firm relationships, it is wise to look at the research on the impact of human nature on cooperation. Research in experimental economics in which people are observed during cooperation and conflict experiments has revealed some general trends in human cooperative behaviour. Gächter and Herrmann (2009), for example, found that:

1. Repeated interactions with the same group members lead to higher individual contributions.
2. People who communicate more also cooperate more. For inter-firm cooperation, this means that frequent interaction between the partners can also foster the propensity to cooperate.
3. People contribute more to the "common good" if they are not anonymous (pointing to a possible "reputation effect"). In alliances, this means that the partner firms' representatives should be known to each other personally rather than only through their functions.
4. Contributions are usually higher in the beginning and decline over time. In order to avoid this declining commitment and maintain cooperation, positive impulses need to be initiated occasionally, thus inviting the cooperation partner to reciprocate.
5. Negative (or free-riding) behaviour tends to be punished, as it triggers negative emotions. However, punishment "turned out to be an inefficient tool to enforce cooperation because resources are destroyed" (Gächter and Herrmann 2009, p. 795) in experiments in which punishment had

material consequences. It is important to be aware of the negative spiral that can develop from negative actions followed by equally negative reactions.

One salient concept in the research on human cooperative behaviour is *reciprocity.* As Tjemkes and Furrer (2011) note, "constructive strategies invite constructive strategies and destructive strategies invite destructive strategies" (p. 241). The special form of *strong reciprocity* is defined by Gintis et al. (2008) as a "propensity, in the context of a shared social task, to cooperate with others similarly disposed, even at personal cost, and a willingness to punish those who violate cooperative norms, even when punishing is personally costly [...] [Thus] it embraces an ethic of treating others as they treat us" (p. 242). People cooperate even if they do not expect to see each other again, and they punish those who act anti-socially even if doing so bears costs (Gächter and Herrmann 2009). Gintis (2000) proposes that strong reciprocity has evolutionary roots, whereby human groups that exhibited such cooperative behaviour had higher chances of survival in adverse environments (such as wars or environmental disasters) than did those that acted in purely selfish ways. Strong reciprocity is distinct from reciprocal altruism, in which people are willing to help others but expect long-term benefits from their positive actions (Fehr et al. 2002).

In experiments conducted in Russia and Switzerland, Gächter and Herrmann (2009) found cross-cultural differences in strong reciprocity, especially in strong negative reciprocity. They noticed that Russian actors punished free riders as well as those cooperating. Herrmann et al. (2008) suggest that these anti-social forms of punishment are more prevalent in societies with weak social norms of cooperation and weak democratic and judicial institutions. Gächter and Herrmann (2009) add the proposition that the punishment of anti-social behaviour may be linked to more traditional societies, which rely on private networks more than on state institutions and which feature active cooperation within closed networks and little cooperation outside them.

When managing cross-border cooperation, it is necessary to understand the cultural cooperation norms of the partners' nations. Besides understanding cultural differences, it is also necessary to manage cultural diversity effectively. There are three options in doing this:

1. *Domination*, in which the culture of one partner is the dominant culture in the cooperation;
2. *Segmentation*, in which a balance between the partners' cultures is found, either by separating different segments of cooperation with their distinct

cultures or through the pluralistic approach of finding the best cultural fit for a certain task;
3. *Synthesis*, which strives to integrate the cultures into a "third culture" that includes the positive aspects of the cultures of all the partners involved (Child et al. 2005).

All three strategies have advantages and disadvantages: domination can create a unified identity but at the cost of possibly creating resentment in the dominated partners; segmentation creates more flexibility for adapting to local differences but may lead to conflicts and a lack of standardisation; synthesis can maximize the potential for mutual learning but takes too much time and effort to implement (Child et al. 2005). To facilitate cross-cultural interaction, employee training programs can (a) raise the awareness and understanding of differences in values, attitudes, behaviour, and communication patterns across cultures and (b) enhance inter-cultural communication competence (Tung 1993). Part of communication competence is learning the partner's language, which can be used as an effective bridge between cultures (Dietachmair and Sternad, 2011).

Communication plays a major role in establishing and maintaining good working relationships between partners. As Elmuti and Kathawala (2001) point out, an alliance "will inevitably dissolve as a result of doubt and mistrust which does not manifest good communication practices" (p. 215). Frequent communication, both formal and informal, can lead to a better understanding of the partners and their values. As Ariño and de la Torre (1998) have proposed, "a firm should not evaluate the alliance exclusively from its own perspective, but supplement it with the partner's angle as well. By appreciating the partner's position, a firm can better understand what the partner wants from the alliance using the same framework" (p. 39). A better mutual understanding between the partners also eventually leads to better cooperation (Spence et al. 2008).

Related to the communication issue is the development of friendly personal contact between the managers of the cooperating organisations (Child et al. 2005). In a study by Spence et al. (2008), SME managers found the personal characteristics of the partners, especially a compatible personality, to be the most important qualitative factor in the evaluation of cooperation.

Fundamentally, building good relationships between cooperation partners can also be seen as a form of capital. Kale et al. (2000) define relational capital as the "level of mutual trust, respect, and friendship that arises out of close interaction at the individual level between alliance partners" (p. 218). They found that relational capital increases information and know-how exchanges between partners and thus fosters reciprocal learning. Building social capital through high-quality relationships between actors within and between firms (Yli-Renko et al. 2002) takes time and effort. Chetty and Agndal (2007) consider this a major reason for the long internationalisation processes in firms without adequate experience in building relationships and networks. Building and maintaining social capital might be costly, requiring frequent social interaction, but it also unlocks opportunities. If a situation with a cooperation partner becomes deadlocked, the personal relationships between managers of the partner firms can help the partners overcome the challenge, while relationships with other potential partners could provide an adequate "best alternative" (Chetty and Agndal 2007).

14.3 Maintaining cooperation

Social exchange theory, following Blau's (1964) foundational work, asserts that people evaluate the quality of relationships by judging each interaction between the partners. This resembles the "balance sheet approach", in which both sides put a value on the inputs and outputs of the relationship and thus judge the overall degree of its reciprocity and fairness.

In addition to reciprocal interactions, in which relationships are built through the exchange of positive actions, Ballinger and Rockmann (2010) also identify "nonreciprocal" relationships, in which key exchange events – also called "anchoring" events – have a salient effect on the relationship. They argue that some events and partner actions make a lasting impression on others and get stored in their autobiographic memory: "Once an anchor is set in a relationship, the parties evaluate exchanges that occur later in the relationship through the prism of the anchoring event. Thus, once the rules for the relationship have been changed, the relationship becomes resistant to reversion to reciprocity" (p. 374). Anchoring events can be positive (an unexpected act of kindness, for example) or negative (like a significant breach of trust). In exchanges with a negative anchoring event, competition (trying to maximise one's gain compared to the counterpart), revenge (trying to minimise the counterpart's outcome), or rationality (trying to maximise one's outcome regardless of the counterpart's outcome), together called 'negative nonreciprocal states' by Ballinger and Rockmann, can become dominant rules that replace reciprocity. In exchanges with positive anchoring events, altruism (trying to maximise the counterpart's positive outcomes) or group gain (maximising the outcome for both sides) might become the prevalent positive non-reciprocal guidelines. These findings have implications for inter-firm cooperation:

First, they reveal the importance of being aware of the repercussion effects that single events can have on the relationship. As events with lasting impacts often occur early in a relationship (Robinson 1996), cooperation partners should be particularly careful while interacting in the initial stages of a developing relationship. It has been found that immediate opposite reactions increased the possibility of overturning the first event (Ballinger and Rockmann 2010): a fast and honest apology when something went wrong served as an important determinant for the likelihood of further fruitful cooperation. Finally, Ballinger and Rockmann propose that, when engaging in cooperative ventures, one should not only gradually build positive exchanges but also make an effort to "create moments, or extreme events, [...] [showing that an] organization is willing and able to go above and beyond expectations toward the relationship" (p. 387).

Dyer and Singh (1998) identify the factors that influence the propensity to uphold cooperation. These are:

- Partner assets that are closely interconnected (for example, an investment of a newspaper distribution company within the printing house of a partner company);
- A scarcity of partners who can offer both the needed resource complementarity and the ability and willingness to cooperate;
- The development of resources or capabilities that are indivisible (for example, a common brand name under which the alliance's products are marketed);
- An institutional environment or social controls that facilitate cooperative partnerships;
- Causal ambiguity about how value is created within the cooperation; and
- The inability to replicate the distinct advantages of cooperation due to time constraints.

Xia (2011) found that partner substitutability reduces the likelihood of a cross-border alliance's survival. According to Lu and Beamish (2006), the stability of an international joint venture is associated with the difficulty of replicating the partner's resources. In addition to resource-interconnectedness and the availability and evaluation of suitable alternatives, interpersonal factors can influence the propensity to maintain cooperation. Continuity in the firms' contact persons plays a particularly important role in this context. If a contact person changes, part of the relationship, especially the personal one, might be lost. As Ring and Van de Ven (1994) point out, constantly changing firm agents means "restarting the clock on the psychological contracts" (p. 104). Cooperation that solely relies on one good personal relationship is therefore built on thin ice.

In addition to building personal relationships, systematic approaches can maintain good cooperation. Formal control mechanisms for cross-border alliances include business plans, financial statements, key performance indicators, internal (transfer) prices, economic efficiency calculations, reports, and service-level agreements (Hoetker and Mellewigt 2009). To maintain a mutually beneficial cooperation, the partners should regularly organise meetings to evaluate their cooperation. A variety of performance factors can be reviewed on such occasions, among them:

- whether cooperation is achieving its original strategic goals (e.g., in terms of efficiency gains or market share);
- whether cooperation partners still share a common purpose and common goals for the alliance;
- whether all partners involved perceive cooperation as beneficial to their businesses;
- whether cooperation provides benefits to all parties involved that could not be obtained individually;
- whether the risks of and returns from cooperation are adequately balanced;
- whether all partners understand the expectations of the other partners concerning their distinct roles in cooperation;
- whether all partners perceive the information and communication policies as well as the alliance's management system as being suitable; and
- whether there is sufficient trust and commitment from all the partners and top decision makers within the organisations.

While it is important to regularly review whether cooperation still makes sense for the parties involved, it needs to be mentioned that cooperation partners too often "worry more about controlling the relationship than about nurturing it" (Kanter 1994, p. 96).

14.4 Managing risk

Embarking on a cooperative strategy is not without risk. Das and Teng (1998) and Das (2005) posit that there are two basic kinds of risks in cooperation: *relational risk*, the risk that the partners may have their own agenda and will therefore not behave cooperatively, and *performance risk*, the risk of failing to reach the cooperation's goals despite fully cooperative partner behaviour.

In some types of cooperation, for example in R&D alliances, firms put their own technological assets and know-how at risk (Li et al. 2008). Firms engaging in cooperative relationships do not want only to obtain resources; they also wish to retain and protect their own resources, especially from the partner's opportunistic behaviour: "Such opportunistic behavior tends to be more severe when it involves tacit knowledge and skills that are not protected by property laws" (Das and Teng 2000, p. 44).

In this context, it is necessary to distinguish between risk and perceived risk. The former generally refers to the objective probability of a negative outcome, whereas perceived risk is an actor's evaluation of this objective risk (Das and Teng 2001). Two factors influence the risk perceived by cooperation partners – trust and control. Das and Teng (2001) distinguish between two types of trust – goodwill trust and competence trust. Goodwill trust refers to the good intentions and commitment of a partner firm and can reduce perceived relational risk; competence trust is a belief in the capabilities and competence of the partner firm and can lower the perceived performance risk in cooperation (ibid.).

The second means of reducing perceived risk is control. There are three types of control mechanisms for cooperation (Groot and Merchant 2000):

(1) *Action (or behavioural) control* occurs through procedures and rules that need to be followed, which can be specified in contracts and checked by the partners or auditors;
(2) *Results (or output) control* are specific performance targets and the requisite monitoring or rewards systems;
(3) *Personnel (or cultural) control* occurs through working with trusted partners, sharing values, and placing loyal personnel in key positions in the cooperative venture.

Das and Teng (2001) suggest that these control mechanisms display varying levels of effectiveness when applied to different kinds of risk: whereas results control is appropriate for managing performance risk, behavioural control is more suited for managing relational risk, as it allows the partners to detect potential counterpart misconduct. Cultural control – or *social control* in the words of Das and Teng (2001) – include socialisation processes and the development of shared goals, values, and trust between the partners, which can reduce both relational risk and performance risk, the latter through a clear orientation towards a common goal. Figure 14.2 provides an overview of the techniques for reducing relational risk and performance risk in cooperation.

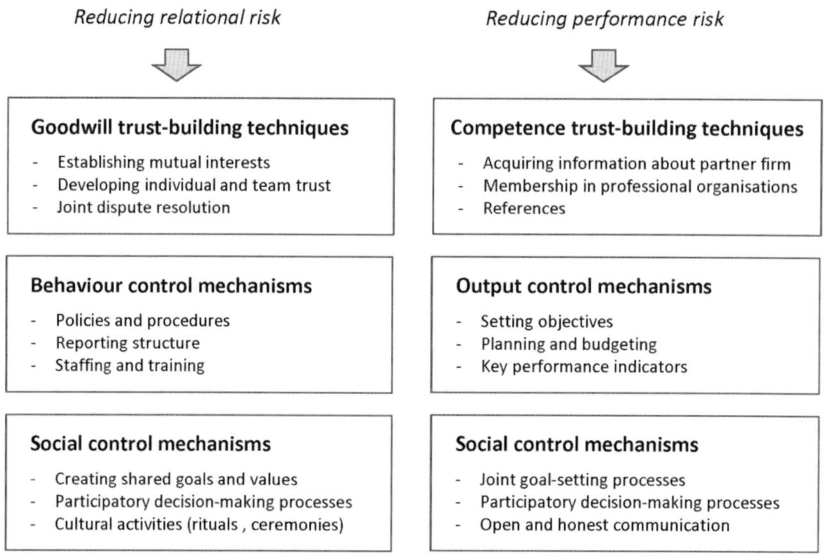

Fig. 14.2 Risk-reduction techniques in cooperation

Source: Graphic presentation by the author based on contents from Das and Teng (2001), pp. 271–276

The following questions based on the alliance risk management guidelines presented by Das and Teng (1999) can help in evaluating whether adequate measures have been taken to control risk in cooperation:

- Are your firm's resources (especially the intangible resources such as patents, copyrights, and trademarks) well protected in all the countries in which the cross-border alliance is operating?
- Have you established security measures against unintended knowledge transfer?
- Has it been made explicit to both your staff and that of your partner firm that unauthorized acquisition of partner know-how is not acceptable?

- Have knowledge barriers been inbuilt to separate the work between the partners so as to minimise the unauthorized knowledge spill-over of unique know-how that needs special protection?
- Is the use of resources, property, and ownership rights regulated in the cooperation contract?
- Are there adequate exit provisions in the contract?
- Is flexibility maintained through an incremental process of commitment to the cooperation?
- Do you have your own personnel in key positions in the cooperation?
- Is behavioural and social control through frequent interaction and communication ensured?
- Are mechanisms in place to ensure cultural and procedural compatibility between the partners?

The answers to these questions will point to potential deficiencies in the risk control of cooperation. As mentioned, one form of risk specific to cooperative undertakings is relational risk, which can manifest itself in opportunistic behaviour. We take a closer look at this issue in the following section.

14.5 Managing opportunistic behaviour

When firms engage in cooperative ventures, they retain their own strategies and interests, which are not always fully compatible with their partners'. Thus, "[l]ike thorns on the stems of roses, the popularity of strategic alliances has been plagued by potential for deceitful behavior by partners" (Das 2005, p. 706). Das (2005) has noted that deceitful behaviour – putting self-interest before the common interest – is a major factor in the failure rates of alliances and can occur in many forms, such as, for example, reluctance to disclose one's abilities or real goals, failure to make a full effort, failing to meet obligations, withholding or manipulating information, and trying to gain knowledge at the expense of the partner.

Wathne and Heide (2000) have classified the forms of opportunistic behaviour in inter-firm relationships: they first distinguish between active and passive opportunism. Partners can either act in a way detrimental to cooperation or be passively damaging by evading obligations or withholding information. Depending on whether opportunistic behaviour occurs under existing conditions or in new circumstances, Wathne and Heide further suggest that alliance partners can engage in evasive behaviour (passive/existing conditions), a refusal to adapt (passive/new circumstances), a violation of an agreement (active/existing conditions), or forcing a renegotiation (active/new circumstances).

Several strategies have been suggested for controlling opportunistic behaviour in cooperative endeavours. Wathne and Heide (2000), for example, propose the following mechanisms:

(1) *Monitoring* of a partner's behaviour or of their outcomes can help reduce information asymmetry, thereby potentially limiting information-based opportunism. The mere fact that the partners are aware of the monitoring could restrain them from acting opportunistically.
(2) *Incentive structures* can align the partners' individual interests if they are designed in such a way that the long-term outcome from cooperative behaviour exceeds the short-term gains from deceitful behaviour.
(3) *Partner selection* can help pre-empt opportunistic behaviour. However, finding trustworthy partners it is not always possible without having prior experience with them. Even reputation is a dangerous proxy, as it can be systematically manipulated.
(4) *Socialization strategies* include efforts to create common values and goals in a partnership to reduce the potential for opportunistic behaviour.

Das (2005) sees monitoring as well as staffing and training (as socialisation strategies) as feasible mechanisms for deterring deceitful behaviour. He further proposes contracts, governance structures, mutual hostages, and participatory decision-making as workable strategies for managing opportunistic behaviour. According to Das, tight and complete contracts are more useful in the short term, as "it is impractical to try to address all future contingencies in a contract" (p. 711). Regarding governance structures, equity alliances such as joint ventures are seen as most effective in controlling opportunism, as they very clearly determine the partners' resource inputs and align their interests in the success of the joint firm. Mutual hostages are cooperation-specific investments contributed by all the partners that would be lost if deceitful or opportunistic behaviour were to occur. Das suggests that managers should beware of "fake hostages", deployed resources that are actually not critical. He also observes that, as hostages can lose value over time, a continuous exchange of hostages should occur as a sign of sustained commitment to cooperation. Finally, participatory decision-making can help align goals and reduce the cooperation partners' tendency to act opportunistically. Adequate negotiation skills are thereby crucial for joint decision-making: "Managers of an alliance firm should search for the root causes for differences in their own goals and those of their partner's. Listening carefully to the partner's arguments is extremely important for this mechanism to work." (Das 2005, p. 715)

Ultimately, it is important to keep a balance when employing tools for controlling opportunistic behaviour. Overly rigorous contracts or intrusive monitoring, for example, are detrimental to the strengthening of the trust between partners. Therefore, it makes sense to weigh the advantages of the mechanisms designed to prevent opportunism against the potential disadvantages of diminished trust and relational capital.

A summary on managing cooperative firm relationships

1. The initial phase of cooperation is crucial for building a good partner relationship. It is essential that the partners are clear about their mutual expectations and commitments from the outset and that they understand that small actions early on can have a significant effect on the development of cooperation. A mutual understanding of the partners' needs and interests is a key precondition for developing trustful relationships.
2. Cooperative relationships develop over time through negotiation and renegotiation, partner commitment, the execution of commitment, and the assessment and evaluation of the execution by all parties involved. To attain high performance, partners must first develop interpersonal and reciprocal trust in each other's competence.
3. Cooperative behaviour is fostered by frequent communication. However, cultural differences may influence partners' notions of adequate cooperative behaviour. Cultural diversity should therefore be actively managed in cross-border cooperation, either through the domination of one culture, segmentation, or a synthesis into a "third culture".
4. Cooperation is maintained because of the resource dependencies between the partners, a lack of substitutes, and the partners' close personal relationships. A regular review of whether cooperation is meeting the needs and goals of the partners can facilitate the early identification of problems or imbalances in the partnership.
5. Cooperative strategies carry both performance and relational risks. The latter lies in the potentially opportunistic behaviour of the partner. The perceived risk can be reduced either by trust or by a control mechanism in the form of behavioural, output, or cultural control. A trade-off is required, however, between trust and control.

References

Ariño, A. and de la Torre, J. (1998) Learning from failure: Towards an evolutionary model of collaborative ventures. *Organization Science* 9(3), 306–325

Ballinger, G. A. and Rockmann, K. W. (2010) Chutes versus ladders: Anchoring events and a punctuated-equilibrium perspective on social exchange relationships. *Academy of Management Review* 35(3), 373–391

Blau, P. M. (1964) Exchange and power in social life. New York: Wiley

Chetty, S. and Agndal, H. (2007) Social capital and its influence on changes in internationalization mode among small and medium-sized enterprises. *Journal of International Marketing* 15(1), 1–29

Child, J., Faulkner, D., and Tallman, S. (2005) Cooperative strategy, 2nd edn. Oxford: Oxford University Press

Dacin, M. T., Hitt, M. A., and Levitas, E. (1997) Selecting partners for successful international alliances: Examination of U.S. and Korean firms (cover story). *Journal of World Business* 32(1), 3–16

Das, T. K. (2005) Deceitful behaviors of alliance partners: Potential and prevention. *Management Decision* 43(5), 706–719

Das, T. K. and Teng, B.-S. (1998) Resource and risk management in the strategic alliance making process. *Journal of Management* 24(1), 21–42

Das, T. K. and Teng, B.-S. (1999) Managing risks in strategic alliances. *Academy of Management Executive* 13(4), 50–62

Das, T. K. and Teng, B.-S. (2000) A resource-based theory of strategic alliances. *Journal of Management* 26(1), 31–62

Das, T. K. and Teng, B.-S. (2001) Trust, control, and risk in strategic alliances: An integrated framework. *Organization Studies* 22(2), 251–283

Dietachmair, B. and Sternad, D. (2011), Cultural and institutional challenges for Austrian expatriates in South East Europe, Proceedings of the 19th Annual Conference on Marketing and Business Strategies for Central and Eastern Europe (1–3 December, Vienna), 53–68

Doz, Y. L. (1996) The evolution of cooperation in strategic alliances: Initial conditions or learning alliances. *Strategic Management Journal* 17(1), 55–83

Dyer, J. H. and Singh, H. (1998) The relational view: Cooperative strategy and sources of interorganizational competitive advantage. *Academy of Management Review* 23(4), 660–679

Dyer, J. H. and Chu, W. (2011) The determinants of trust in supplier-automaker relationships. *Journal of International Business Studies* 42(1), 10–27

Dyer, J. H., Kale, P., and Singh, H. (2001) How to make strategic alliances work. *MIT Sloan Management Review* 42(4), 37–43

Elmuti, D. and Kathawala, Y. (2001) An overview of strategic alliances. *Management Decision* 39(3), 205–217

Fehr, E., Fischbacher, U., and Gächter, S. (2002) Strong reciprocity, human cooperation and the enforcement of social norms. *Human Nature* 13(1), 1–25

Gächter, S. and Herrmann, B. (2009) Reciprocity, culture and human cooperation: Previous insights and a new cross-cultural experiment. *Philosophical Transactions of the Royal Society* 364(1518), 791–806

Gintis, H. (2000) Strong reciprocity and human sociality. *Journal of Theoretical Biology* 206(2), 169–179

Gintis, H., Henrich, J., Bowles, S., Boyd, R., and Fehr, E. (2008) Strong reciprocity and the roots of human morality. *Social Justice Research* 21(2), 241–253

Groot, T. L. C. M. and Merchant, K. A. (2000) Control of international joint ventures. *Accounting, Organizations and Society* 25(6), 579–607

Hoetker, G. and Mellewigt, T. (2009) Choice and performance of governance mechanisms: Matching alliance governance to asset type. *Strategic Management Journal* 30(10), 1025–1044

Kale, P. and Singh, H. (2009) Managing strategic alliances: What do we know now, and where do we go from here? *Academy of Management Perspectives* 23(3), 45–62

Kale, P., Singh, H., and Perlmutter, H. (2000) Learning and protection of proprietary assets in strategic alliances: Building relational capital. *Strategic Management Journal* 21(3), 217–237

Kale, P., Dyer, J. H., and Singh, H. (2002) Alliance capability, stock market response, and long-term alliance success: The role of the alliance function. *Strategic Management Journal* 28(10), 981–1000

Kanter, R. M. (1994) Collaborative advantage: The art of alliances. *Harvard Business Review* 72(4), 96–108

Li, D., Eden, L., Hitt, M. A., and Ireland, R. D. (2008) Friends, acquaintances, or strangers? Partner selection in R&D alliances. *Academy of Management Journal* 51(2), 315–334

Lu, J. W. and Beamish, P. W. (2006) Partnering strategies and performance of SMEs' international joint ventures. *Journal of Business Venturing* 21(4), 461–486

Nakos, G. and Brouthers, K. D. (2008) International alliance commitment and performance of small and medium-size enterprises: The mediating role of process control. *Journal of International Management* 14(2), 124–137

Ring, P. S. and Van de Ven, A. H. (1994) Developmental processes of cooperative interorganizational relationships. *Academy of Management Review* 19(1), 90–118

Robinson, S. L. (1996) Trust and breach of the psychological contract. *Administrative Science Quarterly* 41(4), 575–599

Schoorman, F. D., Mayer, R. C., and Davis, J. H. (2007) An integrative model of organizational trust: Past, present, and future. *Academy of Management Review* 32(2), 344–354

Spence, M. M., Manning, L. M., and Crick, D. (2008) An investigation into the use of collaborative ventures in the internationalization of high performing Canadian SMEs. *European Management Journal* 26(6), 412–428

Tjemkes, B. and Furrer, O. (2011) Behavioral Responses to adverse situations in strategic alliances. In: Das, T. K. (ed.), Behavioral Perspectives on Strategic Alliances. Charlotte, NC: Information Age Publishing, 227–249

Tung, R. L. (1993) Managing cross-national and intra-national diversity. *Human Resource Management* 32(4), 461–477

Wathne, K. H. and Heide, J. B. (2000) Opportunism in interfirm relationships: Forms, outcomes, and solutions. *Journal of Marketing* 64(4), 36–51

Xia, J. (2011) Mutual dependence, partner substitutability, and repeated partnership: The survival of cross-border alliances. *Strategic Management Journal* 32(3), 229–253

Yli-Renko, H., Autio, E., and Tontto, V. (2002) Social capital, knowledge, and the international growth of technology-based firms. *International Business Review* 11(3), 279–304

Yoshino, M. Y. and Rangan, U.S. (1995) Strategic alliances: An entrepreneurial approach to globalization. Cambridge, MA: Harvard Business School Press

15 Adaptive cooperative strategy

Gomes-Casseres (1997) distinguishes between two categories of competitive advantages, firm- and group-based, for companies engaging in cooperation. While firm-based advantages lie in the capabilities that a company controls, group-based advantages are attainable only through cooperation. Economies of scale or synergies from the joint use of resources or capabilities are salient examples of the second category. Under specific conditions, especially when technologies are changing rapidly, small firms can outcompete large entities using their flexibility and highly specialised capabilities (Gomes-Casseres 1997). When group-based advantages become more important, however, cooperation becomes essential for SMEs to stay competitive. Dyer and Singh (1998) argue that firms can create distinct competitive advantages through cooperation (by investing in partnership-specific assets, joint learning, combining complementary resources, and lowering transaction costs), which they would not be able to develop on their own. When firms engage in cooperation for strategic reasons, however, they also need to think about their cooperative strategy (Child 2005, p. 1).

Street and Cameron (2007) note that the literature on small business cooperation strategy "was found to be very slim" (p. 251). Each company that engages in cooperation has its own corporate and business strategies and pattern of decisions affecting the long-term scope and direction of the firm and its individual business units (Thomson and Baden-Fuller 2010). When two or more firms engage in cooperation, they need to reconcile their strategies. Specifically, cooperation partners need to make two critical strategic choices – concerning the resources and capabilities to be devoted to the joint effort and how to control the joint use of resources and capabilities (Gomes-Casseres 1997). Firms operating independently have full control of their resources and capabilities. In cooperative ventures, however, the control of resources and capabilities is shared (Gomes-Casseres 1997). This means that entering cooperation always requires giving up some control.

In cooperative strategy-making, the partner firms must consider their individual strategies and the cooperative strategy simultaneously. Strategic cooperation is effective in the long term only if it continues to serve the strategic goals of all partner firms involved. At the beginning of cooperation, all parties usually see the strategic benefits; otherwise, they probably would not have entered the alliance. Over time, however, the partners' strategic priorities can change. In such cases, "an inability to evolve has led to alliance failure, often to the potential disadvantage to both partners" (Child et al. 2005, p. 409). Therefore, cooperation must be open to constant evolution, especially as "[p]roperly conceived strategies and processes may often be inadequate if they cannot be adjusted to meet changing circumstances" (Lorange and Probst 1987).

In this chapter, we will first explore how partners can develop a joint strategy and how cooperative strategies evolve over time. Subsequently, we will turn to the question of how cooperation can strategically adapt to changes in the environment.

15.1 Developing the cooperative strategy

A good strategy should (a) effectively communicate a purpose or vision to others, (b) connect internal strengths with external opportunities while (c) maintaining current performance and building future potential, (d) increase the stock of resources, (e) employ a coordinating and guiding function for operational activities, and (f) be adaptable to changing environmental conditions (Huff et al. 2009). Developing such a cooperative strategy is often more complex than is crafting a strategy for a single firm, as different strategic intents need to be reconciled.

Figure 15.1 shows an exemplary strategy development process for a cooperative venture. The starting point is the set of individual strategies of the partner firms. If, in their own strategic planning processes, the firms realise that they could most effectively reach their strategic goals in a synergistic cooperation with other firms, they will need to think about a cooperative strategy (Child et al. 2005). In the first step, partner firms thereby clarify their own cooperation goals, focusing on how cooperation could assist in achieving the overall individual strategic goals. Based on these goals, potential partner firms are screened and selected. When two (or more) partner firms with compatible goals meet and agree to engage in cooperation, they need to develop a joint cooperative strategy (while maintaining their own), wherein the partners focus on joint value maximisation (Zajac and Olsen 1993). Ring and Van de Ven (1994) believe that there are two main criteria by which partners evaluate cooperative agreements – efficiency, the most economical way of dealing with each other, and (equally importantly) "fair dealing", which follows a general equity rule. Equity is different from equality: it is not necessary that all parties receive the same outcomes from cooperating; however, the benefits must be proportional to their inputs (ibid.).

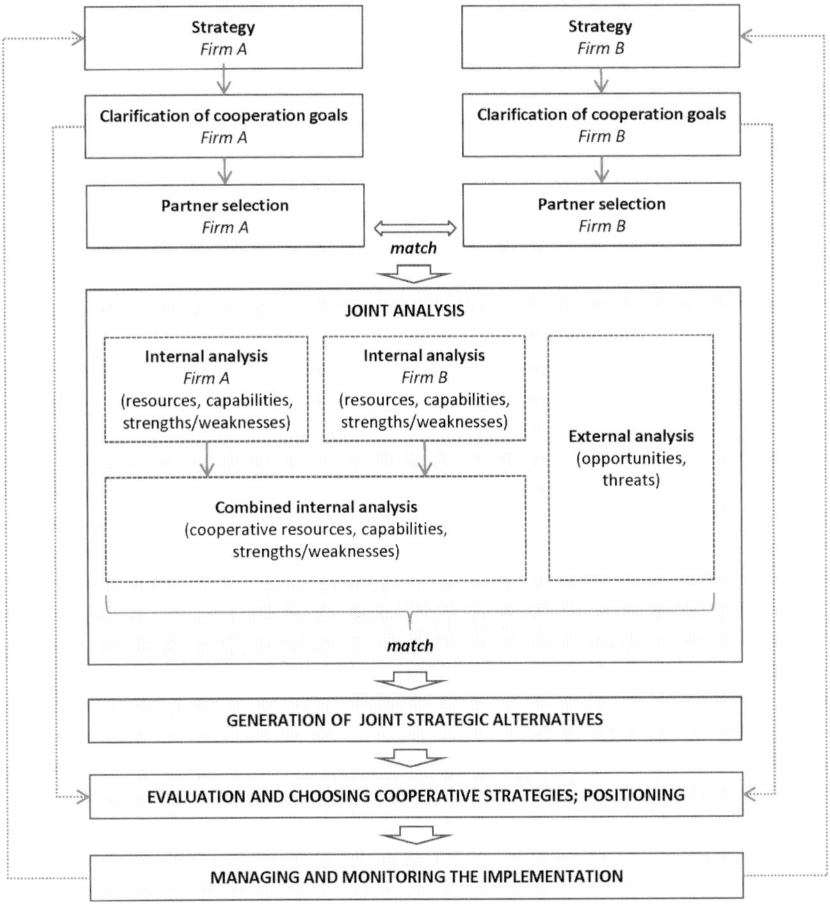

Fig. 15.1 The cooperative strategy development process

Source: Author

As in the case of the strategic planning process for a firm, joint strategizing begins with an analysis phase. In addition to the internal analyses of the partner firms, a combined internal analysis can identify the resources and capabilities that the partners can build and develop synergistically and the strengths and weaknesses the partnership will have relative to the potential competitors. In cross-border cooperation, the technological or process capabilities of one partner are, for example, often combined with the local market knowledge and networks of another partner, thereby creating a value for potential customers that neither firm could have created individually. In an external analysis, major developments in the macro environment (such as the influence of legal, political, economic, socio-demographic, or technological factors), emerging trends, and key success factors in the potential alliance's industry are identified (Johnson et al. 2008). The internal and external analyses are then combined to match market opportunities with the partners' joint strengths. Together, the partners then generate alternative strategic positions for their partnership, evaluate these against their own cooperation goals, and, after deciding on a strategic position that suits all sides, start to implement and control cooperation.

This process does not always follow an exact sequence, as strategic decision-making processes are often iterative and recursive (Sternad 2011).

Likewise, not all cooperation is built on a planned cooperative strategy development process. Strategies often just 'emerge' through the joint decisions that partners make over time (Mintzberg and Waters 1985) as cooperation evolves.

15.2 The evolution of strategic cooperation

Typically, cooperation does not start at full potential from the beginning. Rather, it evolves over time. The first steps in bringing an agreement to life are often crucial to the development of cooperation. Kelly et al. (2002) identify people and relationship problems, operational issues, and strategic agenda matters as the most important challenges faced by the partners in their first year of cooperation, with more than half of all problems attributed to the first category. The main relationship issues concern communication problems, cultural differences, and unclear roles and responsibilities. The following eight steps are proposed to avoid or alleviate the start-up problems that can occur in cooperative ventures (Kelly et al. 2002):

1. Evaluate potential partners' relationship capabilities.
2. Keep relationship issues in mind while negotiating the cooperation agreement.
3. Select cooperation managers and staff for their interpersonal skills.
4. Start with small projects and gain feedback from their performance.
5. Address cultural differences (especially important for cross-border cooperation).
6. Develop strong communication linkages among the partners.
7. Set up processes to monitor and evaluate the performance of the alliance.
8. Be constructive.

Doz (1996) proposes a framework for explaining the evolution of alliances after their initial stages (see Fig. 15.2). Cooperation begins under a set of specific conditions and expectations about partner performance, behaviour, and motives. As an alliance develops, the cooperation partners experience new environmental circumstances, learn from these experiences, and evolve. As the environment changes, so does the value of cooperation to the partners. In light of their new perspectives, the partner firms' managements re-evaluate the alliance's efficiency, equity, and future adaptability, which may, in turn, lead to revised expectations about the partnership and an adjustment of the original conditions. Doz argues that successful alliances continue to go through these learning cycles, developing higher trust, commitment, and alliance capability on the way, while unsuccessful ones fail to learn.

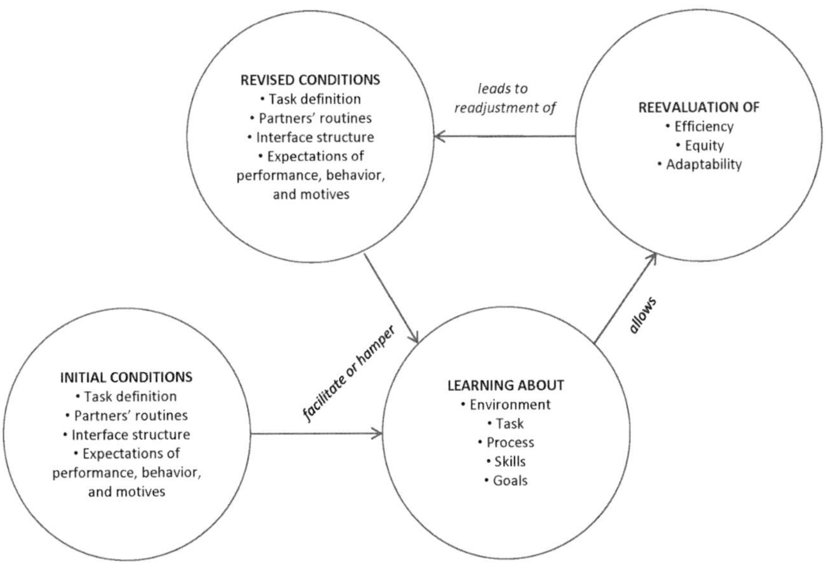

Fig. 15.2 The process of alliance evolution

Source: Doz (1996), p. 64

Ariño and de la Torre (1998) propose that a series of positive learning loops following revised conditions builds goodwill that can increase 'relational quality', which they refer to as "an elusive but important concept [...] [depending] partly on personal bonds between key executives on both sides, on their trust in each other, and on the broader reputation the partners have for fair dealing [...] also affected by more objective assessments of previous contributions made by the partners in the relationship" (p. 307). The authors consider a reserve of relational quality as essential to the survival of cooperation in the face of serious disruptions.

Doz (1996) highlights the importance of immediately setting the conditions for a positive alliance evolution. He finds, for instance, that (a) widely differing skill bases among the partners without overlap, (b) an organisation with overly fragmented levels, functions, and locations and thus many interfaces requiring continuous managerial involvement, (c) overly optimistic expectations, and (d) information asymmetry among the partners can all act as detrimental initial cooperation conditions and hamper evolution. On the contrary, complementary but partially overlapping skill bases, internal partnership "championing" in each partner's organisation, a similar pace of decision-making and issue resolution, continuity in the people managing the partnership, realistic and flexible expectations, concern for common value creation, and limited information asymmetry are identified by Doz as factors that positively influence the mutual learning process and thereby contribute to the capacity to jointly adapt and evolve cooperation. He further notes that alliances that started small and developed over time in the assessment dimensions of efficiency, equity, and adaptability tended to be more successful than those with the highest initial expectations and aims. A stepwise cooperation evolution can lead to repeated positive experiences for all partners, thereby resulting in a more favourable overall evaluation of the alliance's performance.

15.3 Managing the social dilemma in the evolution of strategic cooperation

McCarter et al. (2011) see strategic cooperation as a social dilemma, in which being egoistic at the expense of others can be beneficial. They propose that lack of cooperation in an alliance can happen for two reasons: cooperation partners may choose to "free ride" in an attempt to reap benefits without making considerable investments, or they might underinvest if they believe the other partners will be inclined to do so as well, a stance that McCarter and his colleagues term "defensive defection".

There are two general ways to approach this social dilemma (ibid., p. 623):

- First, in the structural approach, the partners attempt to raise the cost of a party's defection, for example, through contractual fines, cooperation-spe-

cific investments, or by the threat to spread negative assessments of the defecting partner.
- Second, in the motivational approach, the partners attempt to increase mutual trust, for example, through frequent interaction, joint strategic planning, and an open exchange of needs and intentions.

McCarter et al. argue that neither the structural nor the motivational approach is sufficient to resolve the social dilemma in cooperation. Structural solutions might cause mistrust and could be too expensive to enforce. The motivational approach, on the other hand, relies heavily on verbal reassurance, which they do not deem sufficient for a deep, trusting relationship. This is supported by Agarwal et al. (2010), who found that strategic cooperation is more likely to be successful when both economic incentives and good communication among the partners are used, concluding that "[t]hese two mechanisms are thus complements, not substitutes" (p. 431).

An integrative solution offered by McCarter et al. (2011) is termed 'collective real option', defined as an "action undertaken jointly by alliance partners when all partners agree to make a small initial investment of resources to uncover environmental and social information about the possible success of a subsequent larger-scale alliance initiative" (p. 624). Thus, if the partners commit only a limited amount of resources to a pilot project, they (a) create joint opportunities and a "proof-of-concept" (McAdam et al. 2010) for a planned large-scale investment, while (b) limiting the partners' risk and exposure and (c) revealing insights into their reliability and trustworthiness. Serapio and Cascio (1996) propose a similar path when they recommend that partners discover each other's strengths, weaknesses, and real goals through what they call "dating", that is, cooperating on a limited scale before entering into an alliance with a high resource commitment. Child et al. (2005) also indicate that cooperation needs a "symmetric" or balanced development, meaning that one partner should not outpace the others' strategic gains, as this could lead to tensions among them and even to the breakdown of the collaboration.

15.4 Adapting cooperation in the face of a changing environment

Even when cooperation has evolved effectively from its early "dating" stage to a trustful relationship from which all sides reap benefits, the cooperation partners need to ensure that they maintain the joint value in light of changing environmental conditions. Lewin and Volberda (1999) suggest that firms evolve in a coevolution with an ever-changing environment. Lorange and Probst (1987) indicate that, when an alliance wants to survive and evolve within a dynamically changing environment, it generally needs to possess a certain degree of self-organising properties. They identify three joint venture archetypes that also represent three distinct categories of cooperation (ibid.):

- The first, "freestanding" cooperation follows strategies in areas where none of the parent companies is strategically active. In this case, the joint venture carries the main responsibility for adapting to the environmental challenges.
- In the second category, only one partner firm is pursuing strategic interests in the field where the alliance operates. In such a situation, the responsibility to adapt should be shared between the active partner and the cooperation managers.
- In the third category, both partners expect to stay involved in the strategic field where their collaborative efforts are concentrated. In such a structure, both partners will need to be intensely involved in strategic adaptation efforts.

Especially in the latter case, reconciling the partners' strategic intentions can require much effort, as different firm strategies need to be taken into account, as do different perceptions of environmental changes and their potential impact on the cooperative strategy.

Ansoff (1975) refers to environmental trends and events with potentially major discontinuous or destructive effects as "strategic issues". How strategic issues are interpreted can significantly influence the strategic choices of decision-makers, both within firms and in an alliance (Dutton and Jackson 1987). Strategic issue interpretation thus becomes central to strategic adaptation, "the process by which management actively aligns an organization [or, in our case, a cooperative venture] to a changing environment through setting actions which involve high resource commitments and affect the organization's [or alliance's] overall scope and direction" (Sternad 2011, p. 28).

Which strategic issues are attended to and how they are interpreted can be influenced by situational factors (such as the current market situation or the nature of the industry) as well as by the personal characteristics of the decision-makers. Cultural differences can affect how strategic issues are perceived (Barr and Glynn 2004), a factor particularly salient in cross-border cooperation. When the strategic choices of one company depend on the strategic issue interpretations of its top management, it is necessary to develop a joint perspective on a strategic issue as a precondition for developing a feasible cooperative strategy (see Fig. 15.3). Therefore, cooperation partners should make a considerable effort to create a common understanding of major environmental developments and what they mean for their collaborative work. This will enable them to create a joint strategy that permits to adapt cooperation to environmental changes while remaining congruent with the partners' individual perspectives and strategies.

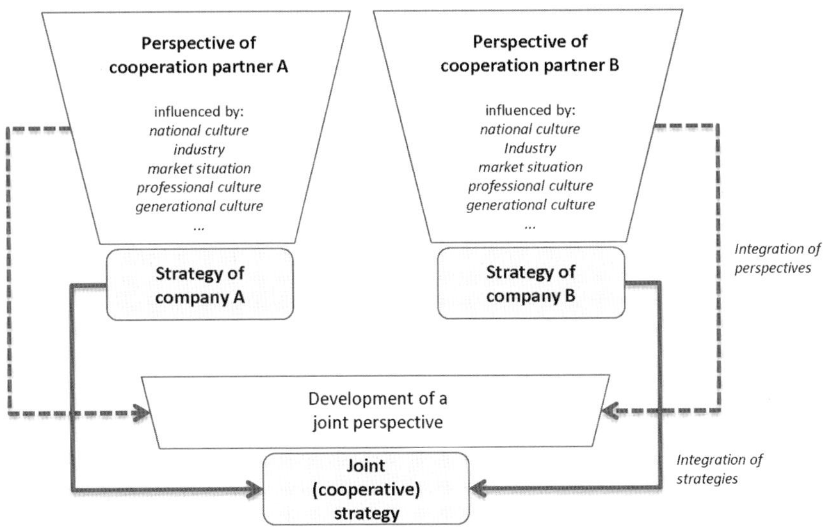

Fig. 15.3 Creating a cooperative strategy through integrating partner perspectives and strategies

Source: Author

Strategic adaptation to dynamic environmental circumstances requires that a certain degree of adaptability be built into the alliance from the beginning. High adaptability can be achieved if the cooperation structure is designed to allow a high degree of flexibility and reactiveness (Green et al. 2008). It is especially important that SMEs build in enough flexibility in their cooperation contract: due to their limited resources, smaller firms are less likely to be able to adjust their contractual agreements once the alliance is in operation (Ariño et al. 2008).

A summary of how to strategically adapt cross-border cooperation in a dynamically changing environment

To be sustainably successful, cooperation should have a long-term direction and scope with which all partners are comfortable: a joint cooperative strategy. As cross-border cooperation usually operates in a rapidly changing environment in which the partners' individual strategic goals and preferences also change, cooperative strategies must adapt over time. In this context, it makes sense to consider the following points:

1. In a joint strategic planning process, the partners can determine their group-based advantages based on the synergistic use of resources and capabilities and ways of jointly positioning themselves to exploit these advantages to create value.
2. Partner firms need to keep both their own and the cooperative partnership strategies in mind. If a discrepancy between them occurs, the strategic direction must be renegotiated with the other partner(s). Cross-border cooperation needs to develop in a balanced way, ensuring that the strategic goals of all the partners are met.
3. Strategic cooperation evolves over time. Rather than operating at their full potential from the beginning, alliances need to go through cycles of learning and building trust. The relational quality, developed over time, is a major precondition for the long-term strategic success of cooperation.
4. A stepwise strategic cross-border cooperation evolution, starting with smaller, low-risk projects, provides partners with the opportunity to create a proof-of-concept and gain information about the other partners' reliability before entering into larger investments. Such a gradual commitment building also enables a more realistic assessment of mutual expectations and can thus lead to a more trustful long-term cooperation.
5. Before creating a joint strategy, partners in cross-border cooperation also need to develop a joint perspective on the strategic issues facing the alliance, particularly as the cultural and institutional differences among partners from different countries can produce very different views on strategically relevant events and developments.

References

Agarwal, R., Croson, R., and Mahoney, J. T. (2010) The role of incentives and communication in strategic alliances: An experimental investigation. *Strategic Management Journal* 31(4), 413–437

Ansoff, I. (1975) Managing strategic surprise by response to weak signals. *California Management Review* 18(2), 21–33

Ariño, A. and de la Torre, J. (1998) Learning from failure: Towards an evolutionary model of collaborative ventures. *Organization Science* 9(3), 306–325

Ariño, A., Ragozzino, R., and Reuer, J. J. (2008) Alliance dynamics for entrepreneurial firms. *Journal of Management Studies* 45(1), 147–168

Barr, P. S. and Glynn, M. A. (2004) Cultural variations in strategic issue interpretation: Relating cultural uncertainty avoidance to controllability in discriminating threat and opportunity. *Strategic Management Journal* 25(1), 59–67

Child, J., Faulkner, D., and Tallman, S. (2005) Cooperative strategy, 2nd edn. Oxford: Oxford University Press

Doz, Y. L. (1996) The evolution of cooperation in strategic alliances: Initial conditions or learning alliances. *Strategic Management Journal* 17(1), 55–83

Dutton, J. E. and Jackson, S. E. (1987) Categorizing strategic issues: Links to organizational action. *Academy of Management Review* 12(1), 76–90

Dyer, J. H. and Singh, H. (1998) The relational view: Cooperative strategy and sources of interorganizational competitive advantage. *Academy of Management Review* 23(4), 660–679

Gomes-Casseres, B. (1997) Alliance strategies of small firms. *Small Business Economics* 9(1), 33–44

Green, K. M., Covin, J. G., and Slevin, D. P. (2008) Exploring the relationship between strategic reactiveness and entrepreneurial orientation: The role of structure-style fit. *Journal of Business Venturing* 23(3), 356–383

Huff, A. S., Floyd, S. W., Sherman, H. D., and Terjesen, S. (2009) Strategic management: Logic and action. Hoboken: Wiley

Johnson, G., Scholes, K., and Whittington, R. (2008) Exploring corporate strategy: Text and cases, 8th edn. Harlow et al.: Prentice Hall Financial Times

Kelly, M. J., Schaan, J. L., and Joncas, H. (2002) Managing alliance relationships: Key challenges in the early stages of collaboration. *R&D Management* 32(1), 11–22

Lewin, A. Y. and Volberda, H. W. (1999) Prolegomena on coevolution: A framework for research on strategy and new organizational forms. *Organization Science* 10(5), 519–534

Lorange, P. and Probst, G. J. B. (1987) Joint ventures as self-organizing systems: A key to successful joint venture design and implementation. *Columbia Journal of Wold Business* 22(2), 71–77

McAdam, M., McAdam, R., Galbraith, B., and Miller, K. (2010) An exploratory study of principal investigator roles in UK university proof-of-concept processes: An absorptive capacity perspective. *R&D Management* 40(5), 455–473

McCarter, M. W., Mahoney, J., and Northcraft, G. B. (2011) Testing the waters: Using collective real options to manage the social dilemma of strategic alliances. *Academy of Management Review* 36(4), 621–640

Mintzberg, H. and Waters, J. A. (1985) Of strategies, deliberate and emergent. *Strategic Management Journal* 6(3), 257–272

Ring, P. S. and Van de Ven, A. H. (1994) Developmental processes of cooperative interorganizational relationships. *Academy of Management Review* 19(1), 90–118

Serapio, M. G. and Cascio, W. F. (1996) End-games in international alliances. *Academy of Management Executive* 10(1), 62–73

Sternad, D. (2011) Strategic adaptation: Cross-cultural differences in company responses to an economic crisis. Wien New York: Springer

Street, C. T. and Cameron, A.-F. (2007) External relationships and the small business: A review of small business alliance and network research. *Journal of Small Business Management* 45(2), 239–266

Thomson, N. and Baden-Fuller, C. (2010) Basic strategy in context: European text and cases. Chichester: Wiley

Zajac, E. J. and Olsen, C. P. (1993) From transaction cost to transactional value analysis: Implications for the study of interorganizational strategies. *Journal of Management Studies* 30(1), 131–145

16 Terminating cooperation

Business relationships are always dynamic. In an ever-changing environment, partners' strategies and goals change, as do the people managing the alliance (Tähtinen et al. 2007). Changing circumstances can also lead to changes in partners' expectations regarding cooperation and to re-evaluations of the usefulness of the partnership (Cui et al. 2011).

There is ample evidence confirming that the failure rates of inter-firm cooperation are high. Although some alliances are designed to last only a certain period of time (when dissolution is thus not a failure), several studies indicate that 30 % to 50 % of strategic alliances were terminated because they had been deemed unsatisfactory (Das and Teng 2000). Dissatisfaction with a partnership often leads to an unplanned termination of the cooperation and to concurrent conflicts among partners.

The breaking up of a partnership entails a number of expenses. In addition to financial losses, the termination itself can consume many resources, distract managerial attention from other, more development-oriented endeavours, create emotional strain, and potentially lead to a loss of reputation, especially in the foreign market where the cooperation partner is located. Despite this, planning for an orderly alliance termination often does not rank highly on partners' agendas during the launch phase of an alliance, mainly because talking of a break up during the initiating phase of cooperation might "sour the deal [or] it might reveal the lack of trust of partners" (Comino et al. 2010, p. 719). Thus, talk of termination is often avoided upfront, as the potential partners fear that focusing too much on a possible relationship breakdown might sabotage the initial cooperation talks.

On the other hand, ending a partnership for which no contractual termination arrangements have been formulated can be very costly for all parties. Therefore, it makes sense to think about the dissolution of cooperation and its possible consequences upfront and include clear exit clauses in the cooperation agreement. After all, "amicable dissolution[s] [...] seem to be the exception rather than the rule" (Peng and Shenkar 2002, p. 93).

In this chapter, we will explore the reasons for the termination of cooperation, different ways of ending a partnership, the process of dissolution, and how best to prepare for the "endgame" upfront.

16.1 Reasons for terminating cooperation

Forming partnerships is a "flexible form of accessing resources without making irreversible investments" (Cui et al. 2011, p. 418). This implies that from a resource-based perspective, following a cooperative strategy is often a temporary solution that makes sense as long as it provides resources that the partner firms need to implement their own firm strategies. Once the cooperation partners gain access to all the required resources, the primary reason for cooperating vanishes, thereby leading to a termination of co-operation. In an empirical study of inter-firm alliances in the manufacturing sector, Cui et al. (2011) find that higher marketing and R&D spending by one of the alliance partners led to a higher propensity to terminate co-operation, as the internal availability of resources (e.g., in marketing and R&D) rendered the partnership resources redundant and therefore dispensable.

In addition to this argument based on resource dependence theory, Das and Teng (2000) highlight other theoretical explanations of why cooperative strategic alliances can fail:

- *Relational contract theory* asserts that cooperation is built on mutual trust among the partners. If there is a lack of trust, the relationship can deteriorate, ultimately leading to the failure of cooperation.
- In the *transaction cost theory* view, cooperation partners may choose to behave opportunistically, thus undermining the common interest, which can in turn lead to a breakdown of cooperation.
- *Game theory* sees alliances as games in which partners might find that following an uncooperative strategy yields outputs superior to those that they would gain from behaving cooperatively.
- *Bargaining power theory* asserts that the bargaining powers among cooperation partners shift over time, inducing renegotiations of their agreement and, in some cases, the dissolution of the partnership.
- The *agency theory* explanation focuses on the managers who act in their self-interest. If managers see that more can be gained (in the form of their compensation, for example) without cooperating, it may trigger the dissolution of the alliance.

These theoretical lines of argumentation can be supplemented by a categorisation of the reasons for ending cooperation derived from empirical observations. Serapio and Cascio (1996) propose six reasons for ending cooperation:

(1) *A lack of success of the alliance*: An alliance may simply not have fulfilled the expectations of one or several of the partners. Managing cooperation across two or more countries can turn out to be more difficult than anticipated. The partners might not see the benefits and returns they had hoped to gain from cooperating.
(2) *Incompatibility and differences between the partners*: In cross-border cooperation, differences in national and company cultures (the latter often being more disruptive than the former [Sirmon and Lane 2004]) and differences among the partner firms' management styles can lead to insurmountable conflicts, resulting in a termination of cooperation.
(3) *Breach of the cooperation agreement*: Partners may violate the terms of the cooperation contract. For example, the wind turbine parts maker American Superconductor (AMSC) filed a lawsuit against its former Chinese cooperation partner Sinovel in 2011 for their allegedly illegal use of intellectual property. A former American Superconductor employee was convicted in an Austrian court for transferring a secret source code to Sinovel. The Chinese company in turn accused their former partner of failing to meet the contractual requirements (Reuters 2011).
(4) *Misfit between partners' goals or strategies*: Partners constantly change their strategies due to their constantly changing environment. If a cooperation partner's goals or strategies are no longer consistent with the common endeavour, the alliance might be terminated.
(5) *Financial reasons to end cooperation*: Financial considerations such as the possibility of gaining free financial resources by ending (or selling one's stake in) a cooperative venture or the opportunity to achieve a price exceeding the perceived value of one's stake in a joint venture can also lead to the termination of inter-firm cooperation.
(6) *Cooperation fulfilled its goals*: If the alliance's mission has been accomplished, the partners can initiate a planned termination of cooperation. This is particularly common with project-oriented cooperation, such as in the construction business, where partners plan upfront to cooperate only to erect a single edifice.

Different categorisations of the reasons for terminating inter-firm cooperation are proposed by Peng and Shenkar (2002), who include failures in partner selection, lack of adequate governance, changes in bargaining power, and what they call a "learning race", wherein one party uses the know-how gained from cooperating opportunistically to outperform the other. Ring and Van de Ven (1994) argued that the following factors can play a decisive role in triggering an alliance termination: "(a) excessive legal structuring and monitoring of the relationship; (b) conflicts between role and interpersonal behaviors of organizational parties; (c) conditions for violations in trust; and (d) escalating commitments to failing transactions" (p. 108).

Personal reasons can also play a role in the termination of business relationships. If an important contact person leaves one of the cooperation partner's firms, social bonds developed over the years might suddenly be severed, thereby lowering the "relationship energy" (Havila and Wilkinson 2002) among the partners, which can ultimately lead to the end of the business relationship.

It should be noted that cultural differences can affect what managers from different countries believe is a reason to terminate a partnership. Scheer et al. (2003) indicate that US and Dutch companies showed differences in their perceptions of relationship inequities, which they attribute to differences in societal norms, such as the level of solidarity expected. A relationship perceived as being more inequitable by one partner might end up being terminated.

Figure 16.1 summarises the main factors in inducing partners to initiate the termination of cooperation.

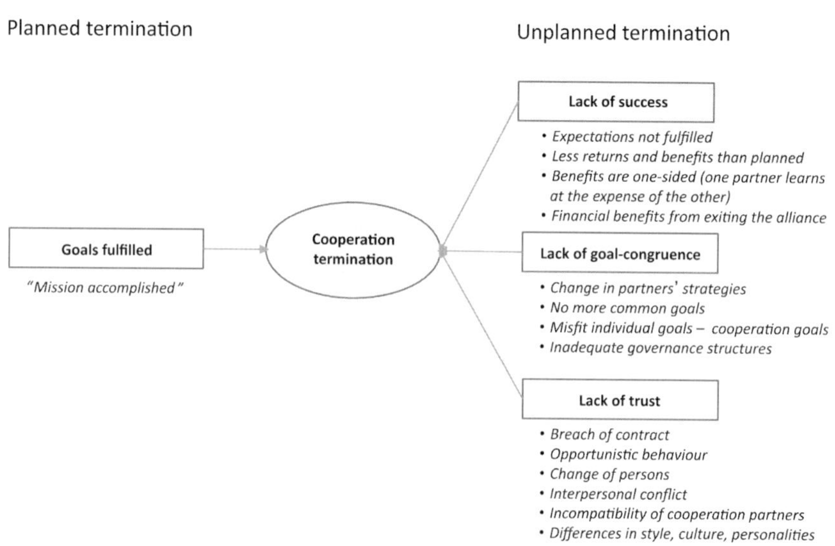

Fig. 16.1 An overview of factors leading to the termination of cooperation

Source: Author

16.2 Ways of terminating cooperation

Cooperation can be terminated in a number of ways: (i) it can be dissolved by distributing common assets and other rights and obligations among the partners; (ii) it can end through a merger and acquisition, when one partner buys out the other(s) or a third party takes over the cooperative venture; and (iii) it can be renegotiated, thus paving the way for a new form of collaboration.

Das and Teng (2000) suggest a theory to explain the circumstances under which partners might choose a certain form of termination. They argue that alliance instabilities are rooted in 'internal tensions', with the nature of these tensions leading to a propensity to end cooperation in a particular way. The theory is based on the proposal that three pairs of competing forces exist in any cooperation:

(a) *cooperation* versus *competition*
(b) *rigidity* versus *flexibility*
(c) *short-term orientation* versus *long-term orientation*

Common goals and interests are the basis for engaging in cooperative efforts. On the other hand, partners still have their own interests, which sometimes run counter to the interests of the alliance. According to Das and Teng (2000), the success of an alliance depends on the right balance between the two factors, as "both cooperation and competition are indispensable for a sustainable and successful alliance [...] If cooperation is lacking, opportunistic behavior will become prevalent [...] [whereas] [w]hen firms are too cooperative, they are likely to transfer their know-how and competence to the partners carelessly" (pp. 86–87). They also believe that it is necessary to achieve a balance between the other factors – between rigidity (the degree of clear structures, systems, and processes binding the partners together) and flexibility, and short- and long-term orientations. Short-term orientation fosters adaptation and fast, visible results, whereas long-term orientation is a precondition for an ongoing commitment to the alliance. From this perspective, cooperation can be sustained only when all three pairs of competing forces are kept in balance, both common and individual goals are in focus, both procedural rules and flexibility are present, and both short-term returns and long-term potential building are sought. If any of these forces begin to dominate, the stability of the cooperation will be at risk.

How do these tensions relate to choosing a way to terminate cooperation? Das and Teng (2000) propose that, if a balance turns into rigidity and long-term orientation, a more hierarchical form of termination (mergers & acquisitions), which enables a more stable governance structure, will be more likely.

On the other hand, if competition, flexibility, and short-term orientation become dominant in an alliance, the relationships among the partners will come to resemble market transactions. In these circumstances, alliance dissolution is a more common strategy than are mergers and acquisitions.

The form of termination also depends on the alliance's original governance structure. In cross-border equity joint ventures, termination by acquisition is most common, whereas, in most contract-based cooperation, dissolving the contractual agreement is more common (Serapio and Cascio 1996).

16.3 The process of termination

The termination of a partnership is usually not a single event but a process that unfolds over time in stages (Pick 2010). Peng and Shenkar (2002) use the metaphor 'corporate divorce' to indicate that the process of dissolving cooperation[2] resembles a divorce, as both corporate and human relationships are built on mutual trust. If this trust vanishes, the relationship deteriorates, leading to dissolution.

A proposed four-phase model for the dissolution of joint ventures is presented in Fig. 16.2 and will be described, following Peng and Shenkar's (2002) account, in more detail below.

In the first phase *(Initiation)* of Peng and Shenkar's model, one partner begins feeling uncomfortable being a part of the alliance, for reasons indicated earlier in this chapter (such as a partner's incompatibility with the firm's goals or perceived insuperable differences among the partners). The increasing dissatisfaction of one partner is often not noticed by the other partner(s). It can begin very quietly; however, the unsatisfied partner usually begins to demand changes to, or even a renegotiation of, the agreement or relationship. In the process, partners may attempt to change their counterpart's behaviour, while wondering whether the relationship is still the right one and finally switching from thinking about *whether* they should terminate cooperation to *how* they should terminate it. At this stage, the initiator may already be searching for alternative partners. An important behavioural aptitude in this first phase of the termination process is a very intense monitoring of the partner, with small events and clues perhaps being attributed very high importance. By the end of this phase, the initiator has the clear intention of quitting cooperation. The partner, sensing the danger, might begin renegotiation and reconciliation efforts.

2 In their research, Peng and Shenkar (2002) focus on joint ventures.

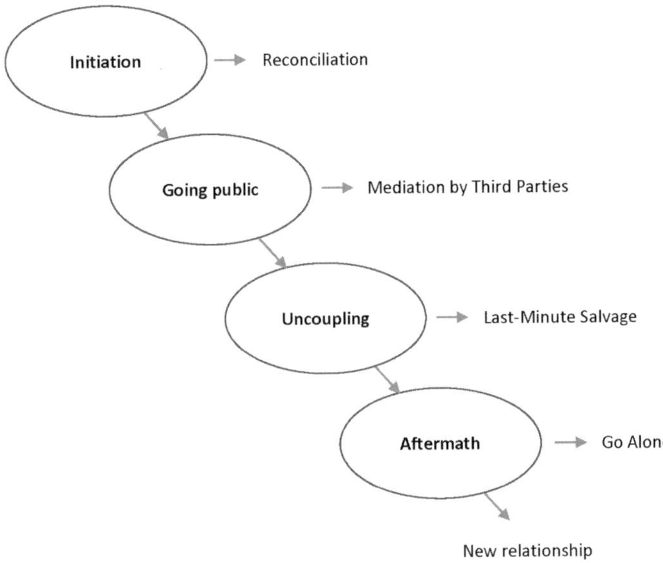

Fig. 16.2 The process of "corporate divorce"

Source: From "Joint venture dissolution as corporate divorce" by M. W. Peng and O. Shenkar (2002) Academy of Management Executive 16(2), p. 95

In phase 2 *(Going public)*, the news of the imminent corporate divorce is publicised. The partner who breaks the news is said to have an advantageous position, being able to provide compelling reasons for the breakup, thereby putting itself "in the most positive light and [..] [securing] coalitions with key stakeholders, such as parent-company executives, investors, and journalists" (Peng and Shenkar 2002, p. 98). This phase is usually also characterised by the inclusion of outsiders such as lawyers or mediators to support the termination negotiation process. The parties are now being closely monitored by the public, and reconciliation is becoming increasingly unlikely. Only the intervention of very powerful external stakeholders (such as the parent-company CEOs or governments) can change the relationship positively.

At the centre of the third phase (*Uncoupling*) lies the formal dissolution process. All the energy here is devoted to attaining a favourable outcome for one's own firm. The distribution of assets, rights, and obligations are discussed in negotiations, usually including (costly) legal advisors before either an arbitration committee or a court. This process can consume a considerable amount of resources and usually takes a long time. Unambiguous termination clauses in the cooperation agreement can be of great help in such a situation.

Last-minute salvaging of cooperation is very rare and possible only if trust still exists in the personal relationships among the key actors.

In the fourth phase *(Aftermath)*, after the alliance has been dissolved, firms generally have two options. They may decide that, given their negative cooperation experience, it is better to proceed independently, or they may learn from cooperation failure and use their experience when entering new and different types of partnerships. Peng and Shenkar (2002) assert that firms with negative cooperative experiences will usually be more cautious in future, demanding more formal rules and monitoring procedures from potential partners.

Attempts to renegotiate and reconcile a cooperative relationship have higher chances of success when initiated early in the termination process. Therefore, a major lesson learned from viewing cooperation through a "divorce lens" is to be watchful for early warning signs, such as frequent complaints about a partner, pointing out partners' faults, or a gradual withdrawal of one of the partners (Peng and Shenkar 2002, p. 98). Like marriages, cooperation can be saved; however, this requires much effort from all the partners.

16.4 Preparing early for termination

Cooperation can also be regarded as a 'Hollywood marriage', with an assumed high risk of divorce and a need to specify in the cooperation contract how to divide assets and other rights and obligations in the case of termination of cooperation (Comino et al. 2010). As Serapio and Cascio (1996) pointedly argue, "[d]ivorce is difficult, but partners to an alliance should be prepared for it, and also be prepared to tackle the sometimes difficult issues in exiting an alliance" (p. 63).

A few reasons have been provided, however, for not including exit clauses in cooperation contracts. Comino et al. (2010) argue that having a contractual agreement without clearly specified rules for ending cooperation might increase the cost of termination for all parties involved, due to the potentially costly litigation. Thus, partners would be willing to expend more effort to save the alliance, as the outcome of a termination is uncertain and potentially detrimental for all partners.

Nevertheless, no relationship lasts forever. This is especially true, as empirical evidence shows (Das and Teng 2000), of inter-firm cooperation. At the beginning of this chapter, a variety of reasons for the termination of partnerships has been discussed; often, only one of them needs to materialize for the dissolution of a partnership. Therefore, in the event of a cooperation breakdown, clear and unambiguous exit clauses in the initial agreement can enable the partners to avoid additional uncertainties and costs in an already unpleasant situation.

Exit clauses in cross-border cooperation contracts usually contain conditions for termination, arrangements for distributing assets and disposing of liabilities, and mechanisms for resolving any conflicts that might occur during the cooperation termination process (Serapio and Cascio 1996). The following questions (at minimum) should be considered in the contract (cf. ibid, pp. 69–71):

- *Under what circumstances can a partner exit or terminate cooperation*? Such circumstances might include a "(1) material breach of agreement; (2) breach of law; (3) repeated (two or more) deadlocks among the members of the board of directors [of the cooperation]; (4) changes in the laws and regulations of the home or host country; (5) failure to meet a specific target; and (6) after a certain period of time period has lapsed" (ibid., p. 69).
- *How will the partners distribute the assets of the alliance? How will these assets be valuated?*
  The applicable valuation procedures might include an independent advisory opinion, an offer from a prospective external buyer, or buy-sell clauses such as a 'Texas shoot-out', wherein both parties simultaneously notify the other (usually through sealed envelopes) of the price they would be willing to pay for their counterpart's assets and the highest bidder is obligated to buy out the other (de Frutos and Kittsteiner 2008).
- *How will the partners dispose of the liabilities of the alliance?*
  Serapio and Cascio (1996) indicate that there are cross-national differences to consider here; for example, some European countries have stricter rules governing the severance payments owed to terminated employees than others.
- *How are rights and obligations distributed?*
  This includes (depending on the type of cooperation) intellectual property rights such as patents, copyrights, brands, and licenses[3], distribution rights, and obligations to suppliers, customers, and banks.
- *How will the partners resolve conflicts? Are arbitration mechanisms provided or will the disputes be carried out before a court? Which country's law will be adhered to? Where is the court of jurisdiction?*
  The choice of legal venue, place of arbitration, and governing law is parti-

3 For a discussion of the special challenges regarding this issue, see also Pearson and Parker (2008).

cularly crucial for cross-border cooperation, as firms often have an advantage when a court case is tried in their country.

- *What will happen to the employees specifically employed for the alliance?* Will their contracts be terminated? Will they be allowed to continue working for one (or several) of the partners?

When formulating the contract for cross-culture cooperation, it is also important that all partners fully understand the meaning of the legal terms in the language in which the contract is drafted and according to the legal system of the country in which the contract will be enforced.

An important issue to consider when terminating cross-border cooperation are the relations with the host government (Serapio and Cascio 1996). The government may have mechanisms to discourage divestment, such as rules which block the repatriation of cooperative investments. Thus, good advice for managers engaging in cross-border cooperation is to "[t]ake the time to study the host government's policies towards divestments by international direct investors" (ibid, p. 71). On the other hand, breaking up cooperation could significantly affect one's ability to invest in other ventures in the host country, if one's relationship with the government has deteriorated (ibid.).

Some types of cooperation are more easily terminated than others. If, for example, a company has associated with a local partner to provide target country-specific market knowledge, termination will affect only one market. If, on the other hand, one partner aims to terminate a global alliance in which both sides have used highly integrated operations to achieve synergies, the split could have major repercussions on the performance of both firms. The paradox of partnerships is that the more integrated and interdependent they are, the harder they are to separate (Tähtinen et al. 2007). In all cases, besides providing detailed exit clauses in the contract, there is another way to end a cooperation reasonably, following Serapio and Cascio's (1996) advice: "Take the time to develop a personal relationship with your new partner that will permit unforeseen issues to be resolved amicably" (p. 72).

A summary of the factors to be considered in case of termination of cooperation

Inter-firm cooperation often fails. Partners who are well prepared for the termination of cooperation and who negotiate the terms of dissolution from the outset do not display a lack of trust, but show that they have a clear perception of the reality of business relationships. At the beginning of their collaborative efforts, partners in cross-border cooperation should therefore consider the following regarding the possible termination of their joint endeavour:

1. Cooperation is terminated for a number of reasons. It can end in a planned way when the partners' goals are fulfilled or in an unplanned way due to a lack of success, goal-congruence, or trust among the partners. Interpersonal problems leading to a loss of trust can also be caused by cultural differences.
2. Cooperation can be terminated through mergers and acquisitions, contract dissolution, or renegotiation of an agreement. The type of termination will be influenced by the original governance structure and the relative strength of the competing forces within the cooperation (with cooperation, rigidity, and long-term orientation favouring mergers & acquisitions and with a tendency towards competition, flexibility, and short-term orientation more likely to result in agreement dissolution) (Das and Teng 2000).
3. Corporate "divorce" is a process rather than a single event. Being attentive and responsive to early warning signs such as frequent complaints or criticism and avoidance behaviour can save cooperation partnership from breaking up.
4. Exit clauses in cooperation contracts will usually save money and time and can enable partners to avoid ambiguous and conflict-laden dissolutions. Typical basic exit clauses include conditions for ending the contract, provisions for the distribution of assets and liabilities, rights and obligations, conflict resolution procedures, and the applicable laws and courts of jurisdiction.
5. Firms should take all the repercussions of the termination of cooperation into account. In addition to the immediate financial and relational outcomes, the local divestment regulations and the long-term effects on one's reputation and ability to do business in the former partner's market need to be considered.

References

Comino, S., Nicolò, A., and Tedeschi, P. (2010) Termination clauses in partnerships. *European Economic Review* 54(5), 718–732

Cui, A. S., Calantone, R. J., and Griffith, D. A. (2011) Strategic change and termination of interfirm partnerships. *Strategic Management Journal* 32(4), 402–423

Das, T. K. and Teng, B.-S. (2000) Instabilities of strategic alliances: An internal tensions perspective. *Organization Science* 11(1), 77–101

De Frutos, M.-A. and Kittsteiner, T. (2008) Efficient partnership dissolution under buy-sell clauses. *RAND Journal of Economics (Blackwell Publishing Limited)* 39(1), 184–198

Havila, V. and Wilkinson, I. F. (2002) The principle of the conservation of business relationship energy: Or many kinds of new beginnings. *Industrial Marketing Management* 31(3), 191–203

Pearson, C. and Parker, N. (2008) Post-termination use of licensed intellectual property by licensees. *Journal of Intellectual Property Law and Practice* 3(5), 305–313

Peng, M. W. and Shenkar, O. (2002) Joint venture dissolution as corporate divorce. *Academy of Management Executive* 16(2), 92–105

Pick, D. (2010) Never say never – status quo and research agenda for relationship termination in B2B markets. *Journal of Business Market Management* 4(2), 91–108

Reuters (2011) Sinovel denies AMSC's charges of IP theft. http://www.reuters.com/article/2011/09/16/sinovel-americansuperconductor-idUSL3E7KG21B20110916 (date accessed 27 October 2011)

Ring, P. S. and Van de Ven, A. H. (1994) Developmental processes of cooperative interorganizational relationships. *Academy of Management Review* 19(1), 90–118

Scheer, L. K., Kumar, N., and Steenkamp, J.-B. E. M. (2003) Reactions to perceived inequity in U.S. and Dutch interorganizational relationships. *Academy of Management Journal* 46(3), 303–316

Serapio, M. G. and Cascio, W. F. (1996) End-games in international alliances. *Academy of Management Executive* 10(1), 62–73

Sirmon, D. G. and Lane, P. J. (2004) A model of cultural differences and international alliance performance. *Journal of International Business Studies* 35(4), 306–319

Tähtinen, J., Blois, K., and Mittilä, T. (2007) How the features of business relationships influence their endings. *Journal of Business Market Management* 1(3), 231–247

Index

D